Studies in Economic Transition

General Editors: **Jens Hölscher**, Senior Lecturer in Economics, University of Brighton; and **Horst Tomann**, Professor of Economics, Free University, Berlin

This new series has been established in response to a growing demand for a greater understanding of the transformation of economic systems. It brings together theoretical and empirical studies on economic transition and economic development. The post-communist transition from planned to market economies is one of the main areas of applied theory because in this field the most dramatic examples of change and economic dynamics can be found. The series aims to contribute to the understanding of specific major economic changes as well as to advance the theory of economic development. The implications of economic policy will be a major point of focus.

Titles include:

Irwin Collier, Herwig Roggemann, Oliver Scholz and Horst Tomann (*editors*)
WELFARE STATES IN TRANSITION
East and West

Hella Engerer
PRIVATIZATION AND ITS LIMITS IN CENTRAL AND EASTERN EUROPE
Property Rights in Transition

Hubert Gabrisch and Rüdiger Pohl (*editors*)
EU ENLARGEMENT AND ITS MACROECONOMIC EFFECTS IN EASTERN EUROPE
Currencies, Prices, Investment and Competitiveness

Jens Hölscher (*editor*)
FINANCIAL TURBULENCE AND CAPITAL MARKETS IN TRANSITION COUNTRIES

Jens Hölscher and Anja Hochberg (*editors*)
EAST GERMANY'S ECONOMIC DEVELOPMENT SINCE UNIFICATION
Domestic and Global Aspects

Mihaela Kelemen and Monika Kostera (*editors*)
CRITICAL MANAGEMENT RESEARCH IN EASTERN EUROPE
Managing the Transition

Emil J. Kirchner (*editor*)
DECENTRALIZATION AND TRANSITION IN THE VISEGRAD
Poland, Hungary, the Czech Republic and Slovakia

Julie Pellegrin
THE POLITICAL ECONOMY OF COMPETITIVENESS IN AN ENLARGED EUROPE

Gregg S. Robins
BANKING IN TRANSITION
East Germany after Unification

Johannes Stephan
ECONOMIC TRANSITION IN HUNGARY AND EAST GERMANY
Gradualism and Shock Therapy in Catch-up Development

Adalbert Winkler (*editor*)
FINANCIAL DEVELOPMENT IN EASTERN EUROPE
The First Ten Years

Hans van Zon
THE POLITICAL ECONOMY OF INDEPENDENT UKRAINE

Studies in Economic Transition
Series Standing Order ISBN 0–333–73353–3
(*outside North America only*)

You can receive future titles in this series as they are published by placing a standing order. Please contact your bookseller or, in case of difficulty, write to us at the address below with your name and address, the title of the series and the ISBN quoted above.

Customer Services Department, Macmillan Distribution Ltd, Houndmills, Basingstoke, Hampshire RG21 6XS, England

Critical Management Research in Eastern Europe

Managing the Transition

Edited by

Mihaela Kelemen
Department of Management, Keele University, England

and

Monika Kostera
Academy of Management and Entrepreneurship, Warsaw, Poland, and Management Faculty, Warsaw University, Poland

palgrave
macmillan

First published 2002 by
PALGRAVE MACMILLAN
Houndmills, Basingstoke, Hampshire RG21 6XS and
175 Fifth Avenue, New York, N.Y. 10010
Companies and representatives throughout the world.

PALGRAVE MACMILLAN is the global academic imprint of the Palgrave Macmillan division of St Martin's Press, LLC and of Palgrave Macmillan Ltd. Macmillan® is a registered trademark in the United States, United Kingdom and other countries. Palgrave is a registered trademark in the European Union and other countries.

ISBN 0–333–98709–8

This book is printed on paper suitable for recycling and made from fully managed and sustained forest sources.

A catalogue record for this book is available from the British Library.

Library of Congress Cataloging-in-Publication Data
Critical management research in Eastern Europe; managing the transition/edited by Mihaela Kelemen, Monika Kostera.
p. cm. – (Studies in economic transition)
Includes bibliographical references and index.
ISBN 0-333-98709-8 (cloth)
1. Post-communism – Europe, Eastern. 2. Europe, Eastern – Economic policy –1989– 3. Europe, Eastern – Economic conditions – 1989– I. Kelemen, Mihaela, 1968– II. Kostera, Monika, 1963– III. Series.
HC244 .C75 2002
338.947–dc21 2002025141

10 9 8 7 6 5 4 3 2 1
11 10 09 08 07 06 05 04 03 02

Printed and bound in Great Britain by
Antony Rowe Ltd, Chippenham and Eastbourne

To

Rodica and Iosif Kelemen

and

Krystyna and Józef Kostera

Contents

List of Figures

List of Maps

List of Tables

Foreword

This book is the first in *Studies in Economic Transition* that looks at transition in Eastern Europe from a managerial and organizational point of view. *Critical Management Research in Eastern Europe* is innovative in the sense that a cultural perspective is chosen in order to address the progress and its setbacks of the transition from socialism to market economies. *Culture* is the main theme of the book guiding readers through the major issues of the transition: changes of practices, the role of the past for current identities; potential synergies between East and West European ways of thinking.

A main achievement of the book is its contribution to the understanding of how individuals and organizations influence and are influenced by the environmental context of transition. Case studies, discourse analysis as well as observation and introspection, are used. The freshness of the approach is supplemented with the autobiographical disclosures of the editors, who begin by describing their experiences when the Berlin Wall came down in 1989. (At that time Mihaela Kelemen was in Transylvania and Monika Kostera in Warsaw. The editors of this series, however, were in Berlin, albeit on the Western side.) This difference of location implies totally different identities at that time, and this book traces back the interaction between these different cultural backgrounds since 1989.

Although a critical approach is taken, especially in its fields of gender and career developments, the overall tone of the book is overwhelmingly positive. We hope that *Critical Management Research* will help to overcome some of the obstacles of managing the transition and will be read by some of the academics and practitioners alike.

JENS HÖLSCHER
HORST TOMANN

Notes on the Contributors

Iiris Aaltio is Professor of Management at the Lappeenranta University of Technology, Finland. Her research interests focus on organizational culture, gender issues in management and entrepreneurial organization cultures. Her background is in business administration and organization psychology. She is the author of several books, book chapters and her work has been published in journals such as *Organizational Change Management, Journal of Management Inquiry, Human Relations* and *Scandinavian Journal of Management Studies.*

Elizabeth C. Dunn is an anthropologist who is currently Assistant Professor of Geography and International Affairs at the University of Colorado at Boulder. Her work centres on global processes of rule-making and their effects on industries, particularly in Eastern Europe. She is particularly interested in how systems of rules, from accounting to quality control, affect workers' and managers' ideas about personhood. Her most recent work focuses on the European Union's food safety and hygiene regulations and their effects on the Polish meat-packing industry.

Bruno Grancelli is Associate Professor of Political Sociology at the University of Trento. His publications are in the fields of organizational behaviour, management training, entrepreneurship and local development in Russia and Eastern Europe. He is currently involved in a comparative research on the accession strategies to the EU of east-European elites.

Herbert Kalthoff studied sociology at the University of Hannover and University of Bielefeld (both Germany), and at École des Hautes Études en Sciences Sociales (Paris). He currently holds a research position at Frankfurt Institute for Transformation Studies at the European University Viadrina Frankfurt (Oder). His publications include: *Wohlerzogenheit. Eine Ethnographie deutscher Internatsschulen* and *Facts and figures. Economic representations and practices* (edited with Richard Rottenburg and Hans-Jürgen Wagener). His research interests are the sociology of banking and financial knowledge and ethnographic school research.

Mihaela Kelemen is Senior Lecturer in Management and Organization Studies at Keele University, UK. She has a doctorate from the Academy of Economic Studies, Bucharest and a DPhil in management studies from the University of Oxford. Her research covers a wide range of topics such as critical management, postmodernism, gender, community, identity, quality and transitional processes in Eastern Europe, and has been published in journals such as *Journal of Management Studies, Organization, Human Relations, British Journal of Management, Scandinavian Journal of Management* etc. Her book on quality management will be published by Sage in 2002.

Jerzy Kociatkiewicz is a doctoral student at the Graduate School for Social Research at the Institute of Philosophy and Sociology of the Polish Academy of Sciences. He has published in a variety of refereed journals, including *Qualitative Sociology, Knowledge Transfer*, and *Studies in Cultures, Organizations and Society*. He has also presented papers at numerous international conferences, and published chapters in edited books. His current research concentrates on the social construction of space in organizations. He is a recipient of the Foundation for Polish Science Annual Stipend for Young Scientists.

Monika Kostera is a Professor in Management and Organization Theory at the Academy of Management and Entrepreneurship in Warsaw, Poland, and Warsaw University, and, since 2000, director of the Centre for International and Comparative Research at the Academy of Management and Entrepreneurship. She has been a visiting professor and visiting researcher at a number of institutions such as Newcastle Business School, Bolton Business School, Vaxjö University, Wissenschaftszentrum Berlin, Lund University. She has published several books and edited collections and has been the guest editor of a special issue of *Studies in Cultures, Organizations and Societies*. She has published over 20 articles in refereed journals such as: *Organization, Management Learning, Studies in Cultures, Organizations, and Societies*; *Qualitative Sociology, Organization Studies, Human Resource Development International, Journal of Organizational Behavior, Scandinavian Journal of Management*, and others. She is a member of editorial boards of several journals. Her current research interests include: ethnography of organizations, aesthetics and spirituality of organizing, critical perspectives on management in East European countries.

Mari Kooskora graduated from the Estonian Business School in 2001 with an Executive MBA, and Tallinn Technical University with a BBA in 1993. She presented her master thesis 'Ethical Aspects of Decision-making' in June 2001. She is the Editor-in-Chief of *EBS Review*, the head of the business ethics working group and the organizer of international conferences at EBS. Her interest is business ethics in the wider sense and her research includes ethical decision-making, ethics and values in society and companies, and conflicts in Estonia. Apart from research articles, she has written educational and training materials for students and business leaders in Estonia, advised and consulted bachelor dissertations, and is now working as a lecturer of organizational behaviour and business ethics at EBS.

Karin Svedberg Nilsson holds a PhD in Business and Organization Studies. She is a researcher at the Economic Research Institute at the Stockholm School of Economics and associated with the Stockholm Centre for Organizational Research (SCORE). She has published work on organizational transformation and privatization in Eastern Europe. Her research interests further include issues of identity, governance, and accountability within and between organizations.

Aneta Pavlenko holds a PhD from Cornell University, and is Assistant Professor at the College of Education at Temple University, Philadelphia. Her research interests include the relationship between language and identity, language and cognition, and language and gender. Her work has appeared in *Applied Linguistics, Annual Review of Applied Linguistics, Issues in Applied Linguistics, Bilingualism: Language and Cognition, The International Journal of Bilingualism, Estudios de Sociolinguistica, Multilingua*, and *Pragmatics and Cognition*.

Henriett Primecz works at the Budapest University of Economic Sciences and Public Administration, Faculty of Business Administration, Department of Management and Organization, Hungary. She graduated in Business and Economics from Pécs University (Hungary), and in Society and Politics (MA) from the Central European University in Warsaw and received her PhD from University of Pécs (Hungary) in 2001. The title of her dissertation is 'Multiple Paradigm Perspectives on Cross-cultural Management'. She conducted research at the Judge Institute of Management Studies at the University of Cambridge (UK) in 1998 as a visiting PhD student. She has published articles in Hungarian management journals, e.g.

Vezetéstudomány (Management Science), *Marketing and Management* etc., and a review of Mats Alvesson and Yvonne Billing's book *Understanding Gender and Organizations*, in *Organization Studies*. Her research interests concern such areas as: cross-cultural management, critical and postmodern management, Foucauldian perspectives on surveillance, and gendered organizations.

Anna Soulsby is a Senior Lecturer in Organizational Behaviour at Nottingham University Business School and Co-Director of the Centre for Research into Enterprise in Emerging Markets. Since 1992 she has been conducting enterprise-level research in Central and Eastern Europe with her co-researcher, Dr Ed Clark. Her research interests include: processes of organizational restructuring, comparative management and organization, and the transformation of management practices and managerial careers in CEE.

Lembit Turnpuu is Professor Emeritus of the Estonian Business School and Tallinn Pedagogical University. He has worked in various higher positions in high schools, universities in Estonia and in Finland, in town councils, and with the Ministry of Higher and Special Education. From 1983, he has been a docent and from 1991 a Professor of Andragogy and Management. He has written numerous articles and conference presentations. His main research interests are management, education theory, andragogy and managerial consciousness.

Acknowledgements

The most important people in bringing this project to life are Jens Hölscher from Brighton University, the editor of the 'Studies in Economic Transition Studies' series who has been extremely interested in this book form its outset and was instrumental in helping us sign the contract with Palgrave Macmillan, and Nicola Viinikka, the Palgrave Macmillan editor, whom we thank for her enthusiasm, kindness and practical help in getting the book through the usual publishing hurdles.

The creation of this book would have not been possible without the outstanding support provided by all the authors, the invaluable help provided by two Palgrave Macmillan reviewers and the helpful comments provided by some of our colleagues who took the time to read the manuscript and encouraged us along the way. Special thanks are also due to the field actors who have made this book possible in the very first place.

The writing of this book has been an inspiring and intellectually challenging process and we hope we will be able to share these feelings with our readers. Dear readers, thank you for your interest! We hope you will not be disappointed.

MIHAELA KELEMEN
MONIKA KOSTERA

List of Abbreviations

CEE	Central and Eastern Europe
CEO	Chief Executive Officer
ETF	European Training Foundation
EU	European Union
GAAP	Generally Accepted Accounting Principles
GDP	Gross Domestic Product
GDR	German Democratic Republic
GmbH	Gesellschaft Mit Beschraenkter Haftung [Limited Company]
GNP	Gross National Product
HACCP	Hazard Analysis Critical Control Point
HCMS	High Commercial Management School
HR	Human Relations
HRM	Human Resource Management
IAS	International Accounting Standards
IASC	International Accounting Standards Committee
IBS	The International Business School
IMI	International Management Institute
IMISP	International Management Institute of St Petersburg
KIMEP	Kazakhstan Institute of Management
MBA	Master of Business Administration
MT	Management Training
NIS	Newly Independent States
OECD	Organization for Economic Cooperation and Development
PCM	Project Cycle Management
PhD	Doctor of Philosophy
PIP	Productivity Initiative Programs
RBTCA	Regional Bank Training in Central Asia
QA	Quality Assurance
SAA	State-authorized Expert in Accounting
SME	State Managed Enterprise
Tacis	EU sponsored technical assistance program to 13 countries of EE and Central Asia
TDP	Technical Dissemination Project
ToR	Terms of Reference

ToT	Training of Trainees
UK	United Kingdom
USA	United States of America
USSR	Union of Soviet Socialist Republics

1
Introduction: Travelling in Time and Space on the Winds of the Transition

Mihaela Kelemen and Monika Kostera

This is an unconventional book. Hence the way in which we start our introductory chapter. Here is Mihaela's story.

I was living in Romania when the country's communist system was overthrown in December 1989. I was in fact a full time student at Academy of Economic Studies in Bucharest. In November that year, I somehow managed to catch hepatitis and was sent to recover to my parents' town, in Southern Transylvania. I was miles away from the epicentre of the revolt, tucked away in a small town where nothing really happened during that time. As I was not allowed to get out of bed (let alone the house), my only contact with what was going on in Bucharest and other big cities was through radio and television. I remember watching the news with a constant sense of bewilderment and thinking it was not real, it could not be real. There was fear, relief, hope and uneasiness in what I was seeing. It felt as if I was on the edge between dream and reality. One year later, I went to the UK to do a doctorate. A decade later I work and still live in the UK. Thus, my experience of the ups and downs of Romanian contemporary history are not embodied, but rather seen through the eyes of my relatives and friends, and well as through the lens of the people I interviewed and observed in my research. It is not an impressive story to tell and yet it has some fascinating undertones: it is a story about struggle and freedom, equality and inequality, fairness and unfairness, poverty and wealth, corruption and professionalism. Yet, the most fulfilling human projects are inseparable from a degree of torment and pain: we should not be embarrassed by such difficulties, only by the failure to grow anything beautiful from them.

Here is Monika's story.

I was living in Poland when the Berlin Wall fell. Before it happened, the first democratic elections since World War II were proclaimed in Poland, and the anti-totalitarian opposition, represented by Solidarnosc, won overwhelmingly. One by one the countries of the Eastern Bloc were declaring their independence from the Soviet Union and the breach from the totalitarian system. On New Year's Eve 1989, I went out into the streets of Warsaw, shouting 'Free Europe!' together with a euphoric crowd. What was happening seemed impossible, magical, powerful, like an experience of enlightenment shared with thousands, perhaps millions of other people. Everything seemed possible then as we were finally free to live and think, to do things, to invent things, because, as the Solidarnosc people said on the TV, 'We are now in our own home.' Since then many things have happened, mostly disappointing my dreams. Europe is free from Soviet domination but it can be quite a sinister place – the mass murders in former Yugoslavia are a chilling illustration of my point. The Berlin Wall fell but an invisible wall remains, often making it difficult if not impossible to engage in meaningful cooperation with Western partners or to take responsibility for a shared future. The wall is external – we, Easterners, encounter many problems with making our voice heard in the West. It is also internal – we act as if we wanted to appropriate the most orthodox, old-fashioned and dogmatic Western ideas in our countries and as if we had nothing to say on our own. I still live and work in Poland, the country of the raging hypocrisy of the epoch of the First Secretary Edward Gierek, the country of the heroic solidarity of Solidarnosc ... I feel that many aspects of the Polish culture are yet to be revealed, many epochs are yet to come.

The traditional view on transition

Discourses of economic reform in Central and Eastern Europe (CEE) place a significant emphasis on the adoption of mainstream Western management theories and the development of managers whose skills and competences mimic those of the Western manager. Western consultants and academics are called upon to prescribe 'the best way' for managing organizational and personal change as well as the values that are to govern the 'reformed' enterprise, its managers and employees (Jankowicz, 1993; 1994; Kelemen, 1999; Kostera, 1995a,b). However, the 'best way' does not always account for differences in the economic, political and socio-cultural backgrounds of Eastern

European countries (Czarniawska-Joerges, 1994a; Kozminski, 1993). The too often hegemonic vision of American management knowledge, which is the most dominant mainstream approach in Western management, attempts to insert a 'one best way' in Eastern Europe, that overlooks the fact that certain managerial and organizational practices developed locally may be more appropriate and indeed more effective within this particular setting (Kelemen, 1999).

After over ten years of various projects aimed at cooperation, inclusion, mutual understanding or just plainly commerce and numerous conferences, publications, (inter-)governmental actions and plans, can we now speak of a maturation of the East–West integration discourse and relationship? Both East and West Europeans are conscious of the 'other half's' existence and soon the European Union (EU) may embrace its first East European members. Therefore it is important to re-evaluate and rethink the lessons we have learned since the fall of the Berlin Wall. This book is dedicated to such conscious reflections and self-reflections, by Western and Eastern (and borderline: those who are natives of Eastern Europe but work in the West and vice-versa) authors. There still is and there always will be a division between the East and the West. However, this division is no longer an insurmountable obstacle but a resource to be drawn upon in positive and productive ways by both parties.

Making sense of the transition

This book offers, with the help of a cultural perspective, an understanding of the mentality in which management ideas are embedded in the East European countries undergoing what is often referred to as processes of transition. We focus on the role played by knowledge and power in the construction of social reality and are interested in the complex relation between societal and organizational practice and individual and group identity.

The book is based on a model of transition that traces ideas in use to both past and present as well as to Western and local knowledge. Actors interpret ideas in use through an identification of what they do and through attempts at making the existing processes meaningful and recognizable. Through their talk and action, they construct the everyday reality of the transition to a market economy. This book seeks to present these processes and ideas without the normative frame typical of mainstream management literature. In other words, this book is about how things are and how they could be, but not about how they should be. There is no 'one best idea' about how reality should be; in fact, these ideas differ from individual to individual, from organization to organization, from context to context. The role of normative discourse differs from, and indeed may be contrary to the role of understanding. The latter is crucial for reflection. Without understanding there is no reflection or imagination – both are necessary for the art of creative management (Morgan, 1993).

This book brings together a collection of articles that question the centrality of mainstream Western management orthodoxy in the constitution and expression of identity at both organizational and individual level in Eastern Europe. The commonly accepted position that mainstream Western management thought (disseminated typically via consultancy models) is crucial to the success of economic reform in Eastern Europe is problematized together with the universality of such models and the mechanistic ways in which they have been exported to, and tried out in, Eastern European organizations. Generally speaking, we subscribe to the common view that economic policy should be formulated in light of global economic priorities and concerns, but we also argue in this book that economic reform must first and foremost subscribe to and be commensurable with local societal and cultural values. These two types of requirements, one derived from technical rationality, the other one from cultural expectations are not necessarily incompatible.

The structure of the book is based on the model of management in transition shown in Figure 1.1. This view suggests that organizational actors make sense of the transition by constantly juxtaposing ideas regarding the past and the present and drawing on both Western and local knowledge resources. The result is typically embedded in the culture; thus culture is our main epistemological metaphor used consistently in the whole book (throughout this book we use Karl Weick's, 1995a, idea of sensemaking in management). Sensemaking at the crossover between these various ideas is understood here as identification, that is, an active quest for something that is relatively stable and recognizable to the individual.

The process of making sense of the transition presupposes the active translation of many concurrent ideas (Czarniawska and Sevón, 1996; Latour, 1986) that move through space: between their own space (local) and the foreign (Western) space, and through time: between their own time (the present) and the time that has passed (the past). Thus, the transition could be reimagined as a complex pattern of the interspatial and intertemporal travels of ideas.

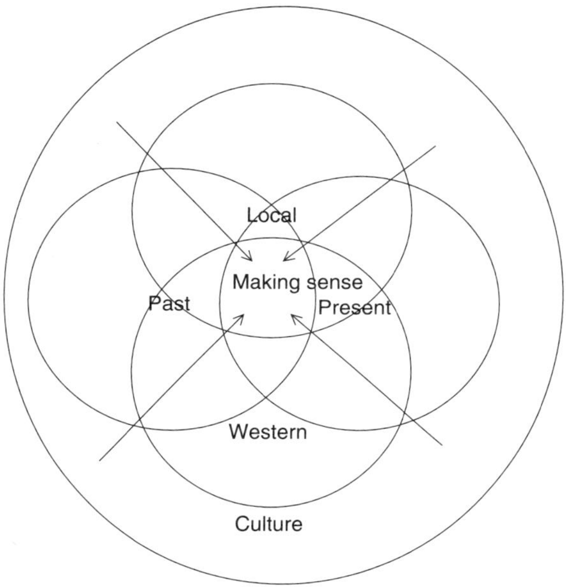

Figure 1.1 Management in transition

The chapters represent a wide geographical spread, including the following countries: Russia and NIS (The Newly Independent States), East Germany, Romania, Bulgaria, Poland, The Czech Republic and Hungary. Some of the researchers are natives of CEE working in Eastern or Western Europe, others are Western researchers. The chapters reflect the current research interest of the individual authors and the international diversity of critical Eastern European management scholarship. The book is focused mainly on the relationship between Western and local ideas and how they influence and are being influenced by current ideologies, power relations, and discourses. Section 1 entitled, 'Stories of Change: Organizing Identities' takes a macro perspective and analyses current changes taking place in organizational and management practices; Section II, entitled 'Stories of The Past: Lost And Found Identities' emphasizes the role played by past and present in the constitution of individual identities. In Section III, entitled, 'Managing the Transition: Crossovers in Practice and Representation', we highlight the potential synergies between local and foreign ways of thinking and organizing.

These three sections correspond with three broad themes. The first theme explores processes of organizational change and their consequences upon organizational identity. The transition to a market economy places a critical emphasis on the development of anti-bureaucratic and flexible forms of organization (Kelemen and Lightfoot, 2000). Thus, the reformed organization is seen to espouse values which are a far cry from those promoted by the socialist enterprise. The latter stressed collective ownership, equality between employees, meeting the requirements of the central plan, and the effectiveness of managers as state administrators. On the contrary, the reformed organization builds upon values emphasizing individual responsibility, market competition and managerial entrepreneurship (Kelemen and Hristov, 1998). The first part of this book explores the processes by which, and the extent to which, organizational and management practices in Eastern European adhere to such values. Both successful and failed cases are drawn upon in order to highlight the complexities involved in cultural change and the indeterminate and unpredictable nature of its outcomes.

Anna Soulsby, for example, in the chapter entitled 'The Impact of Societal Transformation on Czech Managers: A Study of Post-Communist Careers' explores the changing patterns of Czech managerial careers and the ways they have been affected by structural, societal factors as well as individual decision-making. In Chapter 2, 'Geographic Space, Banking Knowledge, and Transformation', Herbert Kalthoff explores the ways in which international commercial banks draw up 'feasibility studies' on which they base their decision to expand their operative network in Central and Eastern Europe through the establishment of branch offices and subsidiaries. He argues that such studies are by no means objective ways of classifying space in economic terms; rather they are highly subjective and rhetorical. Karin Svedberg Nilsson tells a story of how new accounting practices affected the power relationships between two organizations, thereby encouraging organizational reconstruction. Her chapter is based on a case study of a Western acquisition in the former German Democratic Republic. The new accounting practices led to changes in internal power relationships and consequently to a transformation of individual and organizational identities. In the chapter 'From Social Movements to Identity Transformation' Iris Aaltio-Marjosola, Lembit Turnpuu, and Mari Kooskora advocate an identity-based understanding of management education. Their comparative study of Finnish and Estonian values documents the ways in which management education serves as a tool of identity making for the individuals involved.

The second theme focuses on the impact of the transition upon the cultural context and heritage from the past in the experiences of managers, entrepreneurs, and other (more peripheral and marginalized) categories of individuals such as women, the unemployed, and the retired. Competent managerial and entrepreneurial behaviour is considered essential to a successful reform, and so it is important for the way in which individual professional identities are being constituted. Individuals who respond positively and conform to these expectations are constituted as central to the effective functioning of the economy and rewarded accordingly, while those who do not conform are marginalized (via economic and social mechanisms) and pushed to the periphery of the society (women, for example) (Kelemen and Lightfoot, 2000). We do not believe in the division between core and peripheral identities – we challenge the construction of such a division by providing insights into the complex ways in which individuals, be they managers, entrepreneurs, unemployed or women, interpret the transition to a market economy and cope with its complexities on a daily basis.

Aneta Pavlenko in her chapter entitled 'Socioeconomic Conditions and Discursive Construction of Women's Identities in Post-Soviet countries' focuses on the concept of womanhood as it is constituted, transformed and redefined in post-Soviet discourses. The chapter compares the political and economic situation of women in Soviet and in post-Soviet times, linking socioeconomic conditions to the discursive positions assigned to women by existing pre-eminent ideologies before and after 1991. Monika Kostera in the chapter entitled 'Control: Accounting for the Lost Innocence' shows how Polish management students make sense of the term control, often adopting irony, subversion or distrust in the short stories they were asked to write about it. This is related to the recent communist history, where control was by no means a benevolent phenomenon. Mihaela Kelemen in the chapter entitled: 'Re-inventing the Past: Stories about Communism and the Transition to a Market Economy in Romania', organizes her stories in three broad types: stories of regret, emphasizing loss; stories of relief, highlighting optimism for a better future; and stories of uncertainty, contesting whether the path of change from socialism to free-market economy has indeed made a difference to people. This chapter is concerned with the private dimension of the transition, highlighting the important role played by past, present and future in the process of individual sensemaking.

The third broad theme explores the construction of solutions to transitional problems which seem to emerge at the intersection between past and present experiences as well as the interplay between local and imported knowledge. These solutions are in fact ways of coping and work only as long as they allow individuals to place the experience of the transition within their own frames of experience. In most cases, such ways of coping account for both the collective nature of Eastern European societies as well as the individualistic demands of a market driven culture. In 'Local problems and Foreign Solutions: Issues of Management Training in Russia and NIS' Bruno Grancelli explores the problem of whether and to what extent foreign assistance can help form the cultural capital needed for the transition to the market economy in the former USSR. He shows that it can indeed be very useful. Though he believes in the dialogue between East and West, he examines the ways in which East European actors themselves prefer to know about more or less 'orthodox' Western management and to adapt it to their problems. Henriett Primecz presents a case study of an American multinational company operating in Hungary. She focuses on a cross-cultural comparison between expatriates and Hungarians, showing that neither the so-called American business culture nor the authentic local culture has managed to prevail over the other. Thus, there is no integrative culture to speak of. The picture is rather fragmented and ambiguous, but with considerable constructive potential. This culture seems to work well for the actors, therefore the need for 'a strong unified culture' is more of a myth than the desired reality. The last chapter by Jerzy Kociatkiewicz and Monika Kostera shows how Polish actors make sense of the symbolic date of the systemic shift (that is, the collapse of communism in Poland) and how they translate possibilities of change into a space for everyday action. The actors chose to see the shift as something known, under control, rather than discover its innovative potential. The authors look for parallels in the science fiction and fantasy literature – a genre dealing with the impossible and the unheard of. This chapter concludes the book.

An unfinished story?!

As the above overview shows, the book focuses simultaneously on descriptions of practice and representations (what actors do and what they say they do and why (Czarniawska, 2001)), as well as underlying theories. The creative juxtaposition of ideas regarding the construction of the 'transition' is presented as a contextualized yet practically useful process, which allows the authors to trace the role of past and present experiences, local and foreign knowledge in the constitution of the practice and representation of the transition. The chapters are concerned not only with a deeper understanding of the way people act and think in Eastern European organizations; they also attempt to inspire the pursuit of innovative ways of managing and organizing based on a reflexive dialogue between the East and the West. Many of the chapters, without normatively prescribing solutions and telling individuals what they should do, unpack in a creative and reflexive way the context of the transition.

Management recipe books are mainly based on representations, that is, they tell the readers about what successful managers say they do. Researchers have repeatedly shown that managers do not do what they say (see, for example, Mintzberg, 1975). The reason why they say one thing and do another is that practice and representation are based on a different kind of knowledge, or, some would claim, on different kinds of logic (Czarniawska, 2001). Barbara Czarniawska explains that the logic of practice is constructionist, 'that is, it creates and recreates its own rules in each instance of use' (p. 256). It is concrete, typically based on tacit knowledge, often uses narrative knowledge and has pragmatic or aesthetic evaluation criteria. The logic of representation tends to follow formal rationality – it employs ostensive definitions (fixed definitions that say 'what reality is really like'). It is abstract, rhetorically accomplished, and uses stylized narrative knowledge, and formal rationality as main organizing devices. Furthermore, theory is different from both practice and representation, even though it may reflect on both. Theory tends to hide its rhetorical dimension, making claims to use formal logic. The burgeoning number of management recipe books, that is, books not acknowledging the distinction between practice, representation, and theory abound on the market and do, in our opinion, more harm than good. At best, the advice they offer could be regarded as nice aeroplane reading, at worst, if taken seriously, they may trigger in the Easter European manager a bad conscience and feelings of inferiority. The way management and organization practices are represented in such books cannot be translated into practice whether we talk about the East or the West.

In this book we avoid telling the actors what they should and should not do. Instead, we present stories of practices, collections of representations (how individuals portray themselves), and theories (how researchers portray their subjects) in order to construct a conceptual model of the transition, which can be used by researchers and practitioners to reflect upon and contextualize their experiences.

If archetypes and stereotypes are embedded in mentality, their understanding require first and foremost an unpacking of such mentality, a position which is very much lacking in mainstream literature on Central and Eastern European countries. This is, we believe, both the conceptual and practical (in terms of innovative practice) value of a critical and postmodern approach to Central and Eastern European studies.

Part I

Stories of Change: Organizing Identities

2
Geographic Space, Banking Knowledge, and Transformation

Herbert Kalthoff

Introduction

This chapter is intended as a contribution to the analysis of those decision-making processes within the banking industry that lead to the structuring of operative units. The chapter's subject matters are 'feasibility studies' on the economic potential of the geographic space ('countries' and 'regions') in which banks plan the structuring of their geographic presence. In the case at hand, this will be exemplified by the situation of international commercial banks in Central and Eastern European countries, the so-called transformation countries.[1] The empirical material for this study was gathered via participant observation in two international banks in Poland and Bulgaria over several months. Further I conducted interviews with senior staff and employees responsible for Central Europe in bank headquarters in Frankfurt on Main and Munich and in subsidiaries and/or branch offices in Warsaw, Prague, and Sofia. Added to these were interviews with the corporate banking department and risk management staff in the headquarters of a French commercial bank in Paris.[2]

From a sociological vantage point, expert economic reports are interesting for several reasons. In this chapter I will concentrate on just one area, namely the production of knowledge in decision-making situations involving a degree of uncertainty. I shall question whether procedures and negotiation processes are implemented in banking practice to enable statements to be made concerning potential economically prosperous regions. More specifically, the problem of generating knowledge for reducing present uncertainty is that banking people operate in a 'boundary realm' of knowledge – in the sense of 'liminal knowledge' (Knorr-Cetina, 1999). This 'boundary realm' is determined by what can already be said and by what is not yet perceptible. The problem of uncertainty lies precisely in the fact that the foundation necessary for making an optimal decision is unknown. (For managing uncertainty within the credit processes of the banking industry in central Europe see Kalthoff, 2000.)

Over and above that, the way the banking industry interprets economic and sociodemographic data is of interest because in modern societies, the banking industry is considered to be the sphere in which the idea of economic rationality has gained particular acceptance. Banks act in a precise, calculated, and foresighted manner on the basis of the efficient and chronologically successive management of the collection and processing of information and decision-making. First, observation of the process surrounding the production of expert reports permits the microanalytical examination of the assumption that we are dealing with a specific information technology that allows rational control of a business enterprise, bringing about rational decisions under highly uncertain conditions. Second, it enables one to gain insight into how uncertain decisions are assigned plausibility. The rhetorical means economic practice uses to convince itself are of central interest in this connection.

This chapter poses questions from a constructivist vantage point: in what way do banks observe economic activities in geographic space? What material do they fall back on and what rules can be discerned according to which this material is ordered? In what way does the manner in which this material is presented produce evidence for the decision-making process? The aim of this chapter is to investigate the ways in which the banking industry appropriates an economic area, and in doing so, to investigate the rhetorical means that make decisions plausible as *ecographic knowledge*.[3]

In economic theory, various answers have been formulated to the question of how decisions, considered sensible ex post facto, can be made under highly uncertain conditions. The introduction of the theorem of uncertainty into economic theory – for instance by Menger, Knight or Keynes (see Beckert, 1997, pp. 60–78; Wubben, 1993) – was directed at the (neo)classical assumption that market participants had complete knowledge at their disposal for their investments. Since then, uncertainty is considered a central dimension of economic activities along with an asymmetrical information structure, which in the extreme case leads to market failure.[4]

From the point of view of system theory, the problem of uncertainty and with this the problem of foreseeing and redeeming expectations originates from the phenomenon of double contingency. The problem of uncertainty is solved by reducing complexity. However, in order to reduce complexity, on the one hand, the economic system relies on rigid methods and selection processes that identify risks; on the other hand, it backs 'programs' that control exchange processes between the economic system and its environment as well as facilitating the interpretation of prices for allocative decisions. In the economic system uncertainty is therefore processed via the medium (money) and through the form (organization) (see Luhmann, 1981, 1994).

Research on decision-making processes within organizations is carried out primarily according to two schools of thought: the school of behavioural science, on the one hand, and the school of neoinstitutional organizational research, on the other hand (see Kieser, 1994). Research based on behavioural science focuses in particular on the analysis of organizational programs and methods that produce meaningful interpretations and decisions. It criticizes the standard model of decision-making theory, according to which organizations exclusively collect relevant information in an efficient manner; this kind of information management then permits the expectation of rational decisions. In contrast, empirical investigations show that the simple model of the way information is used in decision-making processes within organizations ignores the difficulties with which they are confronted even in obtaining information in the first place (see Feldmann and March, 1998; March, 1994).

Contrary to the assumption that organizations are characterized by heterogeneous structures, neoinstitutionalism forces acknowledging the homogeneity of organizations produced by an institutional isomorphism that assumes compulsory, normative, or mimetic character in the field of organizations. 'Coercive isomorphism' results from hierarchical organizational relationships and cultural dependencies; its mimetic form is a reaction to uncertainty in the form of an imitation; and its normative form obtains its validity through the professionalization of occupational characteristics (see DiMaggio and Powell, 1991). Neoinstitutionalism may emphasize those field effects that produce conformism and homogeneity and thus make transactions easier, but at the same time it does not provide answers to questions about organizational dealings with dynamic and complex environments or with the unintended consequences of organizational decisions (see Sackmann, 1991).

Numbers – processed into tables and choropleth maps – are the main means of representing the geography of economic activities and commodities in expert reports. In the following, description and analysis refer to the numeric representation of the economic space and to the associated modes of ordering and evaluating. The geography of socioeconomic data is documented and proved using maps. The cartographic representation of the economic space is analysed as rhetoric that, on the one hand, follows defined conventions of representation, and on the other hand, by emphasizing difference and homogeneity, is capable of producing evidence relevant for decision-making.

The numeric representation of space

It is not new for business enterprises to analyse the economies of countries in which they intend to establish operations. This does not hold true exclusively for the banking industry, but rather for all business enterprises in general, in particular if they operate on a global scale. The basis for geographic expansion are business decisions regarding in which countries and regions business activities shall be intensified, consolidated or reduced. The decisions are part of the economic control of corporate enterprises, who use these decisions to adjust their own geographic network of operative units to new economic opportunities. The political decision by international banks to extend their presence in Central and Eastern European countries is closely connected to the emergence of a uniform European market. The conceptional language of the banking industry says that the geographic space of Europe shall be 'covered' by branch offices, representative offices or subsidiaries. The purpose of this is to be able to 'support' internationally active corporate clients at central locations on the continent as a 'European bank'. The aim is to erect a 'location network' that allows the banks to largely ignore the nation-state borders within Europe.[5]

Apart from a few exceptions, international banks have established subsidiaries in Central European countries according to the respective national law and placed their 'headquarters' in the countries' capital cities. In their general operational plan, the executive boards of the subsidiaries define the 'target clients' and 'target sectors' in the business community and conduct an initial geographic orientation. One plan says, for instance: 'Beside Warsaw, the Bank has to find zones of economic development within the regions of Poznan, Gdansk, Krakow ... Because of the little progress in regions near the Eastern frontiers and Central-Poland, the Bank holds back its engagement in these regions.'[6] The approximate determination of the banking geography shows that the participants have narrative knowledge (see Czarniawska, 1998) that allows them to estimate the relationship between potential banking activity and the regional economy.

Members of the subsidiaries' local management report on the development of activity to the corporate group's executive board who in turn make the pivotal decision regarding the bank's geographic expansion. Thus, the point of departure for the decision concerning 'branching out' is the significance of the geographic space of CEE for business and – linked to this – the orientation of the general operational plan. If the pivotal decision has been made in the worldwide headquarters for the structuring of the 'location network', the expert banking opinions are prepared in the subsidiaries and passed on to headquarters. In one of the cases observed, for example, studies were sent to the responsible members of the supervisory board who themselves occupied senior positions in the worldwide headquarters in Paris and Frankfurt on Main, among other places. In another case, the study was passed on to the responsible board member of the banking group's central management; his staff then checked the study for the completeness of its economic data and for the soundness of its argumentation.

Just what is the problem to be solved by the producers of expert reports? One of money's characteristics is its spatial indifference.[7] When international banks make a decision regarding the structure of their geographic network, they decide at which locations money should be invested, and thus tied up, in a particular area. Thus the decision regarding the localization of money seeks an answer to the question at which locations and at which points in time the allocation of money makes sense or not. In order to provide categories for conferring meaning to investments, countries and regions are dissected, inventoried, homogenized and listed into economic categories and represented in tables and maps. For the banking industry, the significance of expert reports lies in their ability to enhance decisions and to *document* the knowledge that has influenced these decisions.[8] Expert reports achieve this in two ways: first through two forms of the representation of economic prosperity, and second by reducing complex economic developments to a manageable series of socioeconomic circumstances.

Banking knowledge and administrative statistics

When banks analyse regional economies, they normally fall back on publicly available data, which have been collected in a standardized fashion. These data permit the formation of an idea – or objectivizing an existing idea – about how economic activities are distributed throughout the country. Bankers know what they know about regional economies from the observations, surveys and registrations that transform the economic world into a standardized order of numbers. These numbers result from a chain of translations in which a large number of institutions are involved (see Latour, 1990).

Within the context of the discussion on the third 'significance of the space' – the 'fixation' in space – Simmel (1992, pp. 705–16) described the contribution made by the 'public registration' of mobile and immobile objects to finding them in space. Independent of whether it is a piece of real estate or a building, a ship or a car, an individual or a business enterprise – predefined and thus identifiable units are registered in one list or another. On the one hand, registration, which always requires formalization and homogenization through national law (see Desrosières, 1993), facilitates finding an object in public space (for example, with the aid of ordinal numbers); on the other hand, it facilities the clearing up of claims (for example, concerning mortgages); and finally, it facilitates the listing, calculation and classification of economic and demographic data. Besides government offices (for example, statistical offices), other public institutions (for example, chambers of commerce) and private organizations (for example, market research institutes) also collect, store and publish special data.[9] The purpose of public registration is not solely to collect data and to transform them in a specific way but to assign these transformed data to political–administrative units of the country. On the basis of these territorial taxonomies, which are stable and precise, it is then possible to produce a profile of the regions – and this in reference to very disparate dimensions (see Desrosières, 1994).

The problem with the systems of numbers of public registers is that they elude verification and can only be examined with regard to their internal plausibility: although bankers have a reference system at their disposal, what they lack is that, so to speak, which the numbers are intended to represent. Thus the banking industry's observation is founded on fiction to be able to effect economic development solely on the basis of non-verifiable 'large numbers' (Desrosières, 1993), through which the future shall be made predictable and able to be planned (see Porter, 1995, p. 43).[10] Or in Latour's (1999, p. 29) words: public sector economists 'master the [economic] world, but only if the world comes to them in the form of two-dimensional, superposable, combinable inscriptions'.

The documentation departments of the bank headquarters in European capitals now collect all available and relevant data, process them and prepare information dossiers on request.[11] In contrast to this practice, in CEE bankers must manually collect the material they need for the preparation of expert reports from various public registers and if necessary supplement this material. In Bulgaria in particular the bankers (and the visiting observer) were intensely occupied obtaining any information at all for the study. They repeatedly consulted domestic (for instance the statistical office, the agency for privatization and municipal administrations) and international administrative offices (for instance the economic departments of Western embassies). The futile search for material leads, for example, to the inability to verify the positive trend of the GNP or the negative trend of the inflation rate with figures from the previous year (see, for example Table 2.1). The availability of figures does not solely presuppose an open information policy by the corresponding institutions, but rather it is also dependent on the standardization of operative (e.g. bookkeeping) and statistical accounting (data aggregation). From the banks' vantage point, the transposition of the 'reporting' is particularly important so that the economic and commercial categories share the same meaning and the figures contain readable information.[12]

In one case, in which the 'feasibility' of banking shops in supermarkets was investigated, the non-availability of figures was compensated for by an inquiry carried out by a ministry for internal purposes: in order to justify the authorization of supermarkets, the ministry questioned consumers about their buying habits and their acceptance of the new 'hypermarkets'. In another case, the lack of regional figures on the GNP was replaced by a calculation of purchasing power.

The absence of standardized statistical accounting can, however, only partially explain the intermittent flow of information. This is added to by the phenomenon of non-cooperation, which can be described as a 'loose coupling' of organizational units (see Weick, 1995b, p. 161–73). In the cases I observed, the subsidiary banks did not cooperate with the research or documentation departments of corporate groups, nor did the departments of the subsidiary bank cooperate amongst themselves. In one bank in particular, despite support by the managing director, employees attempting to obtain information from the customer service department met with resistance that strikes one as odd: scheduled meetings did not take place or when they did, their duration was restricted; client lists that could provide information on the geographic distribution of economic activities were not made available; and information on bank products in special demand were not passed on.

Table 2.1 A comparison of regions on the basis of incomplete data

Region	GDP (in Bill. USD)		Foreign Direct Investment (in Mill. USD)			Economic Activities 1996 (in %)		
	1996 %	1997 %	up to 1997	No.	%	Industry	Trade	Tourism
Bourgas	18.7		27.891	357	2.32	18.04	13.3	18.0
Haskovo	N/A		37.958	489	3.15			
Lovetch	12.73		77.530	288	6.44	12.50	9.0	3.0

How can this non-cooperation be interpreted? I would like to present two aspects: first, the behaviour by the customer service department corresponds to the principle which is referred to as 'deontology' or 'Chinese Wall' in banking circles. According to this principle, the departments of a bank operate separately and only exchange information within a specified framework. Second, it emerged that at this particular time the customer service department was working on its own recommendation for a branch office network: the dissemination of information would have meant undermining the plausibility of its own recommendation.

Economic inventory-taking and temporal–spatial ordering

The representation and evaluation of economic space is based on the analysis and transcription of data available from official or private-enterprise sources. Banking practice consists primarily of compiling activities, which join together and systematize material from very different sources. These activities are subject to a central topological rule for the inventory-taking of an economy: the geographic space ('region') is treated as an ensemble of surfaces which border one another, but yet are distinguished from each other (see Thrift and Olds, 1996). In referring to this topological rule, two modes of inventory-taking can be distinguished: the first mode is directed at the (simultaneous) distribution of economic commodities and activities to these surfaces and at their localization. The second mode includes those economic processes of exchange that take place beyond boundaries: this involves the mobility of capital and commodities. Both of these modes inventory economic space using categories and figures according to administrative statistics as well as lists drawn up at a local level and oriented towards addresses.[13] A further central condition of economic inventory-taking consists in the temporal order of the figures: for bankers, only in a time comparison do the figures assigned to economic ratios generate a background of economic development that can be read and interpreted.

In the first mode ('simultaneous distribution') the country is divided up into a multitude of socioeconomic categories – categories that document the distribution of a defined value at a calculated amount. However, before the collected figures are compiled and completed code number for code number, the central business segments of the regions are listed. The GNP and the growth rates of business sectors belong to the general economic indicators. The inflation rate also counts as an important economic indicator for transformation countries: its development over time provides bankers with information about a country's economic policy, about the stability of a country's currency and about the purchasing power of the population.

Aside from the total population and the population density of regions, which indicate potential regional 'markets', in particular purchasing power, the rate of unemployment and the infrastructure (for example, transport routes) are listed as human geographic indicators. This also includes the characterization of important regional centres that exhibit exceptional economic features (for example, industrial sub-centres). This is important in so far as it enables identifying remnants of real-socialist economy (for example, chemical or military production facilities), which are excluded as potential branch office locations.

Lists of corporate clients drawn up locally – lists which reflect the specific economic geography of the bank – function as the second column of the inventory-taking of economic space. In one bank, a comprehensive list containing the names of nearly 800 potential corporate clients was drawn up. The list's columns contained the following information: national origin of the business enterprise; name and address of the primary shareholder; name, address ('headquarters'), size and turnover of the business enterprise as well as the geographically responsible bank branch and contact person in the bank (including his/her language proficiency). The list represents a theory of the spatial situating of economic activities as well as a classification of the actors into the bank's concept.

Flows of commodities and capital come into view in the second mode of inventory-taking. Increasing or decreasing export levels or the foreign trade balance are cited because the demand for domestic products provides information about product quality and can lead to increased investments in successful sectors. What is central, however, is the determination of investment activity, which in the expert reports refers exclusively to direct foreign investments for the following reason: they are regarded by bankers to be a reliable indicator of the attractiveness of the domestic economy; they indicate strengthened (or strengthening) growth and thus a growing market as well as 'trust' by international companies. And finally, large direct foreign investments, also mean that these must be financed; they are in turn financed by commercial banks, who finance the clients who want to invest in these countries. By listing direct foreign investments banks inventory the economic-geographic movement of international clients and thus, their own commitment, because as a corporate group, they have themselves become a part of these business enterprises through various forms of outside financing.

Further, perception of the economy also means observing other economic actors, namely the significant others. As a rule, the observation of banking rivals focuses on foreign banks or large domestic banks with a strategic foreign investor. In addition to the tables on direct investments, lists are drawn up of corporate enterprises who appear as strategic investors in domestic banks; the names of the investors and their participating interest are listed. Maps are also drawn up that depict the financial geography of the competition. With this example, the boundaries of documentation activities and depiction strategies become visible as banks are hardly in a position to make statements concerning the planning of other banks. In such situations rumors, hearsay, assumptions and newspaper reports[14] function as sources of information.

Classification as negotiation and interpretation

The banking industry's division of the regional economy takes place according to a three-way classification. According to the chief executive of a bank, the first category comprises those cities or regions 'where the bank has to be'; 'cities where no full banking service is required' belong to the second category; and the third category consists of all those parts of the country 'where no banking activities are necessary within the next years'.

The problem the bank employees who are to recommend 'first choice' locations in the 'feasibility studies' are now confronted with is that the figures by no means lead to the same assessments and decisions, even if their 'aura of correctness' (Douglas, 1991, p. 151) might suggest this. Accordingly, this ambiguity was explicitly formulated in one expert opinion: 'As can be seen in the conclusion, four locations were recommended; of course, even after studying the documents and data one can come to other conclusions.' The ranking lists drawn up require discursive stabilization in which other departments in the bank participate. How do bank employees now solve the task of recommending locations? An employee in the organization department said the following about the selection process in his bank:

> So the first step was to survey the country. Where are the most important points and how can the largest and most important regions in Poland be covered in four or five places by these branch offices? With this preparation, we arrived at four cities. They were

> Katowice for the whole region in Silesia and the south of Poland including Krakow. At the time I wanted Krakow to be extra, but it wasn't approved. The Wroclaw region, which surprisingly is not only the third largest city but also ranks third in Poland for its GNP and revenue from production. It was Poznan, which basically plays a subordinate role for Poland. I wondered about that, it ranked fourth or fifth. But it clearly ranks first as far as large foreign companies are concerned, above all the German companies. You can't pass Posen over either. The GNP was highest in Katowice. So Katowice, Breslau, and Posen are clearly favoured. The question we have, Gdansk was always talked about. In the end we decided in favour of Gdansk, but Gdansk doesn't matter on its own, it's even washed out behind Szczecin and who knows where. But Gdansk has an advantage: It has a round environment. There's Gdynia for the large companies, there are also large German companies there. Also in Sopot. The people who are going to work there should also open up Elblag, Toru and Bydgoszcz. Then it will really make sense that we're also going to Gdansk. Then Gdansk became fourth place.

Two dimensions are addressed in this quote: on the one hand the linguistic representation of the geographic space, which I would like to call locational rhetoric, and on the other hand the method of decision-making based on figures and geographic knowledge.

Rhetoric of the location

When bankers speak or write about the geographic expansion of their operative units, they use military imagery. They speak of 'bases', 'target areas' and 'target clients' as if they wanted to conquer or occupy an area. Accordingly, geographic space is 'occupied' by branch offices. Once the offices have been established, the area is then under the control of the banking industry. This makes reference to a second aspect: when denoting geographic space, bankers fall back on the synecdoche, a figure of speech in which a part is used for a whole. As in political journalism ('London'), the names of cities like 'Gdansk' or 'Katowice' (see quote above) do not only refer to the city itself, rather they always refer to the entire region. For a bank, to be in 'Warsaw' does not only mean its presence in a city or a district, but rather its presence in a region. This spatial perspective is linked to the structure of the business: a commercial bank has a different relationship to the spatial distribution of corporate clients than does a savings bank to private customers in a district. For this reason, too, it is sufficient for banks to be present in those cities that for their part represent the economic space of the country.

This mode of conceiving of economic space as a network can be interpreted as a second topological rule that banks use to order their own map rather than the economy. Accordingly, the 'bases' constitute 'connecting nodes' to corporate clients, to the banks' other operative units, and to headquarters. However, they are also graded hierarchically: the product range of the branch office is arranged according to the quality of the regional economy.[15]

The decision-making process

A city's rank is calculated in the technical process of decision-making. In the above quote, one bank's procedure becomes clear: cities are ranked on the basis of 'large numbers', like for example, GNP or production revenue, that 'cannot be overlooked'. However, it also becomes clear that bankers take other factors that are not necessarily represented in numbers into account. Thus economically weaker cities are upgraded by actors (foreign business enterprises) or a 'wholesome environment'.

In one bank, the regions' ranks were ascertained by a simple process. For ten indicators (including population, investment incentive, industrial production, number of companies with foreign participation) the ranks were recorded in a table corresponding to their values. The results of this table were then summed up in another table, in which the number of the rank 'achieved' was entered into the respective column; the numeric expressions of rank (rank 1, rank 2, rank 3, and so on) were then added up. In this way 'Warsaw' achieved a ranking of '14', 'Katowice' a ranking of '21', and so on (see Table 2.2). The final ranking of the regions results from a comparison of these sums.

The central characteristic of this method, which produces and represents a linear ranking order that is considered objective, is its doing without the weighting of the indicators measured. The assumption of equal weighting assigns equal value to the ranking established for individual indicators in the calculation of the final ranking. In this respect, the participants abstain from the decision concerning the value of for example, 'population density' and 'production output'. The advantage of being able to produce a ranking order by means of a simple arithmetical method is accompanied by the disadvantage of comparing something that is incomparable; however, this is not thematisized in further detail in the expert reports.

Table 2.2 Determination of city ranking by means of simple arithmetic operations

	Population	Population density	Civilian employed gross wage	Average monthly gross wage	Purchasing power	Purchasing power	Number of registered enterprises	Production output	Number of registered enterprises with foreign participation	Investment attractiveness	TOTAL
1 Warsaw	2	2	1	2	1	1	1	2	1	1	14
2 Katowice	1	3	4	1	2	2	2	1	3	2	21
3 Poznan	4	10	3	11	4	4	4	3	2	4	49
4 Gdansk	3	6	14	8	7	5	3	4	4	5	59
5 Krakow	5	4	2	10	12	7	5	5	7	6	63

A distinction must be made between the calculation or determination of ranks and the selection of cities that now come into consideration as locations as the latter does not result exclusively from the established ranking orders. Other considerations have some influence on the decision, such as taking corporate clients or onsite knowledge into account. Thus an important corporate client for instance can influence the bankers' analysis with a decision to invest in a region that occupies a middle position on the bank's ranking list. Thus, 'interesting' GNP figures do not necessarily guarantee an 'interesting target area' for the bank. In the course of the decision-making process the various bank departments formulate interpretations of the current situation and recommendations for the selection of a location that document two different things: first, a variable evaluation of economic data, and second, the existence of different ranking lists circulating within the bank.

An employee in the corporate accounts department writes an intraoffice memorandum in which he recommends a city (or a region) as 'first choice'. His arguments are aimed at the contacts that already exist with international corporate clients, the significance of the city as an industrial centre in the region, the good geographic location, which would also make it possible to support clients in nearby cities. The General Manager makes a handwritten note – 'Very interesting but not the priority' – and passes the memorandum on to the project manager responsible for the planning of the branch network. Nearly two months later the manager of the corporate accounts department writes a memorandum in which he firmly supports the vantage point of his employee. He stresses in particular the activity by the competition, who – or so it is rumoured – intends to open a branch exactly in this city in order to be the first bank there and to acquire 'important' corporate clients. He attaches a short list of corporate clients to the memorandum that contains information about their turnover size, degree of privatization and drawing on credit lines as well as the total volume of credit. A few days later, a senior employee from the organization department sends out a memorandum in which he lists the advantages of another region preferred by himself. The branch had 'the largest companies ... the largest hotels ... the largest agricultural companies' to support. At the same time he named those bank products to be made available in this city and in this way documents the significance of his choice: 'current and deposit accounts for national and international currencies, cash services in national and international currencies ... international transfers (swift) ... treasury transactions.' After the

General Manager had initialed it, this memorandum was also sent to the project manager.

The handwritten notes show that future locations are negotiated and that individual departments attempt to assert their weight in the negotiations. The fact that future locations are negotiated at all, points towards the existence of different maps of economic space that have been created by the individual departments of the bank and which are brought into the decision-making process. However, this example also illustrates that the chief executive comments on the first recommendation against the background of the general operational plan, which already prescribes a relatively exact geographic orientation of banking activity (see above).

Aside from written notes, the bank's local senior staff are consulted verbally. Employees working on the formulation of the expert report attempt to gather the bank's preferences for one or the other region out of comments made by their 'boss', while managers expect expert opinions with plausible recommendations to the deciding committees (supervisory board or executive board) from their employees. Within the context of meetings, however, they also express their doubts: city G. may be interesting, but it certainly does not belong to the first category; an international corporate client who is already being supported by the bank in other countries is present in city B. In this way the employees instructed to carry out the study attempt to discover the 'bank's strategy'. The result is a recursive process of evaluation (see Giddens, 1995, p. 77) that is hierarchically polarized and allows the employees to recommend something they assume would like to be heard at the top.

Interim conclusion

In order for an economy to be evaluated by the banking industry, it must first be placed into an order. The order of the economy adheres to fixed conventions that are self-evident to bankers. This includes the reduction of economic matters and activities to a few values and the 'breaking down' (bankers) of these values to regions. In this way, economic quantities (for example, the GNP) can be ordered and brought together with geographic entities (regions or countries) and time units (calendar years) in the lines and columns of tables. Tables and lists are flexible instruments: they open up a multitude of possibilities of combining and ordering; they bring together things that were previously separate and make things visible that were previously invisible.

For banks, the importance of administrative statistics is that they put the diversity of economic action into a two-dimensional, paper form and thus produce and ensure the unity of a country. Over and above this, official data fulfil the function of being able to make statements about economic space at all. On the one hand, from the vantage point of decision theory the processing of official figures within the context of the banking industry refers to the management of information in modern organizations; on the other hand, from the vantage point of representation theory it refers to the ways in which economic texts, whose central means of representation and review are figures, suggest plausibility.

The ranking list that has been established in an 'objective' manner is institutionally supplemented by negotiations. This process is not characterized by optimum utilization of exclusively relevant information, but rather by its idiosyncratic use. The spatial strategy of the commercial bank arises in this game between different interpretations of the material and corporate policy. Borrowing from Giddens (1995. pp. 199–213) it can thus be said that the geographic positioning of bank branches is a central mediating factor between clients and the bank, on the one hand, and the temporal ranking order of the economically evaluated regions, on the other hand.

Cartographic representation and investment strategy

The economic potential of regions is not solely represented in numeric and table form; in order to depict the spatial distribution of socioeconomic factors, bankers systematically implement cartographic representations for the following reason: the persuasive power of maps lies in their assigned capacity of being able to neutrally depict reality in that they project a three-dimensional world into a two-dimensional form. In this sense, maps are interpreted as a mere depiction of reality: the geography of economic potential corresponds to the way in which the maps show it. The authority of maps is also linked to the idea that they depict reality. This common (not only in the field of geography) way of viewing depictions and neutrality, has been criticized as 'realistic illusion'. According to this critique, maps do not generate a transparent world, but rather a specific form of seeing precisely this world (see, for example, Harley, 1989; Turnbull, 1996).

The maps used in the expert banking reports are not topographical, topological or thematic maps, but choropleth maps.[16] Choropleth maps are a combination of geographic map and statistical data. They take up the concept of national geography which assumes geographic space with stable political borders. According to this concept, the economy is the content or attribute of the territory and its amounts and qualities can be measured in a way that enables making regional profiles visible.

At first glance, the spatial distribution of a specific aspect of the choropleth map becomes obvious: the maps show, for example, a dominance of the service sector in Western Poland, in the capital and in two regional centres (see Map 2.1). When a Western commercial banker looks at these maps, he obtains the unmistakable information that there is 'nothing to get' out of Eastern Poland. In what follows I will deal with the production method of this perspective, two-dimensional order and thus with the production of cartographic images of economic potentials.[17]

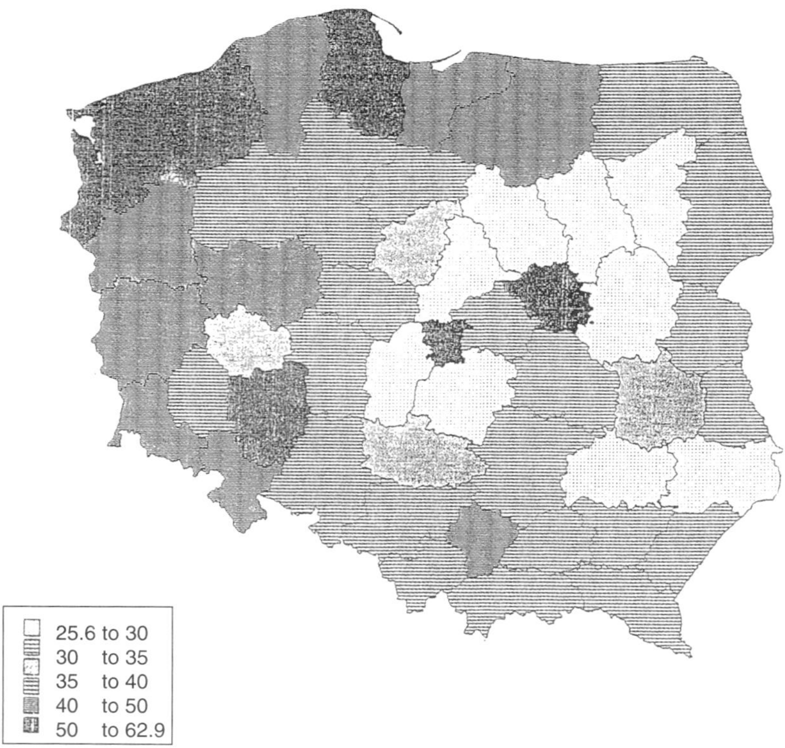

Map 2.1 Map of Poland: the distribution of the service sector (% of the share of the employees)

The production of cartographic evidence

The surface (see Map 2.1) represents the sovereign territory of the state of Poland. The relatively exact representation of the country's borders is carried over into the reproduction of district boundaries (*Woiwodschaften*). The geographic space of the country is completely split up; in this respect it is an 'absolute map' (Geertz, 1996, p. 21). However, at the same time it lacks all of the other characteristics such as the lineal representation of streets, railway lines, rivers, representation of cities or the thematic representation of industry and agriculture.[18] In a choropleth map, the lineal reproduction of the political borders of a country and its political-administrative districts corresponds with the complete omission of the concrete traits of the space; it is mere surface.

Disregarding the socioeconomic geography is the prerequisite for a homogenizing, simplified and contrasting representation of individual socioeconomic factors. On the basis of this decontextualized framework, the choropleth map is vague with respect to the content of the representation: the subject does not follow from the lines or the dotted halftones. Indeed, at first glance one sees only zigzags, arranged symbols and different surfaces, in short: a composition of contoured surfaces. The representation must be recontextualized by a heading before it receives meaning and the reader can understand what he or she sees.[19] What is intended to be shown does not become recognizable until an association is created by means of surface symbols and the heading.

The black and gray shades of the small surfaces ('districts') facilitate differentiation of the density of the characteristics. This ability to differentiate is achieved first through an easily comprehensible number of five or six classes and second through a different dot and line density, which produces the light/dark effects. The map shown here is a classified choropleth map with six intervals.[20] The class intervals begin with the lowest value in the lower stage and close with the highest value in the highest stage. The intermediate stages are at the same distance from each other; the values of the first and last intervals in part greatly deviate from this. Consequently, the medium used to fabricate a spatial pattern of the economy or human geography is not a flawless interval scale. In the next step, for the smaller/larger interval differences, symbols and white and gray shades are established and this is transferred to the administrative-politically defined districts. The transformation of socioeconomic and human geographic data into the surface symbols is done in several steps: data classification of the data symbolizing the data values transfer to the cleaned up map (see Dent, 1990).

The purpose of a choropleth map is to communicate the spatial distribution of economic potential. In order to achieve this, the creation of a choropleth map adheres to a series of set conventions such as, for example, limitation to one characteristic and the negation of any differences within a district and between districts and thus the production of homogeneous economic space. Accordingly, homogeneity is achieved through the selection of all the other characteristics and – linked to this – through a generalizing form of representation that does not produce images of human geographic and economic distributions 'true to location', but rather generalizes aggregated data, and thus suggests the territorial regularity of socioeconomic indicators. This form of representation results in the purely economic interpretation of the political-administrative boundaries, which hardly play a role for banking activities. This means that the depiction of the static surface by means of 'surface symbols' does not illustrate economic differences, but rather it produces them. The graphical logic of the choropleth map, which consists of only being able to identify individual socioeconomic data by concealing all the other dimensions, corresponds with the ability of producing 'visual evidence' (Amann and Knorr-Cetina, 1990), which for its part stabilizes banking decision-making processes.

The choropleth map represents space as a cleaned up and economically surveyed surface; in contrast, a banking group's decision for a location actualizes a dotted spatial model because space is 'covered' by locations and these are linked together to form a network. As is the case with money, a bank actually represents a 'non-spatial object' (Simmel, 1992 p. 693): it is not bound to a specific geographic space, but it never ceases to reconfigure its physical presence through a network of locations and hierarchically ordered relationships.

Investment map and investment strategy

The hypothesis presented here is that the representation of socioeconomic facts in numerical, and, in particular, in cartographic form suggests evidence of economic potential and thus a decision for a location. If this hypothesis is accurate, then the question not only arises concerning how the representations guide the discussion (see above), but also their relevance for determining action. What investment strategies can be observed? Do Western banks adhere to the evidence that they construct themselves?

There is strong indication that the financial institutions of interest here base their decisions regarding concrete investment strategies on a matrix composed of the following elements: number of the bank's clients already in the region, investment and general operational plans of these clients or other clients of the banking group, amount of direct foreign investment, the (suspected) strategies of the competition, and the development of the service sector in the region. Everything occurs on this basis in such a way that it appears as if the actors were orchestrated in the realization of their finance geography, without, however, being led by a conductor.

The international banks orient their 'location networks' in Poland to the following cities: Gdansk and Szczecin (northern, northwestern districts), Poznan and Wroclaw (western districts), Katowice and Krakow (southwestern districts) and parts of Lodz (central Poland). In Bulgaria the following cities are taken into consideration for possible locations: Varna and Bourgas (Black Sea coast), Plovdiv (southeastern district) as well as Rousse and parts of Lovetch (northeastern districts). There is nevertheless a certain amount of variation regarding decision-making: one bank decides for Gdansk and against Szczecin, the other for Krakow and against Katowice and Lodz. These different decisions do not call the matrix into question, rather they are an example of the fact that relatively similar pieces of information (can) lead to different decisions at a local level.

The division of a country into city regions has the advantage that these can be combined with or disassociated from one another. The result of this dividing practice is a three-stage classification of the regions: there are 'directly covered' regions, 'indirectly covered' regions, and regions not linguistically described in the expert reports, but which are represented on the maps as lighter surfaces. From the vantage point of the participant, the regional division and classification of a country is not only necessary in order to be able to bring about decisions, but rather to make the geographic space of a country manageable and controllable in general. A network of selected points originates in this way; the spatial distance between them is the function of banking geography.

What is striking about Poland is that the new locations – with the exception of Lodz – are all in a geographic space with a strong occidental tradition. Moreover, a semantic intensification can be observed in banking evaluation practice: the selected locations represent positive economic development, education and modernity, whereas the eastern part of Poland with its agricultural structure is identified with a pre-modern way of life.

Conclusion

The point of departure for these considerations were empirical observations which indicated that international commercial banks draw up 'feasibility studies' on which they base their decision to expand their operative network in CEE through the establishment of branch offices and subsidiaries. Compared with other expert banking reports, these expert opinions are not particularly polished, nor are they limited exclusively to the 'branching out' of Western commercial banks in CEE. New methods that operate on the basis of electronic databases (as, for instance, 'Geographic Information Systems', see Leyshon *et al.*, 1998) also promise more exact matching of population profiles and bank products. However, expert banking reports also represent a specific form of economic reporting and scrutinizing within the context of decision-making processes in organizations. These organizational procedures are an example of how diverse facts are transformed into figures that, however, for their part also allow looking at the economic 'facts' they represent from a new perspective.

This is a perspective that one can take up with Latour (1999, pp. 69–74). It allows the deciphering of the chain of representations, the transformation of facts into figures and the crossing over of their movements. The representation process moves in successive steps as a movement of reduction and a movement of intensification. However, how bankers can 'see more' through general economic ratios remains a phenomenon which is still not quite clear. This gap is created by the orientation towards translation processes on the one hand, and the production and circulation of documents on the other hand. In order to close the gap I fall back upon the phenomenological notion of 'appresentation' (see Husserl, 1950/1992, pp. 111–23; Schütz, 1971). It appears suitable for expressing the specific phenomenon, in fact the competence of the bankers' economic interpretation.[21] In this sense bankers not only see the numbers cross-tabled with ratios and periods of time, which are unable to state anything without these relations, but rather also that which is not present nor ever will be. This means that bankers always see more than what is actually being represented. Because the economy will always remain inaccessible in its totality, it requires semiotic representation; bankers (and other economists) process their knowledge and their decisions more and more on the basis of a numeric representation of the external world. These number symbols are appresenting objects that refer to appresenting economic activities.

Appresentation is based on the stock of knowledge of the actors. In this case it is in particular the theoretical knowledge about the meaning and the mathematical definition of general economic ratios that has some influence on the representation of the economy, accompanied by an understanding of how the numbers are to be read. In the case of the interpretation of numbers by the banking industry, the background of the practice of economic interpretation is the economic theory that leaves its mark on the ratios.

What is central for banking ecography is the simplicity of the database which is uncertain and cannot be scrutinized. However, it is precisely these carefree and simple forms that allow decisions to be arrived at and justified. This does not imply that the actors falsify or substitute economic reality. Rather the methods described are ways of using economic representation that are central to the successive reduction of complexity. A further aspect is linked with this: it is characteristic for bankers to have infallible belief – the doxa of the field according to Bourdieu (1979: pp. 318–34) – in the meaning and importance of expert opinions. Without verification of the asserted evidence through material, it is decided for example, that the bank must go to Poland or to this or that city. The 'success' of future business then confirms the decision and thus the pattern: the bank had to go there in order to be able to show that the bank had to go there. In other words: the banking industry systematically participates in making its own predictions come 'true'. The decisions are nonetheless not 'once-and-for-all' decisions, but rather they are linked with a self-fulfilling prophecy that does not correspond with the standard model of organizational rationality. The determination of the location network is not irrational because of that; rather in its concrete realization it adheres to an independent rational logic.

Notes

1. In this chapter, the terms 'Central Europe' or 'Central and Eastern Europe' are used as approximate geographic descriptions. There is therefore no presupposition of 'mythical coherence' (Bourdieu, 1982 p. 231) as if there were 'a Central Europe' or anything like a cultural or economic unity of different countries. See Schultz (1989) for a critique in this regard.
2. Within the scope of my field research, in the first bank (Warsaw) I was assigned, among others, to the member of the executive board responsible for management control and thus for the structuring of the branch office network and the so-called 'banking shops'. In the second bank (Sofia) I was assigned to an employee responsible exclusively for the structuring of a new branch office network and whose supervisor was the managing director.
3. This term describes those methods employed to make an inventory of, classify and interpret economic facts. This involves the analysis of concrete

market activities, but not a market theory. The topic of this chapter is the practice of *ecography*. In particular McCloskey (1994) has investigated the ways economic discourse employs rhetorical methods and narrative strategies to effect persuasion.

4. In reference to the phenomenon of 'information asymmetry', the information economy in particular has modelled various modes of behaviour (such as 'adverse selection', 'principal agent' or 'moral hazard') which provides the participants with a lead on information to play their advantage off against the business partner (see Schumann, 1992).
5. The introduction of new communications technologies in many of the banks' business segments has had a lasting impact on the function of the branch office to control market access and generate knowledge (see Leyshon *et al.*, 1998). The closure of operative units in Western European countries and the simultaneous structuring of a new network in Central and Eastern Europe do not, however, represent a paradox, but rather constitute two sides of the same coin.
6. In documents of the banks the names of Polish cities are written in English, Polish or German language. This has not been corrected in this chapter.
7. Following Simmel (1991/1900) who attributes the indifference of money to a 'lack of quality or non-individuality' (Simmel, 1991, p. 127; own translation). However, spatial indifference is not tantamount to a lack of movement; rather the movement corresponds to the dual character of money (Simmel, 1991, p. 211).
8. Baecker (1998) emphasizes the legitimizing aspect of comprehensive information processing. It allows classifying complex decisions as correct at a later date due to their having been made based on accessible information.
9. In the banking industry there is a large number of organizations that observe the individual banks, bank products and banking systems. Auditing firms, rating agencies and even large commercial banks themselves are among these organizations. Merill Lynch, for example, published such a report in May 1996 with the title 'Polish Banks. Polishing Up Their Act'.
10. The numbers are not to be violated and are inviolable. This also applies to reports by other economic organizations, who draw attention to the fact that they publish the numbers 'assuming no liability'. The report mentioned above by the well-known agency Merill Lynch says: 'The information herein was obtained from various sources; we do not guarantee its accuracy.' Thomson's BankWatch ('Banking System Update-Poland' dated 20 May 1996) says: 'The information contained herein is derived from publicly available sources and Thomson BankWatch, Inc. makes no representation as to the accuracy or completeness of such information.'
11. In the case of a French commercial bank, in 1995 18 employees were working in a documentation centre where according to their director they processed more than two thousand inquiries a month coming from various departments and units throughout the banking group.
12. Within this context the countries of Central and Eastern Europe have adopted very different strategies of standardization (see Garrod and McLeay, 1996; Dunn in this volume).
13. According to Klüter (1986, p. 109) an address 'constitutes a code that for that purpose permits making sufficiently precise statements about a posi-

tion in a segmental, linearly ranked structure: first name, last name, house number, street, municipality, postal code, country' (own translation).

14. One headline read, for example, 'Raiffeisen Centrobank To Open Further Branch Offices' (*Prawo I Gospodarka*, 5 November 1997).
15. In one bank the individual branches were differentiated as 'fully operating branches', 'business promotion centres' and 'representative offices'. In a first phase of geographic expansion, the branch offices of Western commercial banks established in Central Europe since 1998 were opened as 'fully operating branches'; a differentiation of the 'bases' is not scheduled until the second phase of 'branching out' activities.
16. Choropleth maps can certainly also be referred to as quantitative, topical maps. The term 'choropleth maps' is 'derived from the Greek words *choros* (place), and *pleth* (value). Choropleth mapping has also been called *area* or *shaded* mapping' (Dent, 1990, p. 146; italics in the original). The investment guides for Central Europe published by market research institutes also make use of choropleth maps for a variety of purposes (for example, Deutsch–Polnische Wirtschaftsförderungsgesellschaft (German–Polish Association for Economic Promotion), 1996).
17. Amann and Knorr-Cetina (1990) have investigated this evidence construction based on scientific research in a laboratory for human biology.
18. Mark and Csillag (1989) distinguish between the following geographic lines: mathematical lines (for example, degrees of longitude and latitude), legally defined lines (for example, political borders), linear characteristics (for example, streets, railway lines, rivers), lines on the earth's surface (for example, coastlines) and boundaries of aerial distinction (for example, climatic regions).
19. Following Wittgenstein (1984, p. 519): 'But we can also *see* the illustration as one thing and then as another – Thus we interpret it and *see* it in the way we *interpret* it.' (Italics in the original; own translation.)
20. See Coulson (1987) for a summary of the discussion on the formation of classes and intervals in the field of cartography.
21. Referring to economic interpretation as practised by foreign exchange dealers, Knorr-Cetina and Bruegger (2002) have used the term 'appresentation' to offset the idea of a separation between market activity and the representation of this market on the dealer's monitors.

3

Accounting for Change: Accounting, Finance, and Changing Methods of Economic Regulation in Post-Socialist Eastern Europe[1]

Elizabeth C. Dunn

> 'Many of the interconnections and interdependences between accounting and the wider context in which it operates go unobserved and are seldom articulated, having become part of accounting as it is. Constituting the silent realm of accounting, their salience becomes apparent only when more radical discontinuities puncture the world of accounting, raising questions about the adequacy of the craft ... Accounting change is therefore never an unproblematic endeavour but rather a process that occurs amidst a complex of other influences that sometimes provide the possibility of such change and sometimes constrain the possibility of it.' (Hopwood, 1992)

The collapse of state socialism and the promises of the postsocialist era have made 'accountability' an acutely felt issue in Eastern Europe, both in the broad senses of 'good governance' and 'transparency,' and in the narrower sense of visible, verifiable financial records. Under socialism, accounting (and, more broadly considered, finance) was a central method of economic and political regulation. As a key technology of the planned economy, socialist accounting promised that its new methods of tracking the movements and uses of property were the keys to both economic development and social equality. Of course, it was a spectacular failure: socialist accounts were notoriously unreliable (Verdery, 1996, pp. 20–1).

The revolutions of 1989 promised greater accountability on the part of government and industry, and hence greater efficiency, more productivity, and a rising standard of living. Yet, despite the mandate for greater accountability, Eastern European governments have been largely unwilling to make radical changes in accounting standards, even though privatization practices and other economic reforms often seem to call for them. Why are the Eastern European governments so reluctant to adopt international accounting standards? Why do national accounting standards show so little change from methods developed under socialism?

In this chapter, I argue that the Eastern Europeans' reluctance to fundamentally reform their accounting systems is not the result of mere obtuseness or national pride, but instead stems from the inherently political nature of accounting in general. Battles over the ostensibly mundane world of accounting, I argue, reveal a great deal about the ways in which various social actors constitute authority, create standards of judgement, and exercise power in the postsocialist context. To make my point, I review the history of Eastern European accounting practices, examine current practices engendered by socialist accounting, and speculate on what the enduring legacy of state socialist accounting means for postsocialist politics, economy and culture. The role played by the past in the construction of the present is a recurring theme in the book.

I frame my argument in the ongoing investigation into accounting as a social (rather than technical) practice. Anthropologists, philosophers and social theorists are finding that far from being neutral reports of empirical facts, accounts and audits are integral and negotiable parts of identity formation and self-presentation among organizations. Producing 'auditable performance' in the name of accountability and transparency affects the members of these organizations, both as they change their practices to produce 'visible' results in these accounts and as they seek to produce accounts that 'bulletproof' themselves by obscuring actions and deflecting criticism (Miller and O'Leary, 1993; Power, 1997; Rose and Miller 1990; Strathern, 1999). The 'audit explosion,' or the introduction of accounting practices into ever more domains of social life, has had a profound influence on the governance of individual action and on the symbolic production of corporate identity, not to mention the overall regulation of the socio-economic system. This is nowhere so true as in Eastern Europe.

The politics of accounting: a case study

In the early 1990s, the economic transformation of Eastern Europe was largely phrased as a problem of property transformation (Major, 1993,

p. 2). In Poland, the problem was diagnosed as one of turning state-owned enterprises into private firms, and then creating a legal and financial framework for the protection of this kind of private property (see Ajani *et al.*, 1992, p. 127; Staniszkis, 1991). This, it was assumed, would jump-start the market economy. However, the Minister of Privatization, Janusz Lewandowski, rapidly discovered that turning state-owned assets into private property was more complicated than in first appeared. 'Privatization,' he famously quipped, 'is when someone who doesn't know who the real owner is and doesn't know what something is worth sells it to someone who doesn't have any money' (cited in Stark, 1991, p. 39).

Although all of the issues that Lewandowski highlighted – ownership, value and capital formation – were problematic, the question of value was perhaps the major stumbling block for the privatization process in Poland. Among the first privatizations to make the technical or economic issue of determining value into a political controversy was that of Alima, a small food-processing company in Rzeszów, where I conducted field research involving interviewing, participant observation and document examination. The controversy centred on the 'true value' of the firm, in terms of an appropriate price to be paid to the Polish state by the foreign companies who were potential purchasers of Alima (see Dunn, 1998). In 1992, when the Ministry of Privatization announced that Alima would be sold for $11 million to the Gerber Products Company of Fremont, Michigan, USA, Alima employees were furious.[2] They accused the Ministry of selling the company at a price far below its 'true value', arguing that $11 million did not reflect the value of the firm's physical assets, much less its brand equity and trained personnel. They also argued that $11 million was not adequate compensation for the firm's future earning potential: after all, they often told me, Alima was one of the most profitable firms in Poland. Some employees questioned the logic behind privatizing and selling the firm at all: 'Why would anyone sell a company that was doing well and making a profit?' asked one Alima employee. 'It just doesn't make sense!' Others accused Lewandowski of corruption. Another Alima worker told me, 'It is absolutely certain that Lewandowski took bribes from Gerber in exchange for accepting their bid for Alima. Why else does Lewandowski keep coming to Rzeszów, and why else would that American from Gerber [Al Piergallini, the CEO] keep coming here? Lewandowski is coming here to accept the latest installment of the bribe!'

When I went to Michigan to interview Gerber executives, I heard a much different version of events. A senior Gerber executive explained Gerber's radically different estimate of Alima's value as a problem of accounting. He argued that although many Poles both inside and outside Alima believed that Alima was profitable, Polish accounting standards had in fact distorted information that would lead to the conclusion that Alima was losing money. He argued that Polish accounting standards booked state subsidies as income rather than investment, that the true costs of production were concealed by state-subsidized prices for inputs, and that Polish accounting methods booked obsolete machinery as still worth its purchase price, thereby concealing its worthlessness. Add in the firm's potential liability for environmental damage, he told me, and Alima wasn't even worth what Gerber paid for it.

These quarrels over accounting may seem trivial, but they are in fact deeply consequential in two ways. First, they have obvious political side effects. After the Alima privatization and several others were called into question, Lewandowski's programme of trade-sale privatizations was halted, and Lewandowski himself was called in front of a Sejm (parliamentary) tribunal and asked to defend himself against charges that he had defrauded the Polish state and betrayed the national interest by selling enterprises at less than their 'true value'.[3] As important as these dramatic side-effects were, however, there were a second set of more subtle and long-term political economic effects. These were not mere side effects of accounting *qua* neutral and objective technical process, but stemmed from accounting's innately political nature and its relation to enterprise governance. 'Political' here is used in the broadest sense of the term, relating not only to the state sphere, but to the organization of power in society. As a political process, accounting thus plays an important role in the reorganization of society and economy in postsocialist Eastern Europe.

Accounting as political practice: West and East

To understand the relation between accounting and politics, it is important to begin with the difference between bookkeeping and accounting. Like bookkeeping, accounting serves a recording function. Bookkeeping is the recording of inventory and transactions – a relatively straightforward, if not particularly illuminating, practice. However, accounting goes beyond bookkeeping to become 'the language of business' (Silbiger, 1993, p. 78). Organizations can use accounting and financial reporting to communicate to shareholders, creditors, employees, government planners and suppliers. Perhaps more importantly, accounts can serve a self-referential function for the organization itself, acting as a self-descriptive means to control, evaluate and plan operations (Silbiger, 1993, p. 78). As such, accounting is the primary tool through which organizations regulate themselves and/or are regulated by others.

Accounting practices and accounting facts, however, are often less self-evident than they present themselves to be. Accounting is deceiving on two levels: the technical and the programmatic (Power, 1997). The technical level is the concrete practice of accounting, as it is carried out in real organizations and real social contexts. The programmatic level, on the other hand, is an idea and set of commitments about a means of problem-solving. On the programmatic level, accounting is an idea, an 'idealized, normative projection of the hopes invested in the practice, a statement of potential rather than a description of actual operational capability. Defining audit is largely an attempt to say what it could be' (Power, 1997, p. 4). The deceptive – and seductive – aspect of accounting arises on the technical level, where accounting facts such as numbers, values and classifications present themselves as empirical realities, despite the fact that they are eminently negotiable artefacts of social relations. Even more deceptive is the fact that there is always an 'expectations gap' between what accounting or auditing is actually capable of and what it is called upon to do, that is, between the programmatic and technical levels. This indeterminacy makes accounting amenable to being imported not only into new institutional contexts such as schools or governments, but into new sociopolitical contexts. This fact is of primary importance when considering how accounting and the idea of accountability are being transformed in the postsocialist era.

The practice of accounting and the production of financial reports depend on questions that – at least in the West – have relatively stable answers. The intended audience for financial reports, the kinds of data required, the uses to which various parties put data, the financial transactions reported, and the forms in which data are recorded are all seemingly predetermined, legitimate and self-evident – if not always technically optimal.[4] Yet, in situations of dramatic economic upheaval such as the transition from state socialism in Eastern Europe, these 'self-evident facts' are revealed as complicated dilemmas. Debates over accounting systems, therefore, reveal not only changes in the economic system but political debates over how the economic system should be reformed and who should be allowed to set the standards for determining value.

During the Cold War period, the answers to questions such as for whom data were created and how they were produced were relatively stable in both East and West. In Eastern Europe, accounting rules were prescribed by government agencies such as planning ministries or ministries of finance. Although there were some differences among countries of the region, accounting rules were generally codified and slow to change (Bailey, 1988: p. 11). For enterprises within each country, accounting rules were rigidly uniform, including regulations pertaining to accounting records, names and content; definitions of accounting terms; valuations of assets; depreciation methods; cash-based budgetary accounting; incomplete accrual enterprise accounting;[5] conservatism in valuing stocks, valuation of capitalized fixed assets; rules for deferred costs and reserves; and the content, format and frequency of financial statements (Bailey, 1988; Jaruga, 1996; Pankov, 1998). In Western countries, although accounting practices could be changed to fit the needs of the enterprise, procedures were also generally stable. Although accounting methods were not prescribed by law, professional accounting organizations prescribed standards and methods, such as GAAP (Generally Accepted Accounting Principles, which vary among countries) or IAS (International Accounting Standards).[6] As new business situations developed, organizations such as the FASB (Financial Accounting Standards Board) wrote new procedures and requirements.[7]

The situation is quite different in post-1989 Eastern Europe, however. The basic objectives of the economic system have changed, but neither the socialist accounting system nor the wholesale adoption of GAAP or IAS standards addresses the problems of the shifting economic terrain (Sochaka and Malo, 1996). The fundamental premises of accounting and financial reporting have been transformed into the following five sets of questions, which are not only heuristic devices with which to analyse accounting systems but matters of both urgency and uncertainty in transition economies:

- *Who are financial reports for?* Particularly in countries undergoing economic transition, the answer to this question is far from obvious. Accounts may be for small investors, for capital markets, for companies themselves, for employees, for investment fund managers or for government planners, each of whom use the data for different ends.
- *What kinds of data do various parties require, and in what form?* As accounting practices become increasingly codified (either by state

decrees, professional organizations or practice), the form that financial reports take is shaped to varying degrees by the demands of different recipients of such data. When one party is more powerful than others, it may have the ability to shape accounting practices in such a way that the data is useful to it and not to others, thus influencing both the capital market and those who can gain entry to it.

- *Why do different parties require different kinds of data?* The answer to this question reveals a great deal about the economic system and its level of development. Is accounting data provided in such a form that it can only be used for macro-economic planning by the government? Can company managers use the data to make decisions about resource allocation or improving efficiency? Do the financial reports make it possible for outsiders, such as fund managers or the capital market, to discipline the company or its managers?
- *How are basic accounting units defined?* This question is more complex than it may appear, and will be addressed at greater length below. Here, suffice it to note that the basic entities contained in a financial report are not necessarily well defined. What is the organizational unit that is reporting? For example, there are substantial differences in accounting depending on whether the reporting organization is a self-financing enterprise, a semi-autonomous business division, or a budgetary entity. Who are the 'stakeholders' in the company, who may assert rights to financial information? What kinds of revenue count as 'income'? How are assets valued? What counts as 'debt'? In the postsocialist context, the definitions of these units are so contestable that in certain circumstances, it is difficult to ascertain whether a certain sum should be booked as asset, debt or income (this was the problem at Alima, where it was unclear how state subsidies should be booked). The way in which these terms are defined is both the product of power relations among different social groups and constitutive of them.
- *Who is authorized to create credible financial reports?* While there were accountants and planners in enterprises throughout Eastern Europe, relatively few of them have the professional training and expertise to create financial reports according to either the methods outlined by International Accounting Standards Committee (IASC) or according to standards recently demanded by government legislation. The question of who has the power to train and certify accountants and auditors is still open in many Eastern European countries, as is the question of what standards and procedures an accounting curricu-

> lum should teach. Moreover, the shortage of qualified accountants has led to an influx of Western accounting firms, many of who have vested interests in defining accounting standards and certification procedures (Euromoney, 1994).[8]

The sections that follow use these five questions to analyse the state socialist accounting system (in its classical and reform incarnations) and postsocialist accounting practices. The analysis reveals that accounting reform is not well-coupled with other elements of the reform process, and suggests that despite omnipresent rhetoric from politicians, bureaucrats and enterprise managers about increasing transparency and economic efficiency, accounting is being used to mask the real operations of firms and mystify emerging power relations.

Socialist accounting: the classical model

> Accounting should be understood not only as a technical exercise but as a social phenomenon in a ... socialist society (Jaruga, 1996, p. 25)

Although each of the Eastern European countries had its own accounting rules, all of the countries in the Bloc based their systems on the Soviet system, which was largely developed between 1945 and 1956 (Brzezin and Jaruga, 1988). In this section, I homogenize the differences among Eastern European countries in order to focus on problems arising from the pre-reform era Soviet model of accounting (see Pankov, 1998, p. 57). I focus on the relationship of accounting practices to the 'classical' or ideal-typical model of state socialism (Kornai, 1992).

The ideal-typical model of central planning was premised on a particular notion of accounting. Because the goal of state socialism was to replace horizontal market coordination or feudal hierarchy with bureaucratic coordination, the planned economy depended upon the vertical flow of accounting information from enterprises to central planning authorities and back (not, as is the case in a capitalist economy, horizontal information flow among enterprises, autonomous financial institutions, and shareholders). In this sense, planning represents a programmatic level of financial reporting and management, while accounting represents the technical level. Accounting was the means through which planning tasks including resource allocation, investment, consumer supply and price setting took place (Kornai, 1992, p. 98).

Although the ideal-typical model of bureaucratic coordination was never realized in any of the Eastern European countries, its use as a model led to a two-cycle financial reporting cycle in which an internal accounting cycle both made use of data from and reported data to agencies outside the enterprise. In the absence of the market, many enterprises used 'net accounting', in which they generally reported only the final results of their budgetary cycles, that is, increases in inventories, finished goods and work in progress. Even enterprises that were required to report more than net results reported little in comparison with similar capitalist enterprises. For example, the Uniform Accounting method in Poland, introduced in 1976, required enterprises to submit only six documents: (1) a balance sheet; (2) a comparative income statement used for macro-accounting purposes which showed costs by nature and revenues by nature; (3) a net income account statement which reported the amount the firm had above or below the inputs provided by the state, as well as extraordinary expenses or revenues; (4) an income distribution statement; (5) a funds flow statement; and (6) a social activities statement. Of these, the balance sheet was perhaps the most important, yet it, too, was remarkable for its lack of detail.

The balance sheet found in Table 3.1 illustrates a fundamental problem in socialist accounting: information flows in two-cycle socialist accounting systems were designed primarily for the use of central planners, not enterprise managers. Because large portions of the managerial function, including production, planning and investment decisions, were carried out by government planners rather than enterprise managers, the data reported on balance sheets was oriented towards macro-economic planning rather than towards the micro-management of enterprises (Bailey, 1988). In general, accounting data were required by four state agencies, each of which carried out an aspect of macroeconomic control. First, the Central Statistical Office required data to produce the statistics used for macroeconomic control. Second, the Ministry of Finance used aggregated enterprise data to set financial policy. Third, national banks used accounting data to set monetary policy. Finally, central and local supervisory agencies, such as national federations of enterprises and province-level administrators used data to set new production targets and to allocate resources for the next budgetary cycle (Jaruga, 1996, p. 16).

Net accounting, of course, is one example of data that are useful to central planners but not to enterprise managers. Data reported in natural units is another. In contrast to Western accounting systems, which trans-

Table 3.1 Balance-sheet structure

Assets	Liabilities
Investment operations	Investment funds,investment bank loans, and payables
Fixed and detached	Statutory fund for fixed assets
Inventories and prepayments	Statutory fund for current assets
Receivables from customers	Short term bank loans, payables to suppliers
Cash and other receivables	Other payables
Profit allocated	Financial result (profit)
Assets for special purpose activities	Funds and liabilities of special purpose activities

Source: Brzezin and Jaruga (1988, p.56).

form all units into monetary values, socialist planners generally required that data be reported in production units. At Alima, the factory discussed above, socialist planners required a statement of the number of cases of baby food jars produced instead of requiring the value of all the baby food produced by a factory. Instead of requiring a statement of the value of labour required to produce that baby food, planners required Alima to present a statement of the number of man-hours to produce the baby food, and so on. The arbitrariness of value in the command economy, which made prices useless as planning and management tools, was one reason central planners requested data in natural units. However, planning in natural units was also the logical outgrowth of socialist planners' ideological commitment to increasing output rather than profitability. It was also the logical outgrowth of an economic system that was resource-constrained rather than demand-constrained (see Buck and Cole, 1987, p. 14; Kornai, 1992).

The difficulty is that data collected for net accounting in natural units does not lend itself to decision-making at the operational level. Because net accounting data are not broken down by steps in the production process and their associated costs (as in western 'cost accounting' or 'activity based accounting'),[9] it is difficult to eliminate wastage, implement cost-reduction measures, or carry out strategic planning in the sense of altering product mixes or production methods (Tintor, 1997). Accounts developed for planners rather than managers rendered it virtually impossible for a firm's management to handle issues of profitability, cost containment, resource allocation, or investment at the enterprise level.[10] Accounts served a control function rather than an operational decision-making function.[11]

However, net accounting on the basis of natural units was a double-edged sword. It revealed the 'expectations gap' between the perfect rational control that socialist accounting promised and its operational capabilities. Because social prices masked the true cost of producing goods, it was virtually impossible for either enterprise managers or central planners to determine if products were producing revenue for the state or draining state coffers. Because the degree to which individual goods produced revenue or required subsidy was impossible to determine, net revenue ('the bottom line') was an extremely poor index of a firm's profitability, in the Western sense of that term. Yet, in the absence of other data, central planners quite often managed enterprises on that basis.

Reform economics and accounting

The complications that socialist accounting systems presented for enterprise management were among the most important factors which led Eastern European governments to institute reforms, such as the Polish reforms of the 1970s or the New Economic and Financial Mechanism, instituted in Romania in 1979. Most of these reforms were designed to allow the market to play a role (albeit a limited one) in enterprise management. As part of these reforms, some enterprises were reclassified as 'self-financing', and charged with producing goods at 'maximal economic efficiency'. In contrast to budgetary units, self-financing firms were supposed to make contributions to the state budget, not take subsidies from it.

Despite the mandates for efficiency and profitability, accounting systems and the planned economy made it difficult for enterprises themselves to determine if and how much profit they were producing (Borda and McLeay, 1996). First, the problem of social prices (in which prices are determined by what consumers can afford rather than what it costs to make the product) made it virtually impossible to determine the true costs of inputs. Then, the relationship of ostensibly autonomous self-financing enterprises to the state concealed a variety of subsidies. The lack of a capital market meant that enterprises had to rely on capital provided by state banks. Rates of interest were, of course, determined arbitrarily, which again made the problem of costing complicated. Moreover, because state banks were the only source of credit, the state *de facto* retained the managerial capacity to determine the amount and type of investment in an enterprise. Enterprise managers did acquire some power with which to oppose state banks, however: although most reform laws contained provisions for bankruptcy, in practice few firms ever went bankrupt. Enterprise managers were therefore able to default on loans to state banks without penalty, which turned loans into subsidies.

Inter-enterprise debt was another form of covert subsidy concealed in socialist accounting practices (Federowicz, *et al.* 1993; 1994). 'Self-financing' enterprises could fall significantly in arrears on their payments to other enterprises, including budget-subsidized enterprises such as power and water companies, thus in effect using inter-enterprise debt as a form of state subsidy. These covert forms of state subsidy defeated the purpose of market reforms, which was to instill discipline and demand-constraint into investment-hungry enterprises.

Another important issue in reform socialist accounting was the problem of asset valuation – a problem which later became acute for those who sought to determine the value of state enterprises such as Alima after 1989. In order to determine how efficiently resources are being exploited, it is necessary to determine the value of the resources. However, in most cases, the worth of an asset declines over time, either because it becomes technologically outdated or because it begins to wear out and become less efficient. Western accounting systems deal with this problem by using accelerated depreciation, a method for recording the value of fixed assets that reflects their 'declining service potential' and the increasing costs of maintenance and repair (Shim *et al.*, 1986). Accelerated depreciation 'front-loads' the depreciation: that is, the asset depreciates most in its first year, and in lesser amounts thereafter.[12] Socialist accountants, on the other hand, did not use accelerated depreciation, instead relying on one of two other methods to calculate asset value. In many cases, they used 'historical cost'. This means that the value of the asset recorded on the books was the price paid for it – even if the asset was in fact becoming increasingly worthless. Assets were occasionally revalued, but only every 15 to 20 years (Jaruga, 1996). In this case, assets whose real value was zero (because the technology was outdated, for example) were reported on the balance sheet as having positive value for years.

To address this issue, some socialist accounting systems introduced the straight-line depreciation method. In this method, the purchase price of the asset is divided evenly over its useful life, so that a 30,000 zloty tractor that would last ten years, for example, was listed as a 3000 zloty asset each fiscal year. This had the advantage of providing a more realistic estimate of the costs of production. Rather than charging a 30,000 zloty tractor to the books in one year and thereby skewing profit margins, an enterprise could spread the cost of production over the time that the asset was used to produce. However, like historical cost, straight-line depreciation distorts the profitability picture of an enterprise, because it does not factor in obsolescence. For example, if a baby food factory producing goods for export had a machine that could cap 5000 jars of food per hour, but competing factories in the world market had machines that could cap 15,000 jars per hour, the first baby food factory was in fact losing money by using the old capper, even though it could technically be used for several more years. If the capper cost 10,000 zloty in 1980, and the capper was expected to last ten years, then according to the straight line depreciation method of asset valuation the capper was recorded in 1985 as an asset worth 5000 zloty – even if the income lost by not producing more baby food with a faster capper were to be factored in, the capper would in fact be a liability.[13] The only way to shield socialist enterprises from this disadvantage *vis-à-vis* more technologically advanced capitalist producers was to erect trade barriers around the socialist enterprises markets. To the extent they could, this is what socialist planners did.

The complex mix of depreciation rules led to profound distortions in estimates of firm value. In Hungarian enterprises, intangible assets could be written down by the straight-line method if they were classified as current assets, but if they were classified as fixed assets, they could not be depreciated at all (Borda and McLeay, 1996, p. 127). Moreover, neither bad debts nor obsolete inventory could be written off. This led to phantom assets whose real value was nil, but which were booked as assets indefinitely, which in turn led to overstatement on the balance sheet. The problem extended to properties which were listed as assets, but which were in practice liabilities. For example, if an enterprise built an apartment building for its workers, it was usually required to list the apartment block as an asset at either the historical cost of building it or at its (straight-line) depreciated value. However, given the costs of maintenance and the fact that rents rarely covered maintenance costs and repairs, and the fact that there was no market for the building, the apartment block was in fact an ongoing cost, not a productive asset. Yet, when listed as an asset at historical value or even at a value determined by straight-line depreciation, it inflated the book value of the firm substantially (Borda and McLeay, 1996, p. 136).

Another factor that distorted an enterprises financial picture was the socialist systems reliance on accrual accounting rather than cash-flow accounting. In accrual accounting, the accountant lists a sale as income, whether or not the purchaser has actually paid for the item. This can mask serious problems in an enterprise: if, for example, Alima sold 10,000 zloty's worth of baby food to a distributor in June, but the distributor did not pay until October, Alima might not have the cash on hand to pay wages or to buy raw materials. Given the state of inter-enterprise debt under socialism and during the immediate postsocialist period, many companies using the accrual method were counting receivables as income when, given that it was unlikely that the purchasers would ever pay, those receivables should have been written off as losses. Needless to say, this significantly distorted the financial picture of enterprises using the accrual method. The problem of non-paying customers was so endemic under reform socialism and in the early postsocialist period that after privatization in 1992, Alima enacted a draconian credit policy. New customers had to pay cash on the barrel until they had built up a reliable record with Alima, and long-time clients had their credit privileges immediately withdrawn the moment they did not pay for shipments within a short period of time (usually less than 30 days).

Reforms of the socialist accounting system notwithstanding, pressures on accountants were severe. As accountant and social theorist Michael Power points out, accounting facts and auditing procedures are inherently negotiable. Despite the ostensible rigidity of accounting rules, the manner in which facts are reported, how they are classified, and how regulations and terms are interpreted are all matters that are negotiated not only between accountant and employer, but also systemically in terms of the boundaries of accounting or auditing knowledge. In essence, although the first order rules, which specify how particular accounting facts are to be treated, may be rigid, the second order rules, which determine how and when particular first order rules apply, usually leave a great deal of room for the accountants discretion (Power, 1997, p. 24). In socialist accounting systems, accounting rules were, in practice, negotiable on both the first and second order, primarily due to the absence of independent audits. An enterprise director, other management personnel, and employee groups might put a great deal of pressure on an accountant to report higher output levels and lower resource-usage levels in order to assure that plans were met and bonuses awarded. In an attempt to 'bargain the plan', managers and employees might press the accountant to provide higher estimates of resources needed and forecast lower output levels. On the other hand, the Ministry of Finance or the Central Statistical Bureau might press a firm's accountant to provide highly accurate data for planning purposes, to forecast higher output and lower budgets for the coming production cycle in order to create a more ambitious plan, or to report higher output and lower costs in order to make it appear that plans were being met or exceeded. As the primary link between the enterprise and the central planners, accountants' relationships with both parties were necessarily strained.[14] This 'no-win situation' for accountants, combined with relatively low levels of training, compensation and prestige led to an acute shortage of accounting professionals in the Eastern Bloc before 1990.[15]

To summarize the discussion of both budgetary and reform accounting practices and problems, it is useful to return to the five basic questions asked in the first section. To the question of for whom financial reports are written, the clear answer is 'for government planners'. Although the socialist accounting system did not generate data that planners could use effectively to determine profitability or to improve efficiency, and although the accounting regulations made fraud and 'plan bargaining' eminently possible, the system did generate the type of data needed to control enterprises, allocate decision-making power to the centre, and focus on increasing output. This is the central paradox of socialist accounting: if the goal of the economic system was control rather than profit, the socialist accounting system functioned reasonably well, at least for a time. Yet the same system played a major role in the erosion of state socialism before 1989, not only because it led to economic inefficiencies, but because it opened the door to fraud and inaccuracy.

The separation of control and profitability meant that the endeavours of planners and managers required different kinds of data. This in turn leads to the question of the nature of data and the manner in which they are reported. There are two answers to this question. In an ideal-typical bureaucratically controlled system, the data required were basically net accounts in natural units.[16] In reform accounting systems, particularly when market-oriented reforms were introduced, most accounts were reported in currency units rather than in natural units. The goal of this change in procedure was not only to make it possible to compare economic effectiveness across industries, but instill the profit motive in managers and to make it possible for enterprises to retain a share of their profits. Accounts in currency units are, of course, of doubtful utility as an index of 'profitability' due to the problems of social prices and covert subsidies (Buck and Cole, 1987, p. 14).

The fourth question, which asks how basic accounting units are defined, is both simple and complex. *De jure*, accounting units under socialism were defined by the state. *De facto*, however, accountants had considerable latitude in defining units and determining the applicability of rules. This discretionary power led to opposing pressures from inside and outside the enterprise to skew data in a favourable manner.

The fifth question, 'who is authorized to create credible financial reports?', is one touched on only lightly here, but which will become a matter of considerable import in the discussion of transition or postsocialist accounting. As a profession low in material rewards and prestige and high in headaches, accounting did not attract large numbers of the best and brightest. Certification standards for accountants continued to drop throughout the socialist period. For example, in Poland, a State-Authorized Expert in Accounting (SAA, the highest professional certification for accountants) was established in 1959 by the Council of Ministers and administered by the Ministry of Finance. Although formal requirements for SAA certification included a university degree in economics or law and at least three years' practical experience, shortages of educationally qualified accountants led the Ministry of Finance to grant certification to accountants with only a secondary school certificate and ten years relevant experience. The reason for this shift was that individuals with higher education simply sought better paying, less politically vulnerable jobs, and it led to a shortage of enterprise accountants. In other parts of Eastern Europe, particularly in rural areas and in agricultural collectives or state farms, labour shortages and generally low levels of education made the requirements for accountants even lower. On Soviet *kolkhozy* in 1960, for example, only one-half of one per cent of the Head Accountants had higher education degrees. The majority of them – 64.8 per cent – had not completed secondary educations but had merely attended agricultural schools for *kolkhozy* accountants or extension accounting classes. A full 22.1 per cent had no secondary education, and had only attended short-term classes for bookkeepers, and 2.1 per cent had no training at all. The obvious explanation is that those with higher educations sought to escape the rigors of collective farm life (Stuart, 1972, p. 185; see also notes 15 and 16).

Accounting in – and for – transition

One of the promises of the end of Communism was that 'rational [that is, capitalist] management' would improve enterprise efficiency and therefore improve the quality of daily life. Changes in accounting methodology were key components of this promised upswing in efficiency, productivity and profitability. Accounting systems useful for managing operations and transparent to the investor were supposed to be the means to ensure effective management and managerial oversight.

However, changing accounting systems was not as simple as it seemed. One of the first questions concerned the desirability and feasibility of importing Western accounting systems into postsocialist countries. Debates hinged on whether the appropriate legal and economic context for Western accounting existed, whether an adequate number of trained personnel existed in the Eastern Bloc to implement such systems, whether or not continuity in bookkeeping is important for government or for enterprise management, and whether Western accounting systems were adequate to the particular economic and social problems of the postsocialist era.

It is unclear whether the necessary economic and legal context for Western accounting exists in Eastern Europe, or whether it will exist in the foreseeable future. This problem is directly related to the enduring problem of the audience for financial reports. The contrast between postsocialist accounting systems and Western accounting systems is stark, primarily for political reasons: Western accounting systems do not need to recognize the wide variety of stakeholders that Eastern European systems, because of their peculiar historical and political circumstances, do. In the West, the International Accounting Standards Committees objectives for financial reports only view investors as main users of accounting data. A contrasting example can be found in the preface to the Slovene Accounting Standards, which identifies interested parties as 'present and potential owners, capital investors, employees, creditors, suppliers and commodity creditors, customers, the government and its institutions as well as the public at large' (Garrod and McLeay, 1996). For historical and political reasons, postsocialist governments must take the interests of all these diverse groups into account in order to enact reform.[17] As various sets of stakeholders fight to obtain information in a manner that reflects their interests, accounting practices become reflections of larger debates over postsocialist property rights (see Dunn, 1998).

However, even as stakeholder groups push for new accounting standards, and despite the introduction of capital markets, guidelines for accounting written by Ministries of Finance and other government bodies still emphasize data collection for the purpose of government control and – most importantly – for tax collection purposes (Pankov, 1998; Toma, 1998). Not only does this make management decision-making more difficult, the lack of information easily comprehensible to the individual investor hinders the development of stock markets or management pressure exerted by employee stockholders. Similarly, investment fund managers and corporate investors are unable to accurately judge management's stewardship of the enterprise, a problem that retards foreign investment and capital market expansion. New accounting standards rarely reflect a shift from government macro-management to capital market discipline (Pankov, 1998).[18] For these reasons, foreign investors and NGOs have been particularly aggressive in demanding changes in accounting methodology.

However, some analysts argue that although postsocialist accounting standards emphasize data for government use, they do so rightly. These writers argue that systems such as US GAAP or IASC are not adequate to the postsocialist economic situation, in which the survival of the enterprise may take precedence over market discipline for political reasons. Speaking of Romania, Feleaga (cited in Sochaka and Malo, 1996) writes:

> I believe that the objectives of financial statements and the hierarchy of users of accounting information in Eastern European countries can be quite different, for some time, from the IASCs conceptual framework ... the principal objective of corporate financial statements in the coming years will be to provide information on the resources, needs, and performance of enterprises, in order to ensure that they remain 'going concerns.' In the same way, the privileged users of information may be the firms managers, staff who hold shares, and relevant government agencies, with the least important in this list being the investors, who, in the IASCs framework, have the predominant role.

Feleaga's remarks point out the fundamental dilemma in Eastern European accounting: Western accounting standards such as IASC or GAAP cannot reflect many of the unprecedented economic dilemmas of postsocialism. The paradigmatic example is fixed assets such as land, which were considered valueless (or were at least not reported as assets) under socialism. According to official policy in Poland, for example, land was not a commodity,[19] and was therefore not subject to valuation. This posed a problem when the worth of enterprises was valued for privatization plans in the early 1990s. Not only was there no historical value for industrial land, there were no market values with which to estimate the value of land. Similar problems were attached to intangible assets such as goodwill or brand equity, which clearly had a value but which had never been subject to valuation. Alima, for example, had produced baby food and juices under the 'Bobo Frut' brand name since 1968. The brand was known for its adherence to the strict quality and purity norms prescribed by the governments Institute for Mothers and Children. Bobo Frut quickly gained a reputation as one of the best products a child could be given, which led to consistently high demand for it for over 21 years (Welc, 1994, p. 28). This strong brand equity was obviously of enormous importance to Gerber, since it was entering a market in which mothers trust in the brand was the most important selling point. Yet, there was no way to determine the monetary value of brand equity, at least not by using Alimas books.[20]

How debt (either payable or receivable) should be valued was another sticky question, particularly given the hyperinflation of the early 1990s. In early privatization programmes, many foreign investors discovered that the equity value of enterprises had been severely inflated either by counting receivables that were unlikely to ever be received as assets, or by not counting payables as liabilities.[21] In some cases, interenterprise debts became less relevant as inflation eroded their real value; however, in other cases inflation-adjusted debt overhang has threatened many enterprises with liquidation (Federowicz, 1992). Inflation has also plagued the valuation of fixed assets and slow-moving inventory, particularly in countries where the currency has changed or been revalued or where hyperinflation has made historical value ridiculously low. For example, a machine bought for 90,000 Polish zloty in 1989 was worth approximately $10,000 in 1989 according to official exchange rates. In late 1999, 90,000 old zloty were worth about $2.25. If the straight line depreciation method were used without adjusting for inflation, the current value of the machine would be 9000 zloty or about 46 cents, assuming a 20 year depreciation period. Clearly, this does not accurately reflect the value of a fixed asset.[22]

Enterprise restructuring also poses difficulties for the introduction of Western accounting principles. Many state-owned enterprises are being or have been split into smaller units. Assigning assets and liabilities to each of these units is highly complex, and in some cases, management has taken advantage of this fact. Because managers know better than anyone else which parts of the company are likely to be profitable, they can assign assets to cost centres they themselves are privatizing, while assigning liabilities to the portions which remain state-owned. For reasons described above, the book value of assets and liabilities – even if an attempt is made to translate the books into a Western system – does not provide an accurate guide for outsiders who might wish to stop this 'cherry picking'. Likewise, because asset valuation is so complex, managers involved in privatization often are able to take advantage of the 'liquidation' form of enterprise restructuring to assign low values to assets, which they then purchase for themselves. This form of cherry-picking was institutionalized in Germany, where the Treuhandanstalt, the state organization responsible for privatization, sold the assets of the former East German state to East German enterprise managers or to West German firms at fire-sale prices (Drost, 1993, p. 471). Western accounting systems, which assume that assets have a determinable market value based on a history of market transactions of similar assets, are powerless in these circumstances – they simply can not cope with the arbitrariness of value in postsocialist economies.

The inability of many Western accounting methods to deal with post-socialist dilemmas merges with other considerations to create strong arguments against the adoption of Western accounting practices and for continuity in accounting practice. In Poland, for example, the Department of Accounting Affairs in the Polish Ministry of Finance has advocated maintaining the 'Accounting Principles of Correct Bookkeeping', which were developed before 1989, as this would allow the 130,000 Polish accountants to continue practising without costly retraining. Jerzy Sablik, the chairman of the Association of Accountants in Poland, commented:

> The former system served – and it was impossible to do otherwise – the needs of a centralized planned economy. There was only one way forward: to rebuild and modernize this system with the help of new contributions. It was not possible to suddenly abandon the system in order to replace it with a superior system, already validated in the West at the methodological, organizational and technical levels. An economic entity is a living organism, and that kind of change could destabilize it. Therefore changes in the running of the system are to be introduced progressively. (cited in Sochaka and Malo, 1996, p. 40)

Even if there were broad consensus about the need for accounting systems oriented towards the needs of investors – and there is not – several factors make such changes difficult. In considering the issue of feasibility, the issue of legal, social and economic infrastructure appears again. In terms of the legal infrastructure, dramatic changes in accounting practices depend on reforms in accounting laws (where accounting practices are prescribed by the state), and tax laws that influence reporting practices. Legal changes related to privatization programmes and laws affecting foreign direct investment are particularly important, since foreign investors often pressure both enterprises and governments to adopt Western accounting standards. In the arena of economic infrastructure, changes in the finance sector are highly important. Particularly in countries where there are few strong private banks, the state may retain a monopsony over the use of financial information.

In terms of social infrastructure, the composition and training of the labour force affects changes in accounting practice. The shortage of accountants trained in Western accounting methods such as IASC makes it unlikely that a wholesale transition in accounting methods could happen quickly. Pankov (1998) argues that given Eastern European accountants' lack of experience in Western accounting systems, any attempt to introduce them rapidly would lead to accounting chaos, not an orderly transformation of accounting practices. However, some commentators see the dearth of trained accountants as a factor mitigating for the introduction of Western accounting standards. Speaking of Romania, Feleaga (cited in Sochaka and Malo, 1996, p. 39) argues that the only alternative to importing an accounting system such as GAAP or IASC would be for Romanians to create their own system. Given the lack of accounting expertise, he argues, this is an impossible task.

Given these considerations, changes in Eastern European accounting systems are happening, but as gradual evolution rather than as a 'transplant' of Western systems. Adaptations and deviations from international accounting standards must be made not only to cope with the unique economic circumstances, but in response to the unprecedented demands of both the postsocialist polity and the global market. These multiple pressures shaping accounting mean that changes in accounting systems will affect not only postsocialist economies, but politics, organizations and persons.

Accounting, accountability and the corporate self

Power (1997) defines four levels of auditing practice. The first is 'official knowledge', the public face of audit which is reflected in laws, regulations and textbooks. Official knowledge is only partly descriptive because it is often written *ex post facto* rather than *ex ante*. That is, it often reflects changes in practice rather than driving them (Power, 1997, p. 37). The next level is 'training and education', in which future practitioners are taught not only official knowledge, but uncodified practice, 'judgment', and self-presentation. It is the process of socializing auditors into a community of practice. The third level is that of 'practice', in which auditors negotiate facts, make judgments and write them down (not necessarily in that order). Practice is not only action, it is a form of knowledge embedded in a community of practitioners and in a wider social order. It is an inherently political process through which authority is constituted, judgment created, and discretion exercised. Finally, the fourth level is that of 'quality control'. This level is built into all the above levels, and into all audit practices. It is made up of the institutionalized mechanisms of peer review, which exist to provide comfort about the production of comfort (that is, they provide surety about the mechanisms that assure investors and other consumers of financial data of the integrity of the data). Quality control mechanisms emerged from criticisms of auditing and a recognition of the need to regulate firms rather than individuals.

Although these four levels are certainly loosely connected – producing phenomena such as the 'expectations gap' between official knowledge and actual practice – they are connected. As a whole, this system exerts constant pressures on organizations to become more auditable, or to create more auditable performance. This may or may not lead to more efficiency, effectiveness or better goal setting, but it does lead to more 'accountability' and more visible performance (Power, 1997, p. 49). Auditing systems place increasing pressure on organizations to create self-definitions and self-portraits in terms of measurable outputs, which then become self-fulfilling prophecies, not only measures but targets (Strathern, 1999). Immeasurable outputs (in a university setting, for example, the degree to which students think independently, for example, versus their scores on standardized tests) become invisible and hence unimportant, while measurable targets and performance can be emphasized disproportionately.

Socialist accounting systems failed precisely because they could not induce organizations to produce auditable performances. This is partly due to the failure of the quality control function. State external auditors investigated the management practices not only of enterprise managers but of the ministries that employed the auditors, problematizing the ideal of external objective audit free from political considerations. The other main form of quality control came in the form of accountants from one firm acting as auditors of another, a practice which was surely influenced by social networking and 'connections'.

If, in the state socialist context, we take 'official knowledge' as state-decreed accounting systems, 'practice' as the creation of accounts, and 'quality control' as audit, it is clear that one of the reasons that socialist accounts were inauditable was the radical disjunction between these three levels. Given the importance of both activity in the grey market and fulfilling the plan, books had to be 'cooked', which led to a disjunction between official knowledge (the way accounts should be done according to official instructions, textbooks and so on) and practice (the way they were in fact done). Likewise, because of the interpolation of political considerations in between practice, official knowledge, and audit, what was audited and how it was audited often bore little relation either to the prescribed standards for audit or to the books that actually existed.

Aside from the disjunctions in the audit system, there was a crucial and fundamental difference between socialist and Western audit: socialist auditors audited transactions, whether all the transactions of an enterprise or only a sample. Western accountants, who are less concerned with output volume than with value and profit, audit the systems that a firm uses to audit and regulate itself. That is to say, rather than auditing transactions, Western auditors verify the self-auditing management system. This leads Western organizations to place increasing emphasis not on output, but on the production, elaboration and presentation of systems of self-control. Auditable performance comes to be seen as a more important goal than production itself, not only in the financial domain but all domains of business. A paradigmatic example of this in the West can be found in the ISO quality standards, which do not measure product quality but the production process (Power, 1997, p. 91). Another example is the Hazard Analysis Critical Control Point (HACCP) system, which has been widely touted by ex-Vice President Al Gore. HACCP aims to ensure food quality not by setting standards or norms for nutritional value or biological contaminants, but by dictating the process through which the food is processed. Like all such quality assurance (QA) programmes, it 'has less to do with high standards than with a certain style of management process in which it is not the product which is evaluated but the practices and procedures of manufacture and provision' (Power 1997, p. 59). Western audit is not observation, but the observation of observation.

Auditing (and, as a variety or subsystem of audit, accounting), is therefore not only a means of making organizations more 'transparent' and their activities more visible, but also a means by which internalized systems of governance or regulation are installed. When organizations do not have clear measures of productivity which relate their inputs to their outputs, the audit of efficiency or effectiveness is not just a verification or description, but a process of defining and operationalizing measures of performance for the audited entity. That is, audit 'functions do not only verify what is already there, but also install an internal control system which embodies auditable performance measures' (Power, 1997, p. 52).

Concluding remarks

Changes in socialist accounting practices, even if they are state-initiated, might therefore be seen as a process of shifting control of the enterprise from the state to the enterprise itself – for example, installing internalized self-control. By forcing enterprises to become 'accountable', both in the sense of being auditable and in the sense of conveying a description of their activities outside the firm, Eastern European states and markets are asking enterprises to develop systems of self-assessment and monitored self-discipline.

Because the forms of assessment and discipline are carried out by the enterprise itself but not defined by it, internal control systems become quasi-public objects (Power, 1997, p. 83). The many faces of audit and auditable performance connect the enterprise to regulatory levels outside it such as the state, the capital market, the industry and non-governmental regulatory bodies such as the International Organization for Standards. Audit is therefore an important means of economic regulation, and a way for the state to coordinate the economy without visibly coordinating it. In this sense, battles over accounting reform are not so much battles about state control versus enterprise freedom, but struggles to replace direct control by state bureaucrats with indirect control over managerial regulation and the managerial environment (see Rose and Miller, 1990).

Accounting and audit are 'rituals of verification', tools that produce comfort (for investors, the polity or the market) rather than critique. They produce comfort because they mask the real operation of the firm in favour of a facade of auditable performance. Accountability, the battle cry of postsocialist economic reformers, can therefore be broken down into three aspects. First, accountability is a form of discipline that is internalized and that generates specific self-descriptions from organizations. This kind of identity production, perhaps even more than less quantitative forms of identity-building, influences how managers interpret information, make decisions and create corporate strategy. Both corporate identity and the self-perceptions of industrial managers can have profound effects on the fortunes of enterprises (see Schoenberger, 1997).

Second, accounting is mystifying as much as it is revealing. It obscures power relations, such as those between the firm and the state or the firm and the capital market, in the production of an auditable face. Accounting and audit are rituals which produce the social institution of trust, a substitute for knowledge and a force which mystifies both the workings of the firm and the social relations which surround it. Because accounting presents negotiable facts as empirical realities, accounts often aid managers in presenting less palatable decisions (such as layoffs) as necessitated by the business environment rather than as managerial dictates.

Finally, accounting and audit are legitimating, in so far as the auditable surface provides the illusion of information, control and choice. Legitimacy is intimately related both to the production of trust and the production of comfort. Even though the figures in a stockholder report are the product of negotiation, and even though many stockholders are probably incapable or unwilling to decipher them, they produce comfort and trust by adhering to a ritual form. This encourages investment, enhances the identity of the company, and legitimates institutions like the stock market.

Shifts in accounting and auditing practices are therefore important and integral parts of postsocialist transformation. In some senses, they do make enterprises more penetrable and more transparent, which attracts foreign capital and loans from international agencies. In doing so, shifts in accounting practice make it possible to forge regulatory links between Eastern European enterprises, transnational regulatory bodies (such as the World Bank or the International Bank for Reconstruction and Development), and the global market. In other senses, they are integral parts of the process through which the visible power of the state under socialism is transformed into the 'hidden hand' of market society (Burawoy and Lukács, 1992).

Notes

1. Earlier versions of this chapter benefited from comments by Katherine Verdery, Michael Power, Monika Kostera, Mihaela Kelemen and Barbara Brown, and I thank them very much. Research was funded by a grant from the National Science Foundation for which Katherine Verdery was the principal investigator. Writing was completed under the auspices of the Wissenschaftskolleg zu Berlin. I am grateful to both these institutions for their support.

2. Gerber paid $11 million to the Polish government in exchange for 60 per cent of Alima's shares, but later spent an undisclosed amount to buy almost all the outstanding shares from Alima's workers and agricultural suppliers, who had purchased them under the terms of the privatization deal. Gerber also agreed to invest another $14 million in Alima (Nowy Swiat 1992, Zycie Warszawy 1992, A-Z Rzeszow 1992).
3. Lewandowski was made to answer to charges of selling enterprises for less than they were worth so many times that he told me 'I should be in the Guinness Book of World's Records under "Person Appearing Most Often in Front of a Sejm Tribunal".'
4. Thanks to Michael Power for pointing out the difference between legitimacy and optimality in this situation.
5. In the USSR, Bulgaria, Yugoslavia and Poland.
6. IAS standards are spelled out at the International Accounting Standards Committee website, http://www.iasc.org.uk/frame/cen2_1.htm
7. For example, FASB rule 90 was developed in 1987, to provide guidelines to regional power companies who had to account for closing and abandoning billions of dollars' worth of unsafe and unnecessary nuclear power facilities.
8. See also Garrod and McLeay (1996).
9. Cost accounting is a system in which the costs of each input are calculated in such a manner that managers can precisely determine the aggregate cost of producing each finished good. During various periods of economic reform, socialist systems attempted to introduce cost accounting methods along with a greater role for the market. Activity-based cost accounting, a recent trend in US and UK management, takes cost accounting principles even further. Not only are raw materials and labour considered as costs, but also inputs formerly booked to 'overhead', such as energy real estate and administrative costs. These 'overhead' costs are minutely calculated and distributed differentially to different products. For example, if the value of storage space were to be calculated in terms of present real-estate values and opportunity costs, boxes with a 12 cm^2 base would be 'charged' more than jars with a 10 cm^2 base (Barbara Brown, pers. comm.).
10. There were attempts to introduce accounting procedures that would facilitate these kinds of managerial decisions, but they were of limited effectiveness. For example, the idea of normative costing (that is, analysing cost variances by product groups) was introduced in Lithuania in about 1960. Nonetheless, less than seven percent of all Lithuanian enterprises ever used the method. See Mackevicius *et al.* (1996).
11. It seems logical to assume that enterprise managers may have kept their own unofficial books with which to manage the enterprise. I have never been able to find any evidence of this, however.
12. In Western countries, the estimated useful life of most fixed assets and the rate at which they depreciate under accelerated depreciation is usually determined by using standardized tables such as the 'Blue Book' for automobiles. However, the accelerated depreciation rate for some fixed assets is set at the accountant's discretion.
13. This might be thought of in terms of opportunity cost. Even though opportunity costs and obsolescence are terms typically associated with competitive markets, one can think of them as costs in socialist systems, too. If the

value of a productive asset is determined by the amount of output it can generate, than an obsolete productive asset is incurring opportunity costs *vis-à-vis* the productive value of newer machinery.

14. There is a strong contrast between management–accountant relations in a socialist society versus a capitalist one. While there is inevitably a great deal of tension between accountants and senior executives in a socialist enterprise, accountants in capitalist enterprises are in the business of providing data for senior executives' use, and hence tend to become active participants in the management team. See Bailey (1988), and Jaruga (1996).
15. There was, however, a plethora of bookkeepers. Given that bookkeeping was a low-paying, low-status, high-stress job, most members of the profession were of course female. In an ironic twist of fate, these women were ideally placed to be retrained as Western-style accountants after 1989, which gave them privileged access to high-paying, high-prestige jobs in a market with high demand for their services.
16. This is a slight overstatement, since accounting systems did not exist for any length of time in a 'pure' ideal typical state. However, even as accounting regulations were reformed, the amount of data required from a self-financing enterprise was minimal – usually just a balance statement, a profit-and-loss statement, and a statement of social activities undertaken during that planning period.
17. The Polish Ministry of Privatization (1991) compiled a similar list of stakeholders in state-owned enterprises, which suggests that the idea of a broad social interest in enterprise affairs is still current.
18. The exception to this generalization appears to be Slovene accounting standards, which are quite detailed and investor oriented.
19. Land was not considered a commodity except when it was used in private farming.
20. Thanks to Dieter Sadowski for help on brand equity.
21. Romania has recently changed its accounting laws to remedy this problem. Provisions for potential bad debt must be included even if the bad debt is not tax deductible. See Toma (1998).
22. The problem is particularly acute in Romania, where assets must be valued at acquisition cost and can only be revalued when a government ordinance has been issued. See Toma (1998).

4

From Social Movements to Identity Transformation: Comparison of Estonian and Finnish Management Students' Values

Iiris Aaltio, Lembit Turnpuu and Mari Kooskora

Introduction

Students studying management in universities hope to acquire the knowledge and skills required in the positions they will hold later on. Countries characterized as transition economies face especially important questions of identity transformation, because their business life is being shaped in close connection with the political and intellectual developments in society. Estonia is one of the countries currently in transition; its former leaders and managers are giving way to their younger counterparts. The decisions made and the values adopted by the latter will not only affect organizations but also society as a whole. The discussion concerning values is gaining increasing attention in the media and academic journals. Value change is a topic of current interest also among the managers themselves. Education and training are seen to be fundamental means by which values can be affected.

What kind of insights are called for in education to ensure that what we call 'tomorrow's managers' will be able to carry out their work in ways that are both productive and but also meet the cultural requirements of the environment? The crucial elements in our discourse involve questions like 'What is needed?' and 'What are we striving to do?' This requires not only clear thinking about what values to adopt but also a decision about the processes by which such values could become operational.

First, we argue that the basic aim of education is to affect the values, attitudes and capabilities of management students with the view to help them to adapt to the requirements of the new post-Soviet environment. This of course raises many dilemmas such as what rate of change and what ideology to base it on, as well as ethical issues concerning the 'manipulation' of values.

Second, we argue that major emphasis must be placed on an anthropological understanding of the current situation and of local history. The pre-Soviet culture of the country, going back to earlier centuries, is seen as something worth respecting and preserving, instead of exchanging it with Western values and practices of business life.

Students derive knowledge, skills and values through education. In a relatively short period of time, management students will become specialists working in enterprises, on their way to higher positions. The question that arises is whether the values of managers and management students in countries in transition are significantly different compared to Western counterparts. We present some findings of a field study comparing the values of Finnish and Estonian management students, and on the basis of the data, discuss issues regarding the content and the pedagogical solutions of university education for tomorrow's business managers in countries facing economic transition.

Comparing recent cultural developments in Estonia and Finland

Finland and Estonia have always had good cultural and economic relations. Also geographically they are close to each other. Finnish exports have gained a major position in Estonian trade, and tourism between Finland and Estonia, especially between the capitals Helsinki and Tallinn, has increased considerably. At the same time, there are pronounced differences in the recent historical development of the two countries, with respect to both societal and political aspects. The economies of these countries have undertaken different paths of economic development and need to be approached from different perspectives; sometimes, the differences may easily be exaggerated without recognizing the many similarities any national economies nowadays share.

The old mythologies of 'East' and 'West' contrast the ways people think and act in these parts of the world, positing a clear contrast between Eastern and Western identities and personalities, apparently dating far back in history. Basic human questions, such as the idea of ageing in relation to working life, are seen to be dealt with differently in Eastern as compared to Western mythology (see Wada, 1995, pp. 48–75). The modern story talks about people being stuck in a certain time and place, that is, inhabitants of a given culture are rooted in modern institutions, both temporal and local. These myths are strengthened by survey results such as those of Hofstede (1984/1991), which, besides finding differences between countries globally, also found differences between the continents. It is the political, economic and social system that creates these differences, as evidenced by his findings.

The political system has a significant impact on the principles and traditions of a country's economy and, further, on managerial identity, as seen in the centralized system of Soviet enterprises before Perestroika and 1985. A Soviet-style economy was characterized as follows (see Liuhto, 1999, pp. 240–1):

1. The centrally planned system was responsible for the founding of enterprises, determining their activities and also capable of closing down their business.
2. The absence of a real criterion of competitiveness caused quasi-rational managerial behaviour, which sometimes met the external requirements but not the central plan.
3. The enterprise management was sometimes forced to replace the missing enterprise relations of the official system with unofficial enterprise networks.

Overall, Soviet business operations could largely be characterized as being deterministically oriented instead of naturally selected, because activities were extensively determined by centralized planning. This picture acquires new nuances when we see that in the unofficial model the management was much more active, for example, when the Soviet managers' duties expanded from internal production supervision to coping with the deficiencies and chronic shortages of a centrally planned economy. The role of managers was to act as the representatives of the authorities of the centralized system, but simultaneously as rebels of the system using their own imagination and following their own aspirations in this context.

The transition in Estonia began about ten years ago. It has involved some important changes over this period of time. Overall, the change can be referred to as a transition from a planned to a market economy. There are no simple theories that characterize such a transition, and not very much empirical evidence is available on how enterprises survive and what is the role of management in the transition. As Uksvärav and Nurmi (1993, p. 96) note, Estonian managers have been caught between two extremes. They face a new situation where change is needed but where there are no clear answers for how to act in the face of a chaotic situation. Some differences between Estonian and Finnish managers were found at the time when the transition started. The comparison focused on the managers' values and interpretations about how to act in business life (Uksvärav and Nurmi, 1993, p. 98). The study was based on an inquiry conducted in Estonia and Finland in 1990. The Estonian sample consisted of participants in short-term management development seminars for senior managers at the Estonian Management Institute in Tallinn. The participants were mostly people holding top management positions in industry, transportation, trade and construction. Altogether 38 Estonian managers and 20 Finnish managers, all attendees of managerial courses, were included in the sample (Uksvärav and Nurmi, 1993, pp. 22–3). Some illustrative conclusions were drawn from the survey results, at the same time bearing in mind the problems of any cross-cultural research (Nurmi, 1982) as well as the limitations of the samples in terms of scope. Below is a summary of the main findings and of the problems confronted by Estonian managers in their attempts to do their job in the turbulent economic situation of the time:

- Estonian managers stressed the material or the 'hardware' side of business while their Finnish counterparts stressed the human or 'soft' side of the problems.
- The availability of supplies was a matter of primary concern, while marketing problems were of little concern to Estonian managers, whereas Finnish managers considered sales-related matters a major problem, and the availability of supplies and materials did not matter as such.
- Lack of concern for the details of marketing was typical of Estonian managers, whereas Finnish managers attached great importance to markets and people.
- As a result of the long period of access to international markets, Finnish managers knew the market mechanisms and the related details, whereas Estonian managers found the international market a completely new field.
- For Estonian managers, travelling abroad to other countries meant a possibility to earn foreign currency and buy commodities rather than learning new things about the international business culture.
- Finnish and Estonian managers both considered good relations and personal contacts important in finding solutions to problems.

In general, the results showed that Estonian managers were not very well prepared for successful operations in a market economy. As Nurmi and Uksvärav argue (1995, p. 12):

> older people, who remember the basic rules of a market economy, are in general too old to be active in business ... the younger generation may have been spoilt by attitudes and procedures from the Soviet system ... the transition from the old to the new era is hard for them ... they have to forget old habits and learn new ways of thinking and doing.

Their principal handicap was a lack of knowledge of the market economy and the details of the associated operating principles and technology. This is a direct result of their training in accordance with the old state-controlled system. The earlier environment was one where the production process, machines and materials were most important. People, their aims, desires and needs, were important in principle but not in practice. The period during which this kind of business culture had evolved lasted 50 years. The ethics of business were dubious as blackmail, bribery and corruption were acceptable practices.

The findings above show that Estonian managers faced profound challenges when the transition began ten years ago. Management is not only about the material environment but also about values, meanings and understandings. In many Eastern countries during the past decade, the ideologies carrying the Soviet type ways of managing started to crumble (for example, Czarniawska, 1986; Liuhto, 1999). The new situation lead to a change in how managers grasped the economic world that surrounded them and found ways to cope with it. The identities of business managers, that is, their way of identifying themselves as actors in business life, transformed significantly.

Management education does not only deliver knowledge but also offers elements for identity building to enable students to cope with the changing environment. It is not merely a marketplace for economic and money-based facts and applications, but is based on the social and human sciences, providing insights and skills for acting in society. It is worth noting that management education has become universalized in many ways – students read the same books all over the world, student exchange continues to expand, and international programmes are under way in a great number of universities where teacher exchange is practised (Ingersoll and Adams, 1987). Education, especially at university level, has become globalized to a great extent, even though there still are many country-specific programmes at the same time.

Changes have evidently taken place in business life values in Estonia over the 15-year transition from the Soviet period, and business managers have developed new skills during that time. In the 50 years of Soviet domination, many traditions and values gained a solid foothold in business culture in ways that are not easy to transform: we may ask whether there are some values, traditions and habits that continue to persist in spite of the apparent transformation – only in new clothing? How can we evaluate the changes in ethical concerns, often seen as a continuing problem of the Estonian economy as well as of other transition economies? We now discuss some of the findings of a survey comparing Estonian and Finnish students in terms of their values concerning business life and management behaviour in that context.

Comparison of Estonian and Finnish students' values

The values and value orientations of Estonian and Finnish management students concerning managerial behaviour in business life were compared by means of a field study that we carried out in 1995. A 150 item questionnaire was given to 75 Estonian and 94 Finnish students who had just started their management studies in that year. The students were asked to evaluate the items in terms of how much impact they thought the factors had on managerial success. The value categories behind the items were: 1) everyday life in the organizations; 2) business ideology; 3) business ethics; 4) managerial ideology; 5) social values; 6) juridical aspects; 7) special business area; 8) personality issues; 9) professional issues; and 10) organizational culture. The scale ranged from 1 to 5, where 5 meant extremely important and 1 meant unimportant. Despite the fact that the results were preliminary, that the survey was conducted among first-year students and that the applied survey method has certain limitations regarding the interpretations of managerial identity, some conclusions can still be drawn from the data about how business management students identify themselves as future business actors. Overall, in the light of the findings it is possible to picture how management students identify the business sector as part of society and what kind of ideals they have with regards to management and leadership.

We found some similarities as well as some differences in the ways the students responded to the questions. First of all, there were no great differences between the two nationalities: the mean rating in the various value categories was between 3.82 and 3.12 among the Finns, and between 3.82 and 3.23 among the Estonians. Individual differences that were not dependent on the country were found in addition. Some details could be observed which do, however, imply differences in values and in the ways of grasping the surrounding economic reality and business organizations. When comparing the ten value categories, both the Estonians and the Finns ranked the top four as follows: social values (Estonians 2nd, Finns 1st), values related to the personality of manager (Estonians 4th, Finns 2nd), managerial ideological values (Estonians 3rd, Finns 3rd), and values of business ideology (Estonians 1st, Finns 4th). By analogy, the bottom 3 according to the estimated averages were: values related to the everyday (Estonians 10th, Finns 8th), organizational culture (Estonians 8th, Finns 10th) and ethics (Estonians 10th, Finns 8th). The differences in the specific ranking of the value categories proved insignificant. Nevertheless, the Finns rated ethical values, the personality of the manager as well as organizational-juridical and professional values somewhat higher than the Estonians, and the values of business ideology, professionalism in general and values related to organizational culture somewhat lower than the Estonians.

The top ten specific value items included in the questionnaire according to the highest average score are shown in Table 4.1. The ranking shows no major differences between the countries in terms of the quality of goods and services and the professionalism of managers. However, there are many differences in the set of top values of would-be CEOs and businesspeople of the neighbouring countries in general terms.

Indeed, the unstable economic situation in Estonia makes Estonian businesspeople think more about the future and the security of their company and pay more attention to continuing economic progress, as compared to their Finnish counterparts. This calls for stability, teamwork and clear-cut orders. The Finns consider a positive microclimate and the communication between the manager and the subordinates most important.

In terms of the lowest average scores, the bottom ten value items are seen in Table 4.2.

The data in Table 4.2 show the antipathy of the Finns towards strict measures (like rigorous discipline). Both Estonian and Finnish students appear to be calculated atheists, void of sentimental feelings. Showing a tendency towards 'cold calculation', they place hardly any value on nobleness. Neither the Estonians nor the Finns were found to recog-

Table 4.1 Top ten value items of Finnish and Estonian management students

Estonians	Finns
1. Aspiration for something better	1. Entrepreneurial spirit
2. Investing in the future	2. Positive microclimate among colleagues
3. Quality of goods and services	3. Quality of goods and services
4. Continued economic progress	4. Manager–subordinate relations
5. Entrepreneurial spirit	5. Honesty
6. Clear working orders from managers	6. Manager–subordinate communication
7. Professionalism of managers	7. Professionalism of managers
8. Fluent team-work	8. Professional skills
9. Positive microclimate among colleagues	9. Efforts towards common goals
10. Manager–subordinate communication	10. Reputation of company

Table 4.2 Lowest ten value items of Finnish and Estonian management students

Estonians	Finns
God	Employees' membership in professional associations
Employees' membership in professional associations	Strict discipline
Ideals shared with colleagues	God
Love of the homeland	Myths shared with colleagues
Stylish company vehicles	Manager's composure
National identity	Care about promotion of newcomers
Facilities for sport and culture	Love of the homeland
Nobleness	National identity
Sufficient fuel supply in the company	Professional activities of the intelligentsia at the level of society
Critical attitude of the manager towards the environmental issues	Nobleness

nize national boundaries in business. National identity and love of the fatherland do not seem to have much to do in their value orientation.

Values related to the democracy and friendliness of the Finnish business students are reflected in the ranking inside the value categories. The Finns gave a higher rating to communication between the owners and the employees, managers' self-development, and delegation of working duties to lower levels of management, than their Estonian counterparts. The self-management capability of the team, the unique individuality of each employee and the development of control into self-control were rated much higher by the Finnish than by the Estonian students. The Finns were also found to be more tolerant towards disabled persons than the Estonians.

When evaluating employees, both the Estonians and the Finns gave similar ratings to the high performance of the company, but the Finns considered the punctilious observance of laws much more important than the Estonians. Indeed, the supremacy of the law and obedience to the law are counted among the foundations of democracy. However, the Estonians and Finns alike are against anarchy and formalism. The differences of principle between Estonian and Finnish students with regard to managerial consciousness are disclosed by a cluster analysis of the values of the studied contingents. In terms of value orientation, five basic clusters were found, namely (see Turnpuu *et al.* 2000):

- *Maximalists*, who rated all value groups extremely high.
- *Minimalists*, who rated all value groups extremely low.
- *Professionalists*, who rated the values related to speciality and profession more highly, and the values related to business ideology and the everyday life somewhat more highly than the others.
- *Liberals*, who gave a high rating to the values related to business ideology, the everyday, and organizational–juridical values.
- *Anthropocentrists*, who gave a high rating to the values related to personality, managerial ideology and social values.

Table 4.3 shows the differences in the value orientation of Estonian and Finnish business students.

Against earlier findings to the effect that transition management newcomers highly appreciate material rewards (Uksvärav and Nurmi, 1993), the Estonian business students in our survey gave them relatively low value. It seems that material resources and rewards such as luxury cars were not understood as playing any major role in gaining success in business. With respect to religion (God) there were similari-

Table 4.3 Differences in the value orientation of Estonian and Finnish business students

	Maximalists (%)	**Minimalists (%)**	**Anthropocentrists (%)**	**Liberals (%)**	**Professionalists (%)**
Estonians	21.6	11.5	12.8	28.7	25.4
Finns	13.1	3.0	43.4	21.2	19.2

ties in the way in which both Estonian and Finnish students disvalued it as having an impact on business success, showing an antipathy towards determinism. This can be associated with the idea of human voluntarism and the belief that the individual is responsible for his/her success. A national identity and a sense of the fatherland were not valued highly by either of the groups, which may be surprising when we think of Estonia's economic and political context in 1995. Low ratings in these aspects give clues about an antipathy towards any ideology, implying that business life and its principles are independent of politics and also indicating an unwillingness to obey any ideology, be it religion, politics or any kind of social movement.

Ethical values and honesty were rated higher among the Finnish students compared to their Estonian counterparts. Ethics appears to be seen differently by the Finns and the Estonians. Values like honesty received a clearly higher ranking (4.18) from Finns compared to Estonians (3.89), as did democracy (Finns 3.71, Estonians 3.49) and sincerity (Finns 3.74, Estonians 3.32). Estonians gave a low ranking to national identity (2.49) as well as to patriotism (2.29).

The position of firms has been different in Estonia compared to Finland. Estonian firms – like firms in the other Soviet countries – had a monopoly status and the opportunity to bribe, blackmail and give preferences to selected customers, which provided a favourable ground for corruption to grow and flourish (Uksvärav and Nurmi, 1993, p. 102). It was a reasonable way of management in the then prevailing economic circumstances. As noted earlier, the centrally planned system was responsible for the founding of enterprises, for determining their activities and also for their possible closing down. Inter-organizational relations were vertical rather than horizontal, and the enterprises were more closely related to the ministry in charge of their operations than to other enterprises (Liuhto, 1999, pp. 240–1). The environment of the enterprises was extremely closed. Dual management developed in the Soviet times divided into official and unofficial management methods.

The question of business ethics is problematic in the context of our survey. What does it mean that Finnish students value ethics higher in business behaviour? We also ask whether business ethics has the same meaning for the respondents, without any connection to their cultural background and past experiences. Estonian students understandably see such ethical principles as orders that one has to obey, hence, they view them in a negative light because of the ideological connotations they embrace.

The findings of the study can also be discussed in terms of their relationship with the history and the life experiences of the respondents. Learning new ethics means to Estonian management students adopting a sensitiveness towards international relations and building trust. Trust between organizations and between individuals has several dimensions (Mishra, 1996):

1. Competence-based trust appreciates the skilfulness and abilities of the partner;
2. Openness and sincerity in communication is based on trust.
3. Shared interests mean a sort of trust that the partner is not aiming to take advantage of the other but takes account of the interest of the partner or the broader society;
4. Credibility means a logical relation between what one says and how one acts, belief in the other's words or promises.

Depending on their attitude towards these dimensions, managers can see each other either as a threat or an ally. Adopting a new ethics in Estonian enterprises also means learning new ways of trusting each other in social affairs. At least it requires that they:

- unlearn the former practices according to which other enterprises are a threat, and instead, see them as parties to learn from;
- adopt practices by which one learns to become a partner who earns trust, acting in ways that take account of the other's interests as well as those of society as a whole;
- learn openness and unlearn the withdrawal from social affairs in business life; and
- find competent partners and learn from how they do things.

If clan-style directors were typical in the Soviet era, pure friendship and unofficial relations appear to be losing their grip in post-Soviet business cultures (for example, Lehmbruck, 1999, p. 5; Liuhto, 1999, p. 80), as managers are increasingly using official agreements and formal alliances.

Educational aspects of identity transformation

The findings of the study show that obeying ethical rules is considered among Estonian students less important compared with the Finnish students. At present, there seems to be little interest in regulation and obligations and more emphasis on individual understanding, ciritique and values.

The discourse of 'hard' facts as opposed to 'soft' aspects (for example, people and social affairs) is a problematic dichotomy. Focusing on identity questions disrupts the polarity that comes from using these two concepts. According to Kavolis' definition (referred in Czarniawska-Joerges, 1994b, p. 197), the concept of identity encompasses the following elements:

1. It is an overall coherence between the individual's experience and the way this experience is expressed.
2. It is a memory on the part of the individual and others of a continuity in the course of the individual's life.
3. It is a conscious, but not excessive, artificial or manipulative commitment to the manner in which the individual understands and deals with his or her 'self'.

The concepts of opinion, memory and self-awareness are important in understanding how individuals, through self-narratives, achieve a modern identity that is independent of other people's reactions. Autobiographical literature appears to give good illustrations of this modern identity and, in fact, transforms personal life into private property that is capable of having exchange value (Lejeune, 1989, pp. 161–2).

University education is a way of shaping and reshaping individual identities, both personal and organizational. The process by which identities are created is relevant, as well as the content of identity; the pedagogical solutions that any student is presented with in university education, become relevant as well. The ideas of organizational identity create space for narrating autobiographical acts that contribute to the construction of organizational identities (Aaltio-Marjosola, 1994). However, what is even more important, identity transformation as a basic understanding of organizational change in transition economies like Estonia breaks down the two-headed dichotomy of the development story. Thus the meaning of education is questioned; that is, we either see education as a change agent towards a better future, or something that should restrain from manipulative actions, respect the 'old' and search for new country-specific cultural forms. An identity-based understanding of university education reaches out beyond the dichotomy and sees management education as a process by which the students are given the materials for acting as business professionals in the society of the future, in other words, building identities that fit a given situation. We suggest that identity transformation is of crucial importance in university education among business students in transition economies such as Estonia.

The idea of professional identities of business managers is relevant when we try to understand the acts they are expected to perform and the challenges this poses to education. With respect to the content of business education in Estonia this means:

- The autobiographical experiences of the students are of relevance in their education. When individuals and teams discuss issues concerning their experiences of business life and management issues of Estonian enterprises, they bridge from their previous experiences to new ones and find ways and words for describing these facts. Such processes, and the students' personal involvement in them, are significant. When expressing their experiences, students find their own way to stand and face the realities they need to face, that is, they adopt an identity as business life professionals.
- The discourse on old and new business life values as well as the need to change them is problematic. It refers to the idea of a business life ideology like that of the centralized system, which is disliked by the inhabitants of Estonia today. Instead of rejecting the old completely, bridges must be built between the old and new periods of time and to reach for the future together with the past.
- It is important to transform new self-images at the individual level. This means that at the individual level, in the way people reflect and talk about themselves, they find confidence in doing what they do. Education can support this building of identities at the student level as well as at the managerial levels.

People as actors in the world of management create and change their identities and their cultures. The creation of culture is a dialectic process between subjectivity and objectivity. According to the classical ideas of Berger and Luckmann (1966, pp. 8–15), the creation of culture is due to objectification, a process in which the individual acts both as an assimilator of ideas and a creator of new ideas. Subjective experiences of success and failure develop into collective descriptions about the reality which then starts to take on an objective nature. The dialectic interaction between the self and the sociocultural world is fundamental in the creation of social reality and a world of shared meanings. Economic reality is an institutional reality, a shared reality with connections to these subjective interpretations held by the actors.

As seen in the survey findings, the differences between the values of Estonian and Finnish business students were not necessarily great. Part of these differences find their interpretation in the cultural and economic surroundings and the history of the two countries. The transition from a state-determined enterprise activity to a privately driven business activity represents the special context of the Estonian students' values and value orientations. The former economic system with large economic units has become dominated by small enterprises. In Estonia, more than half of the industrial companies employed over 200 workers in 1987, whereas approximately a decade later only four percent of all companies had more than 50 employees. While Soviet economic thinking overvalued the importance of organizational megalomania and focused on heavy industry (Liuhto, 1999, p. 252), there has been a major shift from domestic-market centricity towards open interaction between the post-Soviet economies and the world economy, and a reorientation in the transition from industry-domination to service- and trade-orientation.

As a result of these macro-economy changes, the identity of the manager and the organization had to change as well. Questions such as: Who am I as an actor in this environment?; What are my experiences?; How do I interpret them for myself and express them to the community outside?; and What kind of sense of continuity do I have during the course of my lifetime in the context of the economy and organizations? become very important. These questions are challenges to Estonian university education. It is university-level business education in particular that carries forward ideas for future ways of management in organizations. Combining technical, cultural and social knowledge is of importance in the processes of identity building of future managers.

Part II

Stories of the Past: Lost and Found Identities

5

Socioeconomic Conditions and Discursive Construction of Women's Identities in Post-Soviet Countries[1]

Aneta Pavlenko

Introduction

What happens when certain identities are no longer legitimized or validated by society? The goal of the present chapter is to understand the impact of radical historical and socioeconomic changes on discursive construction of identity, in particular, on subjectivities available in a specific society at a specific point in time. The current situation in post-Soviet countries provides a unique opportunity to explore this issue by examining lives caught in a rapidly shifting social reality. I will focus my analysis on the concept of womanhood as it is constituted, transformed and redefined in post-Soviet discourses. I will begin by comparing the political and economic situation of women in Soviet and in post-Soviet times, linking the socioeconomic conditions to discursive positions assigned to women by the preeminent ideologies before and after 1991, since at all times notions of acceptable femininities are closely tied to economic conditions and the distribution of wealth (Burr, 1998; Gal, 1978).

In search for new representations of womanhood, I will analyse two types of post-Soviet narratives: public and private. The public narratives consist of interviews and articles published in post-Soviet magazines between 1991 and 1999. While focused on women, these texts are created for and by the media, and at best can claim joint authorship; thus, they are mainly representative of attempts made to position women in specific roles. In order to consider women's own positionings, I will examine the private narratives, women's life stories, collected in the summer of 1997 in Kiev, Ukraine and St Petersburg, Russia. I will look at how these women reminisce, talk about and negotiate in everyday life the multiple meanings of being a post-Soviet woman. The comparative analysis of the two types of narratives will allow me to investigate how various discursive positions and subjectivities prescribed through the media are being adopted, negotiated, contested and resisted by contemporary Russian and Ukrainian women struggling to occupy a place in societies undergoing drastic changes and transformations. Based on the evidence presented in the chapter, I will argue that looking at both sociopolitical and socioeconomic conditions is critical for understanding the range of subjectivities available to women prior to and following the collapse of the Soviet Union.

Research methodology

Recently, reconstruction of gender identity in the former Soviet Union, and, in particular, the concept of post-Soviet womanhood, was subjected to a number of theoretical discussions and empirical investigations (Edmondson, 1992; Marsh, 1996a; Pilkington, 1996; Posadskaya, 1994a). Pilkington (1996) employed various methodologies popular in the fields of social psychology and sociology, such as analysis of the media texts, questionnaires, surveys and interviews with participants. The current project extends this methodological variety by adopting a narrative or life history approach. Narratives and, in particular, stories that people tell about their lives, have recently become the focus of the evolving field of narrative study, which posits narrative as the central means by which people give meaning to their lives across time (Gergen and Gergen, 1993; Josselson and Lieblich, 1993; Rosenwald and Ochberg, 1992; Sarbin, 1986). Life stories are seen in this framework as coherent systems in their own right; they may be contested, negotiated and reconstructed, reflecting changes in speakers' values, understandings and situations. Bringing human subjectivity to the forefront, the study of life stories clarifies how individuals make sense of their lives and what tacit cultural rules, implicit assumptions and belief systems allow this sense making to take place (Linde, 1993; Ochberg, 1994). Until recently, however, Russian discourse and, in particular, narratives have been overlooked as an object of analysis (see, however, Ries, 1997), being overshadowed by the study of post-Soviet politics, sociology and economy. Thus, the present study, while building on the previous scholarship, presents a new development for the field of post-Soviet studies, as well as for cross-cultural feminist investigation of women's lives and for sociolinguistic study of ways in which discourses constitute human subjectivities, allowing people to narrate and renarrate themselves.

Magazines and, in particular, women's magazines have also come to the fore recently in research conducted at the intersection between feminist cultural studies and discourse analysis (Hayashi, 1997; Hermes, 1995; Talbot, 1995). Scholars argue that the study of the meanings and positions offered to the readers of women's magazines allows us to define specific cultural discourses and uncover master narratives which often serve to legitimate and naturalize currently existing social practices and gender relations. Thus, the arguments about subjectivities currently available to Russian women come from the interviews with prominent women and men, as well as articles on women's identities and male–female relationships in a number of post-Soviet magazines published between 1991 and 1999 and available both in Russia and Ukraine (where the Russian press still dominates the market). In the present study, the magazines analysed consist of random issues of several Russian women's magazines (*Lisa, Natalie, Good Housekeeping, Cosmopolitan, Zhenskii mir* (Women's World), *Ona* (She), *Gorozhanka* (Urban Female), *Rabotnitsa* (Female factory worker) and *Krestianka* (Rural female)), one men's publication (*Egoist*) and a few 'gender-neutral' magazines and newspapers (such as *Argumenty i fakty*/Arguments and facts). Content analysis of the data has entailed a hermeneutic task of locating patterns through exploration of recurring arguments, habitual remarks, juxtapositions and oppositions, and the use of metaphors.

Many authors also suggest that any study of subjectivities prescribed by the media is limited without consideration of the readers' opinions, whereby new narratives, meanings and positions are either contested or jointly constructed. In line with this argument, first hand data were also collected for the project. The data come from semi-structured life story interviews, conducted in Kiev, Ukraine and St Petersburg, Russia, in the summer of 1997, as a part of a larger study of meaning-making systems of former Soviet citizens. In order to diversify the choice of informants, several factors were considered as important for women's positioning: age, class, ethnicity, socioeconomic background, degree of professional success and embeddedness in existing social networks. Thus, the ages of the five informants range from 35 to 83; ethnically one woman is Jewish, one Ukrainian and three are Russian. With regard to the socioeconomic position one is a retiree, living on social welfare, one a homemaker wife of an upper-class 'new Russian' businessman, one a clerical worker in a Russian-American mission, one is an unemployed librarian and one is a former scientist turned patent consultant. The tape-recorded interviews with the informants were conducted in Russian, all were one to two hours long. The data were analysed through an interpretative method that entailed multiple readings and listenings of the interview texts, a search for patterns through exploration of recurring arguments, and a comparison of the arguments to the ones identified in the media narratives. All excerpts from the interviews included in the chapter are translated from Russian into English by the author.

Gender politics in the USSR and in the post-Soviet states

While consequent waves of the feminist movement swept over the Western world, the Soviet Union regarded these upheavals with contempt and amusement – in the 'greatest country in the world' the 'woman question' (*zhenskii vopros*) had been solved and women enjoyed an unprecedented equality with men in their legal, political, social, economic and cultural status. The collapse of the monolithic Soviet state in 1991 led, among other things, to the slow dissolution of the myth of Soviet women's emancipation and equality. On the surface, 'women *did* have equality in law, and there *were* women in all the professions, some of which like, the judiciary, still remain virtually closed to women in Britain' (Clark, 1994). At a closer look, however, gender equality under socialism turned out to be one of the most refined social mystifications of the era (Voronina, 1994a, p. 37). Women in the USSR were marginalized and exploited in a variety of ways:

- Gender asymmetry was very visible in both vertical and horizontal *division of labour*: women were segregated into feminized areas of low-paid low-prestige jobs, often with poor working conditions and no possibility of advancement; the average pay for female labour was 30 per cent less than for the male (Voronina, 1994a). The so-called equality also resulted in the infamous 'second shift': women were forced to carry the double burden of work and domestic chores. It has been estimated that the average workload for working Soviet women was about 76 hours per week (Mezentseva, 1994).
- This asymmetry was even more acute in *social and political affairs*: the public sphere belonged almost exclusively to men and the private to women who were continuously absent from decision-making bodies: 'on the one hand, it is considered that they do not have any special political and social interests distinct from those of men; on the other hand, men are fully convinced that politics is not a matter for women' (Voronina, 1994a, pp. 39–40).

- In the sphere of *ideology*, traditional patriarchal attitudes were reinforced through all social mechanisms including mass media by portraying men as the main owners of the public sphere and women as reigning in the private sphere. Severe social problems – women's appalling working conditions, increasing divorce rate, single parenthood, male alcoholism, wife-beating, child abuse, rape, sexual harassment, increasing violence and impossibility to display an alternative sexual orientation – were dismissed as private or personal issues and considered taboo subjects by the press.

In her perceptive analysis of Russian women's history, Marsh points out that the conservative values of Soviet and post-Soviet leaders go way back to the patriarchal attitudes to women in tsarist Russia: 'whatever the political system in Russia, it has always had predominantly negative consequences for women' (Marsh 1996b: p. 4). While outwardly praising the outstanding achievements of independent and equal Soviet women, the Communist leaders were bent on keeping them in secondary positions, using women's labour-power as a means to solve the problem of economic growth. Moreover, not unlike the US during and after World War II, the USSR alternatively introduced the ideology of gender equality and the ideology of women's 'natural mission' depending on what suited the country at the time. Officially, however, the ideologists of the Soviet state promoted one and only one gender identity for women: that of a glorified socialist worker, mother and wife, who, supported by the state, enjoys combining the three roles. Any existing discrimination was 'carefully concealed by the absence (or fabrication) of statistics' (Posadskaya, 1994c, p. 10).

Currently, in the post-Soviet times, the socioeconomic situation of women not only did not improve but became significantly worse. Numerous studies demonstrated that women have been particularly disadvantaged by the political, social, and economic changes, which accompanied the end of the Communist rule.

Difficulties of the economic transition to the free market resulted in the *masculinization of paid labour*, the *displacement of women* and the *feminization of poverty*. For those currently employed, these trends translate into increases in job segregation and discrimination in terms of wages, career promotion and participation in industrial management. For the unemployed they lead to a continuous lack of job opportunities and training programmes. Most importantly, the transition to the free market resulted in unprecedented unemployment rates with almost 80 per cent of the unemployed being women (Marsh, 1996b;

Posadskaya, 1994d). In 1996 most of the working women were concentrated in a limited number of trades and in comparatively junior positions with the average pay one-third lower than that of men (even though the educational level of working women is higher). Correspondingly, women's pensions were only 70 per cent of men's (Marsh, 1996b). The new trends in employment are very visible to the study participants, one of whom pointed out that men are displacing women in all kinds of paid labour:

> The situation changed ... yesterday we were driving and everywhere in the streets, everywhere there were only men doing road construction ... before there were only women ... here the situation changed drastically, I don't know why ... probably because it is difficult to find a job ... probably because it pays well ... that's why men chased all the women out of these jobs. (L, 47, a clerical worker in a Russian–American mission, from an interview with the author)

New legislations, social entitlements and preferential terms, supposedly geared towards women's 'liberation' and 'protection', in fact legitimize the trend to shift women from paid labour to unpaid domestic labour, making female employees an extremely unattractive proposition for employers. As a result, new economic structures, such as joint enterprises, cooperatives and private firms, employ women mostly in a very narrow range of jobs: secretaries, consultants, low-paid service staff and office personnel (Posadskaya, 1994d). Many women have no other choice but to accept any job offer: about 20 per cent of Russian women are single mothers, who are forced to take low-paying positions to support themselves and their children, and who, in view of the scarcity of child-care, are often at the mercy of relatives and friends with regard to baby-sitting. Feminization of poverty is also evident in the case of the elderly women living on their own. The process of housing privatization not only led to continuous violation and infringement of their property rights but also to a new type of crime: blackmail and murder of elderly women by either relatives or mafia gangs interested in taking over their apartments.

In the *public sphere*, women are not just marginalized but 'squeezed out of legislative and executive power' (Posadskaya, 1994b, p. 4). The negative stereotype of an 'iron lady', 'not elected by anyone but appointed by the Party and state apparatus, obedient to the will of the top bosses, always ready to vote "in favor" and carry out directives "from above" (Khotkina, 1994, p. 105) is alive and well and works against the few existing female politicians. In the recent years, public attacks on politically and socially engaged women became verbal as well as physical: the infamous ultranationalist Duma Deputy Vladimir Zhirinovskii had attacked at least two female correspondents and one female deputy during Duma sessions, justifying his behaviour by the victims' 'lack of femininity' (*Russian Life*, March 1998, p. 9; *Russian Life*, May 1998, p. 13).

Finally, with regard to ideology, the post-Soviet states are characterized by the '*patriarchal renaissance*', or, in Attwood's (1996) terms, 'the aggressive re-masculinization' of society. On the one hand, this trend is evident in massive exploitation of sexuality through commercialization and objectification of the female body by the media, the appearance of new social practices such as beauty pageants, erotic shows, mail-order brides' catalogues, and dramatically increased hard-currency prostitution. On the other hand, the return to patriarchal values is evident in the intensified calls for women to return to their 'natural womanly mission' and traditional gender roles.

Thus, democratization in the post-Soviet states, in particular, in Russia and Ukraine, is, as suggested by Marsh (1996b, p. 5) 'a "gendered concept", granting men and women equal rights in the formal sense, but suggesting that their duties were to be very different: women's would be firmly rooted in the moral, spiritual and thus private sphere'. It is by now evident that political, socioeconomic and ideological transformations in the post-Soviet society resulted in a dramatic reconceptualization of women's identities, whereby their previous 'emancipated' subjectivities are severely disparaged, and the new ones – wife, mother, homemaker, on the one hand, and prostitute/object of male desire, on the other – strongly encouraged.

Reconceptualization of womanhood in the post-Soviet times

It is interesting to note that transformation of the image of a Soviet woman was initiated in the Soviet times, in Gorbachev's (1987) infamous appeal to women to return to their purely womanly mission:

> We are proud of what the Soviet government has given women: the same right to work as men, equal pay for equal work, and social security. Women have been given every opportunity to get an edu-

> cation, to have a career, and to participate in social and political activities ... But during our difficult and heroic history, we failed to pay attention to women's specific rights and needs arising from their role as mother and home-maker, and their indispensable educational function as regards children. Engaged in scientific research, working on construction sites, in production and the services, and involved in creative activities, women no longer have enough time to perform their everyday duties at home – housework, the upbringing of children and the creation of a good family atmosphere. We have discovered that many of our problems – in children's and young people's behaviour, in our morals, culture and in production are partially caused by the weakening of family ties and slack attitude to family responsibilities. This is a paradoxical result in our sincere and politically justified desire to make women equal with men in everything. Now, in the course of perestroika, we have begun to overcome this shortcoming. That is why we are now holding heated debates in the press, in public organizations, at work and at home, about the question of what we should do to make it possible for women to return to their *purely womanly mission*. (Gorbachev, 1987, p. 117; my italics)

The climate of *perestroika* and *glasnost* made it possible to question the Soviet ideals and to challenge the accuracy of previous portrayals of women's life in the USSR. Thus, a number of publications attempted a discussion of previously obscured and denied aspects of the 'woman question': difficult and often dangerous working conditions, the double burden of work and home, high rates of divorce and resulting single parenthood (or rather motherhood), lack of contraception, the horrifying conditions in abortion clinics and maternity hospitals, high infant mortality rate, male alcoholism, domestic violence, child abuse, high incidence of rape and gang rape, sexual coercion and sexual harassment (in particular, in the workplace), female sexuality and lesbian sexual orientation. The press also attended to more sensational cultural and ethnic aspects of the woman question, such as the self-immolation by Muslim women or an extremely difficult situation of Vietnamese female *gastarbeiters* (foreign workers). However, while these and many other issues were hotly discussed and examined, and the problems revealed, defined and deplored, the acknowledgment of the still-existing and unresolved woman question did not result in improvement in any of the areas. Moreover, soon the discussion took a rather unexpected turn, and 'turned into a debate on the nature of the

Soviet woman and what she should be in order to be a "real" woman, not a "Soviet" woman' (Voronina, 1994b, p. 135). Premised on Gorbachev's appeal and on earlier concerns that female emancipation in the USSR led to appearance of 'unfeminine' women, this 'discursive explosion around what constitutes femininity' (McRobbie, 1994, p. 158) opened up a space for the creation of new positions and subjectivities for post-Soviet women, often fashioned explicitly in opposition to images, discourses and ideologies of the past. The past is a powerful resource mobilized by various parties in an attempt to legitimize a version of the present aligned to current political and social agendas (see also Kelemen's chapter). Through the media, in particular, the state invaded all spheres of women's lives propagating particular images of femininity and sexuality, promoting preferred gender narratives and patterns of behaviour in the public and private spheres (Bruno, 1996). The predominant images of a socialist worker and a collective farm worker were replaced by those of a happy homemaker, a beauty queen and a hard-currency prostitute.

A textual analysis of numerous portraits, profiles and interviews with successful and well-known individuals that appeared in the last decade in popular post-Soviet magazines demonstrated that in the nineties men and women were portrayed – and portrayed themselves – very differently in the media. Men were typically positioned as the breadwinners and citizens of the world and women – no matter what else they may be doing with their lives – as inhabitants of the home sphere, 'providing the background against which men can define themselves and develop their identities as men and as members of the new Russian nation' (Bruno, 1996, p. 43). A short incursion into the Western literature on the role and position of men and women in management and organizational discourses suggests a relatively similar picture. Western discourses have been shown to constitute the 'ideal employee' (and especially the ideal manager) as a disembodied and 'rational' figure, a figure that fits closely with cultural images of masculinity rather than femininity (for example, Acker, 1990, 1992; Gherardi, 1995; Martin, 1989). Femininity, on the other hand, has tended to be associated with embodiment, emotions and sexuality; as such it is constituted as subordinate to 'male' rationality, and possibly as out of place in 'rational' organizations (Fournier and Kelemen, 2001).

The analysis of these media texts allowed me to identify five interdependent trends in the representation of female subjectivities in post-Soviet discourses, all of which both legitimate and obscure recent political and socioeconomic changes:

1. women as secondary citizens;
2. women as homemakers;
3. women as career businesswomen;
4. women as sexual objects and victims of violence; and
5. non-encouragement of lesbian and feminist identities

The juxtaposition of the texts illustrating these trends and the narratives elicited from the participants of the study allows me to suggest that not all of the trends are uncritically internalized by the women in question; an attempt to impose new ideologies of gender, intrinsically linked to the new market conditions, is in many cases met with criticism and resistance.

Women as secondary citizens

The first and the most important trend is to present *women as secondary citizens* and lesser human beings through a variety of means, including contrastive use of the terms 'women' and 'people'. This contrast can be illustrated half-jokingly by a popular saying 'A woman is a human's best friend' (*Zhenshchina drug cheloveka*) and by a quote from a Soviet poem: 'What does a person need? A woman at his side ...' (cited in Lipovskaya, 1994, p. 123). It is significantly less funny when such a contrast appears in public declarations of distinguished members of intelligentsia, such as Valentin Rasputin, one of the leading Russian writers, who stated that 'women should give sustenance to the people' (cited in Klimenkova, 1994, p. 24) or a well-known parliament depute Sergei Baburin, who in his recent interview said:

> That's exactly what I am trying to say, that our parliament employs serious and loving people, who work with love for the Motherland and for their beloved women. (From an interview given to *Lubov'* (Love), a weekly supplement to the newspaper *Argumenty i Fakty* (Arguments and Facts), no. 15, August 1997. Here and further on all texts are presented in the author's translation).

The idea of a woman being a wife, mother and a willing servant to the newly empowered Russian male is about the only issue that unites politicians across a wide spectrum of positions, from Baburin to Gorbachev to Yeltsin to Khasbulatov, who declared that the market is finally creating conditions under which the Russian man can feel like the head of the family. In view of this widely spread ideological campaign, which takes roots in the Communist past, it is not surprising that many women have internalized the ideology of oppression, as seen in a synopsis of an interview with a wife of another young Russian politician, Yevgeniy Loginov, in a women's magazine *Gorozhanka* (Urban Female):

> Men, busy with politics, have their own goals and agendas. And their wives, like all women in the world, are raising children, giving themselves wholly to serving the family. Tatyana, the wife of a State Deputy Yevgeniy Loginov, thinks that family harmony is the most important. (*Gorozhanka*, December 1996)

Persuaded of their secondary status, some women learned to see and present themselves discursively as an appendage to men and/or family and not as independent individuals. Thus, the wife of the country's leading ophthalmologist, Sviatoslav Fedorov, in an interview given to the Russian edition of *Good Housekeeping* (August-September 1995) stated that she sees her husband as a diamond and herself as a setting (*on – moi brilliant, ia – ego oprava*). A similar view is expressed by the young and popular TV hostess Yelena Bal'burova: 'It is well known that a husband is a head and a wife is a neck. It is good when one really manages to be a "neck" (*Gorozhanka*, 1997, 5, p. 7). Similarly, one of the study participants, an English major in college, refused to reflect on the changes taking place in the country saying: 'You think globally, I don't ... I am on a homemaker's level ...' (I, 35, a homemaker, wife of a successful businessman)

Women as homemakers

Consequently, the second important and closely related trend is to present *women as homemakers*, firmly entrenching them in the 'private' sphere by naturalizing their 'womanly' roles as mothers, wives and homemakers and by undermining their professional competence. The former image of women and men as partners in building socialism, so ironically presented in a popular film *Moscow Doesn't Believe in Tears* (1980), is rapidly being replaced by that of the traditional family where men are the breadwinners and women devote themselves to child care and domesticity. This idyllic tableau of a new post-Soviet reality is painted by a young surgeon Andrei Akopian, interviewed as a bachelor-of-the-month by a women's magazine *Krestianka* (Rural Female):

> From my point of view, a man should support his woman financially, whether they are officially married or not. The question is

> whether he is able to ... When the economy is weak, the woman suffers. And she doesn't need that much: her own house, a predictable husband, a child whose future she could be sure about. So that taking care of them would be a joy. From this point of view the future of the Russian family depends on the economic situation. (*Krestianka*, February 1998, 2, p. 81–2)

The attack on women's rights, initiated by Gorbachev in 1987, only intensified with time, fortified by the pressures of the new masculinized market. It turned out that in the Soviet times both women and the workplace suffered from women working outside the home. An article in *Pravd*a suggested that 'women working outside the home means disintegration of the family and a low birth-rate', while an interview in *Kuranty* presents a view that 'women who work outside the home cannot really be called mothers and wives' (Klimenkova, 1994). One recent article in women's magazine *Rabotnitsa* (Female factory worker) went as far as to describe career women who return home dog tired and/or over-excited as sick and in need of psychological counseling (*Rabotnitsa*, 1997, 10, pp. 18–19). The media also attempts to naturalize and essentialize sex differences, as exemplified by a recent article in a women's magazine *Ona* (She), by a certain Petukhov, Ph D in biology. The article starts out with numeric claims that women's brains are generally of a smaller size than male ones and then proceeds to link this 'fact' to differences in reasoning styles, as well as memory power (using the Russian expression *devichia pamiat'*, girls' memory, which refers to forgetfulness). Most importantly, the author also uses neurobiology to explain and justify gender differences in parenting roles and responsibilities, opposing biologically conditioned motherhood to socially conditioned fatherhood:

> Differences between men and women also exist in their attitudes toward children. To a great regret, not all men know that motherly love is different from the fatherly love not only on the emotional level, but also on the deeper, neurobiological one. For a mother it is an ancient instinct, while father's feelings for his progeny are conditioned by the social, moral, and ethic factors, as well as his upbringing and culture. (Petukhov, *Ona*, March 1998, p. 20)

These ideas are echoed in many advice columns, such as the one in a popular women's weekly *Lisa* whereby women are urged to remember that men – unlike women – cannot think about work and home simultaneously, and, thus, should be allowed to relax and watch TV upon their return home, while their loving wives take care of dinner and other household chores (*Lisa*, January 1998, 3, p. 14). An important role model for post-Soviet women is Yeltsin's wife, Naina, who, continuing the traditions of previous invisible first ladies, and challenging Raisa Gorbachev's unseemly attempts to be a public figure, declared in her interview to the newspaper *My* (We) in August 1992:

> I am not the first lady, I am simply the wife of the Russian president ... Everything is just as it was before for us. I've remained a housewife ... I choose his ties, I take care of his shirts and suits ... But there is an unbreakable rule in our family: I must never ask my husband about anything that relates to his work. (as cited by Attwood, 1996. p. 258).

In accordance with the new image, interviews with actresses, TV hostesses, women writers and singers as well as with successful businesswomen and politicians are illustrated by pictures of them with their children (and/or household appliances) (see for example, an interview with a Duma deputy Ella Pamfilova, in *Ogonek*, May 1998, accompanied by the picture of Pamfilova in her kitchen beautifully decorated with traditional Russian porcelain, wood and pottery). Unfailingly, interviews with prominent women include questions about their housekeeping abilities, while interviews with their male counterparts involve statements about their wives 'female', that is, domestic abilities:

> My wife has amazing housekeeping abilities: in twenty five years of our being together we never had a housekeeper. (From an interview with Iosif Kobzon, one of the leading singers of the country in the last 40 years, *Natalie*, August 1997, p. 7).

> He [Mikhail Boiarsky, a well-known movie and theatre actor] was against me working, in women he values above all domesticity, an ability to cook well ... Mikhail Sergeevich likes meat, likes to eat well. Well, a lot, like all men. So I try to give him a lot – tasty and plentiful. Also, I try to diversify what I cook. (From an interview with Larisa Luppian, an actress and Boiarsky's wife *Good Housekeeping*, June 1996, pp. 131–3).

In her analysis of women's portrayals in post-Soviet media, Voronina points out that 'the notion that a woman's culinary abilities are an integral part of her existence and the best proof of her 'real nature' is so deeply embedded in our national consciousness that it is virtually impossible to find anything in the media about women that does not mention the kitchen or the family' (1994b, p. 136). Not only the 'female abilities' are emphasized in these interviews, but also women's professional interests are presented as secondary. This is especially evident in interviews with women who work in the same field with their husbands, be it theatre, movies, television or music: the wife's career is usually presented as less important, while her main role is to 'cater to the great man' in order to keep the family together. It is for performing this latter role well that the woman is usually praised. Previously cited Larisa Luppian, an actress and a wife of a popular movie actor Mikhail Boiarsky, confides:

> During our long marriage, I forgave Misha a lot, mainly, his rudeness. He is very demanding, considers himself the head of the family, who is allowed everything, while a wife is allowed nothing ... I was afraid to remain alone. My mother was alone since about the age of thirty. Maybe that's why in my family life I am used to being patient in order not to remain alone, because loneliness, probably, is more terrifying for a woman than anything else. (*Good Housekeeping*, June 1996, pp. 131–3)

Her views on marriage, housekeeping and responsibilities are shared by many, including Natalia Yegudina, a dancer and a wife of the director of the Bolshoi Theater of Siberia Valeriy Yegudin:

> – Do you cook yourself?
> – Yes, I like it very much.
> – And your husband doesn't help?
> – No, he really doesn't have any time. Theater, conservatory, public responsibilities.
> – Finally, there is something to reproach him for.
> – It never occurred to me to reproach him for that. He has other goals. And the house is my responsibility. Sometimes the older daughter helps. Everything is fine. (*Gorozhanka*, 1997, 5, p. 26)

The traditional views of gender roles are also reproduced in current social practices whereby girls are encouraged to help at home, while boys are brought up to demand. Natalia Cherkasova, the successful head of the Moscow Cosmetology Club and a happy wife of a government official, states her policy on children upbringing in the following way:

> I always try to have order in the house. Because I have sons. And you know that boys try to find a spouse based on their mother's image. So I want my sons to know that a good wife always has dinner ready on time, she doesn't accumulate dirty dishes nor un-ironed pants. (*Ona*, March 1998, p. 32)

Rather then focusing on possible ways to reduce women's workloads at home by redistributing household responsibilities, the predominant discourses legitimize the sexual division of labour presenting it as the key to family harmony and happiness. The Russian language even has a special term for women's happiness, the infamous '*zhenskoe schastie*' (women's happiness), predicated on having and caring for one's husband and children.

The cult of motherhood has always been an important part of Russian society: a childless woman was considered to be 'less of a woman' and was perceived 'more negatively than a woman who has children but has not managed to find herself a husband' (Lipovskaya, 1994, p. 128). In the recent years, attempts at women's 'domestication' led to increased emphasis on the role of motherhood in women's lives. 'Children and cats are the key to reaching harmony', pronounces a popular actress and a single mother Natalia Varlei from the pages of *Good Housekeeping* (June 1996). Nevertheless, despite an abundance of culturally promoted images of happy mothers, this role is no longer aspired to by women unable to support themselves:

> What I am afraid of is to have children, now, in our country, because before perestroika, I knew that if I don't get married by the age of 30, I will just have a child. Now in my most daring dreams I can't afford that, because the moment I have a child, I will lose a job, any job. And won't be able to raise my child, because I won't have a job, I'll be a beggar ... This is the biggest current problem, this is what we lost. Socialist system had its advantages. (E, 37, former librarian, unemployed)

Blatantly ignoring the socioeconomic reality, the media and the politicians, however, continue encouraging women to finally become happy through giving up their independence and workforce slavery, enforced by communism, and by assuming their 'natural' care-giving roles of wives and mothers. Choice has become the key concept in current discourses about femininity. In the past, women had no choice at all: the socioeconomic and political situation forced them into full-time labour, juggling the demands of the 'double burden'. Currently, however they may have a choice: some may 'choose' a career, while others may 'choose' to stay home with children and become homemakers, an opportunity previously denied by the Soviet regime.

From this position, the encouragement for part-time work or for staying at home 'appears not as a retrograde step threatening female emancipation, but as a blessed release from the rigors of the Stalinist past' (Bridger, 1992, p. 191). What is obscured in the declaration of choice, however, is the fact that choices require stable families with sufficient incomes and adequate day care, neither of which is guaranteed in the socioeconomic reality dominated by the feminization of poverty and unemployment. The latter aspect is clearly visible in the participants' narratives where women accept full and complete responsibility for the family and children's well-being in the situation created by the new market:

> In ninety one I lost my job, I worked in a geography department ... I worked and my position was eliminated, despite my two little children, so ... at this moment, there were big changes in my family, because ... the situation was difficult, and my husband started drinking, and drinking hard ... as usual, in our country, male population, they ... um ... give up first, well, women think of family, children, that's why I lost my job and found another one in a different field. (L, 47, a clerical worker in a Russian–American mission)

Women as career business women

In view of the reigning patriarchal attitudes, it is not surprising that even when the media portrays *successful career or businesswomen*, their portrayals are vested with meanings quite different from the ones in the West. According to the predominant ideologies of gender, even a successful career should not detract women – and men – from perceiving women's social roles and public positions as secondary to those of men, and their main destination as being wives and mothers. Often it is women themselves who voice these opinions. Thus, when asked about her outstanding business success, the founder and head of the Moscow Cosmetology Club, Natalia Cherkasova, responded by saying:

> This world is created for men. She is by His side. If you take this as a given, many things will become easy and uncomplicated. Why should you try and prove to Him that you are better, that you are unique and

> born for something special. He is born for something special. And you simply live in His world. (*Ona*, March 1998, 3, p. 32)

Her opinion is shared by Tatiana Koltsova, head of Red Stars, top Russian modeling agency:

> Journalists keep asking me about emancipation, and I tell them that Russian women will never have emancipation in global terms ... For we have been educated to be a wife and a mother. These values are still valued by Russian women. And I think this is good. When Russian women marry (*vykhodiat zamuzh*), they are literally going 'behind their husband'. It is the husband who is the head of the family. So, I think we are pretty far from emancipation. For I have seen what an emancipated woman in America is ... They pay separately for their dinner, for their apartment. For us, this is something weird ... I don't regard the mere fact that a woman is head of a business as meaning that she is emancipated. (*Russian Life*, March 1998, p. 15)

Most importantly, the interviews with these successful women obscure the fact that such success is very rare considering both current market conditions and the difficulty experienced by the majority of the post-Soviet people who have to change their life trajectories mid-life and/or mid-career (or face working at places that can no longer afford to pay salaries). There is no previous tradition in Russia of taking a different path during one's lifetime: typically, specialization started very early, most often with one's choice of a technical school, college or the first job, and often people remained in a same factory or enterprise until retirement. As discussed earlier, the necessity to change careers in the new economic conditions particularly affected women who face the problem of 'the mismatch between the skills they have and the jobs on offer' (Bridger and Kay, 1996, p. 22). Often, they have to accept positions below their educational level and with little societal prestige, and if they get involved in some form of a business, they get blamed for taking advantage of people in an unstable market situation. One of the study participants, herself a businessman's wife, feels that she has to defend her friend's choice to become a 'shuttle' (*chelnok*), an owner of a kiosk, who buys stuff such as soda, beer or chocolates elsewhere wholesale and then sells it in her kiosk for a higher price:

> I know, I have friends who had a kiosk, I know what it involves ... how they carry the stuff, on their backs, they don't have a car, so they

> buy these cases or whatever of coke in cans, or beer, to earn some kopecks ... and where should they go? ... this friend of mine worked with me, at this [research institution] ... how should she live? ... she has three children and a husband who works in a factory ... what should they do? ... they are not being paid salary ... you should blame the government, not the kiosks ... people are earning their bread. (I, 35, a homemaker, wife of a successful businessman)

Women as sexual objects and victims of violence

The fourth key trend of the era is rather new to the society and involves presenting *women as sexual objects and victims of violence*. As pointed out previously, political, cultural and socioeconomic changes in post-Soviet society brought in a reassessment of values in many domains, and, in particular, with regard to the visual image of women. The 'old familiar woman-comrade, dressed in the buttoned-up uniform, modest business suit or sexless gown of the milkmaid, house-painter or collective-farm girl ... [has changed] her representation from positive to negative, from plus to minus' (Lipovskaya, 1994, p. 123). Advertisements for everything from guns to computers are populated by seductive half-naked or barely clothed females. In the past ten years these images flooded movie and TV screens, commercials, billboards, newspapers, magazines, cartoons and, as a result, public imagination. Even job offers blatantly display objectification and ageism, as well as gender-discrimination: many professional vacancy descriptions directly specify that they prefer male candidates, while minimal skills office position ads 'unabashedly stipulate youth and beauty as the chief requisites for applicants. A typical want ad for a secretarial position specifies: "Not older than 25; striking appearance, long legs compulsory"', (Azhgikhina and Goscilo, 1996, p. 114). While all informants agree that young attractive females have an easier time finding jobs than the older ones, all underscore the limited range and the hidden agendas of such positions: often the ads also specify that the woman should be 'without hang-ups' (*bez kompleksov*), that is willing to perform sexual as well as clerical functions (Ries, 1997).

Not surprisingly, ageism and gender-discrimination, especially with regard to the job market, are among the issues most often raised in the interviews with the informants:

> The first question they asked me at the job interview was how old I am and if I was married ... and they were interested in my age to see

> how young I am, how much I can handle in terms of work and whether I am young enough to be the boss's mistress ... and whether I am married, they wanted to know, to see if I have children who would distract me. (E, 37, former librarian, unemployed)

> And, you know, my age is, how should I say it, close to retirement, forty seven, so that with each year the hope of finding a new job is practically disappearing. (L, 47, a clerical worker in a Russian–American mission)

Exploitation of women's bodies is equally visible in the new social practices such as beauty contests, porn shows and exhibitions, mail-order bride businesses and hard-currency prostitution which has been on the rise since the late eighties. Sex equated with the female body is now discovered and used as a marketable commodity and an object of a displaced male violence. The years after perestroika witnessed the legalization and rapid spread of pornography on the screen and in the media: erotic and pornographic publications are on sale everywhere, and video salons are flooded with erotic and porn films. These Western and home-made publications and films link sex and violence, creating a contrast between male aggression and female passivity, blaming women for their own fate and often suggesting that women enjoy their subordination and suffering, often represented as rape and sexual coercion. In the majority of the cases, this debasement of women not only goes unpunished, but is oftentimes presented as a logical development in the process of democratization and Westernization of the post-Soviet society.

However, to accept that Russia at last is having a 'sexual revolution', modeled on its Western counterpart, would be an oversimplification. As pointed out by Shreeves (1992, p. 139), the concern for the liberation of women's sexuality is essentially male-defined: women's sexuality is to be liberated in terms of the male viewer-definer-judge. The tendency to equate women with other necessary or luxurious objects is evident in media interviews with Russian men, including a well-known, formerly dissident, writer Erofeev, who offers high praise to the new social practices:

> Beauty contests strike a blow at the traditional 'Soviet' image of a woman ... a Communist Stakhanovite in overalls whose principal virtue was her modesty. In today's image there is an emphasis on the erotic element, on physical beauty, on initiative, cleverness, elegance and efficiency. (Erofeev, 1990: 17)

A vivid example of objectifying and misogynistic Russian male discourse is an interview with a successful businessman Viktor Bulankin, director of a fashion-show theatre 'Siberia', in a men's magazine *Egoist*, which invited Bulankin to state his opinions on the subject of 'cars and women'. This interview, entitled 'He chose Audi', not only equates the two but gives preference to the car, the only permanent and special object in Bulankin's life, while women, referred to by a derogatory term *'devochki'* (chicks, girls, babes), are portrayed as disposable and secondary at best:

> But most importantly – a car is also erotic! How many chicks were kissed in the car! And not only kissed, there are some other aspects there. I consider it to be particularly cool to have some kind of relations in a car ... In terms of intimate relations, the car also gives a chance to make a mistake ... it is rather difficult [for a chick] to get out of the car while it's moving. Also, there is such a useful little thing as a seat belt. Some people fixate a victim of their love fantasies with handcuffs ... And here it is normal, the girl has a seat belt on, the car is moving at maximal speed. (*Egoist*, 1997, 1, p. 4).

Even more moderate men support a double standard when it comes to gender relations. When asked about husbands cheating on their wives, a 'bachelor-of-the-month' young surgeon Andrei Akopian responded:

> A woman shouldn't focus on cheating. She wants an intelligent, handsome, well-to-do, sexy [man], who would belong just to her. That just doesn't happen. A smart woman wouldn't be scared off by an affair. (*Krestianka*, February 1998, 2, p. 82)

The view that a woman is to blame for everything, including her husband's cheating, is propagated by many women's magazines including *Gorozhanka*, where the following advice was offered in an advice rubric to a woman whose husband was having an affair:

> Try to analyse your relationship with your husband and to see its flaws, what *forced* him to look for warmth and love elsewhere ... You probably take care of housework and the children. You walk around in an old washed out housedress (no money for anything decent) and constantly bump into your husband lying on the couch. A typical and unavoidable situation, but *the key is how you treat your responsibilities* ... Smile, be attentive and tender, call him by his first

> name ... *if you will treat him and the couch on which he is lying as the centre of the universe, he will come back to you.* (*Gorozhanka*, May 1998, p. 15; my italics)

Voicing chauvinistic opinions, like the ones above, in public is quite acceptable in Russia, according to Ilia Bezouglyi, the editor-in-chief of the Russian edition of *Men's Health.* Like many other Russians nowadays, he feels free to say what is on his mind and, in doing so, to make fun of American concepts of sexual harrassment and political correctness:

> People in the States, they watch their mouth much more, they behave themselves, political correctness, all that. Over here, a man is still a man, and it's much easier to be a man here. You can be a total male chauvinist pig here and feel perfectly fine. It's very accepted – by women too. (*Russian Life*, May 1998, p. 12)

In an attempt to resist and challenge these displays of patriarchal masculinity, many post-Soviet women, including the study participants, engage in the ever-popular discourse of male bashing, their only means to deconstruct the image of an all-powerful male, so dear to the establishment:

> [Men] understand that there are less of them, so that they are valuable ... and that there are lines to get them and they are very proud of it ... any scanky guy, riding a subway, unshaved with his dirty cheeks and a runny nose looks at women choosing ... well, which one am I going to choose today? ... how many women will get in line after me? (E, 37, former librarian, unemployed)

However, many, especially younger, women appear to have internalized the woman-as-a-sexual-object discourse: the monetary awards and social privileges of selling one's looks entice constantly increasing numbers of women into beauty contests, Miss Bust or Miss Legs competitions, pornographic modelling and prostitution, at times euphemistically referred to as 'hostessing' and 'performance' at casinos and nightclubs. Moreover, several recent polls reveal that prostitution is regarded as the most prestigious profession by young women. This fact is not surprising as an image of a prostitute, especially hard-currency one, has been promoted and glorified by the media in the last ten years. Presented as a variation on a Cinderella theme, an all-times favourite cultural script in Russia, a series of Soviet and post-Soviet films such as *Intergirl, Upper Class, Showboy, To Die for Love* and others present an idealized and romanticized image of a prostitute, most often a hard-currency call girl, who gets to marry a well-to-do foreigner and to live abroad. And while films like *Pretty Woman* are also made in the US, it is only in Russia that the majority of the young female spectators identify with the female protagonists and crave all that seems to be available to them: 'dollars, cars, fashionable clothes, good food, cosmetics, relationships, the attention and admiration of men. And the most important thing – the chance of catching a foreign husband' (Stishova, 1996, p. 193).

Non-encouragement of lesbian and feminist identities

Finally, in addition to working mothers and female politicians, there are some other subjectivities that Russian women are not encouraged to adopt *lesbian and feminist identities* among them. Since 1917 'feminism' has been a pejorative term in the country, as liberated Soviet women were supposed to be the opposite of the oppressed Western ones. Feminism was officially denounced by the Soviets 'as an example of bourgeois self-indulgence which served to divide the working class' (Buckley, 1992, p. 215). No feminist publications, either translated or local, were allowed in the country, and all attempts at home-grown feminism were suppressed and persecuted as ideologically alien, anti-Soviet and anti-family. Most importantly, feminist questions were usually opposed to 'real problems', shared by men and women in the Soviet society. As a result, Soviet women were very suspicious of Western feminists, the contacts between Western and Soviet women's organizations were few and far between, and fraught with misunderstandings. As one of the few Russian feminists succinctly summarized: 'Soviet women [were] convinced that Western women have no problems and therefore they participate in the women's movement, while Western women [were] bewildered that Soviet women have so many problems, but no movement' (Lissyutkina, 1993, p. 274). Comparing the goals of women in the two societies, a well-known writer Tatiana Tolstaia suggested that while the American feminists were fighting for the right to work in coal mines, Russian women were fighting *not* to do so (Gray, 1989).

As a result of glasnost and perestroika, and the ensuing de-Sovietization, the eighties and, especially, the nineties witnessed an appearance of several women-only and feminist groups, such as Sajudis in Lithuania or Lotus (League for Emancipation from Sexual Stereotypes) in Moscow. The goals of these groups do not always mirror their Western counterparts or even coincide: while Sajudis women attempt to recapture traditional family values denied to them by the Soviet regime, many radical groups in Moscow and St Petersburg attempt to challenge traditional patriarchal values, to inform the public about the feminist movement and to transform gender roles in the post-Soviet society. Since 1990, the new feminist scholars created several Centres for Gender Studies, in order to investigate women's situation in post-Soviet society, to offer academic women's studies courses, to disseminate feminist literature and to open up alternative discourses based on the concepts of *fakticheskoe neravenstvo* (factual inequality), *muzhekratiia* (male dominated bureaucracy), and *podchinennoe polozhenie* (subjugated position) (Buckley, 1992). They have also organized several national and international conferences and events, among them Independent Women's Forums in Dubna. More often than not, however, their efforts are met with the typical mistrust that any -ism elicits from people, who under so many years of the Soviet rule grew suspicious of any kind of organized activity, movement or ideology, especially one proclaiming 'equal rights'. An example of such a misreading is a polemic provoked by the publication of the 'women's issue' of the journal *Inostrannaia Literatura* (Foreign Literature) which, among other pieces, published an extract from Naomi Wolf's *Beauty Myth* (1991). The categorical tone and polemic style of Wolf's article, representative of Western feminist criticism, evoked for the Soviet readers the directives set forth by the Communist Party publications, and, thus, provoked unmitigated resistance (Azhgikhina and Goscilo, 1996).

The post-Soviet media provide little if any unbiased information about the feminist movement, in the recent years they mounted multiple anti-feminist attacks, whereby the authors paint a shallow and sensationalist portrait of feminism (often equating it with lesbianism and men-hating) and argue that for Russian women to become feminists means 'to "lose their femininity" and cease to be attractive to men' (Marsh, 1996b, p. 6). As a result, 'even otherwise enlightened Russians [conceive] of feminists as vengeful, mustached hags or harridans thirsting for the wholesale metaphorical (if not literal) castration of men, intent on crushing or replacing them so as to gratify their lust for power, compensate for their self-doubts, or enact their lesbian inclinations' (Goscilo, 1996, p. 11). Having internalized gendered ideologies of oppression, Russian women resist the concept of constructed identity and often propagate the same inequities that marginalize them and represent social constructs – femininity, motherhood, domesticity – as biological ones. For them, feminism smacks of Soviet emancipation, the main reason behind the double burden, while new femininities represent liberation: the right not to work (previously nonexistent) and the possibility to finally embrace Western consumerism, an important aspect of 'things that were formerly forbidden and, therefore, must be wonderful' (Azhgikhina and Goscilo, 1996).

Often, Russian women's subservient position and self-sacrifice are turned into a matter of national pride in comparison with the 'cold attitudes' of Western women, as seen below in the interviews with a popular TV hostess Natalia Darialova and a successful businesswoman Taisiia Suvorova, the editor-in-chief of *On-Ona* (He-She) magazine. Suvorova suggests that many foreigners are attracted by Russian women because they don't get any warmth, compassion and attention from their own, 'the readiness to get up and guess the desire of one's husband' (*Russian Life*, March 1998, p. 13):

> Nothing similar happens in America or Europe ... Maybe it is because the Russian woman has been faced with the necessity to preserve herself ... to remain attractive in spite of everything, not dare to say to her husband in spite of terrible fatigue the phrase which is on the lips of many Western women: 'Tomorrow, tomorrow, not today'. I don't know of any woman in my country who would allow herself such a phrase. Our woman goes for everything for the sake of preserving relations with the one she chose. Me saying to my husband – give me a break, leave me alone?! We need constantly to do some heroic deed, I don't even call it sacrifice or immolation ... Who else is capable of this? (*Russian Life*, March 1998: 12–13)

Darialova, interviewed upon her return from the US, called the upper-class New York women 'steel she-wolves':

> They are very well groomed, very well dressed, but their faces are so angry and focused that they simply scare you. Even though American women achieved a lot in their fight for equality with men, some strive to be like men too much. For example, they don't allow men to help them with their coats or to open doors for them. It is a mistake. Men and women are created different by nature, and our social roles are different. (*Rabotnitsa*, June 1997, p. 22)

The notion of 'sexual harassment', ever-present in Western discourse, is not warmly received on the Russian soil either. A recent article in the Russian edition of *Cosmopolitan*, entitled 'Sexual harassment the

Russian way'(*Domogatel'stvo po-russki*), ridicules an American feminist who misinterpreted and overdramatized a Russian man's invitation for her to come up to his hotel room:

> Honestly, I don't understand their laws! So, a guy called a woman, invited [her] to come over. Our [woman] would have elegantly told him to go to hell (or not so elegantly, depending on her upbringing) or ... Why not, if a guy is cute? But to imagine a lady who woke up her friends in the middle of the night in order to spend all night writing a stupid complaint, is rather difficult! ... I would venture a guess that our women treat men's interest in them rather positively! (*Cosmopolitan*, April 1998, pp. 85–86)

The female author of the article emphasizes her point by telling an apocryphal story of another American feminist who came to Russia as an angry emancipee, rejecting all male attempts at gallantry, and then met a macho Russian man who turned her into a happy feminine woman, who couldn't make a decision without his advice or put a coat on without his help.

Nevertheless, despite the ideologies and attitudes propagated by the media, and without associations with any feminist movement, the women in the study were able to draw on their own discursive resources to pinpoint and analyse the problems of gender-discrimination, marginalization and feminization of poverty in the post-Soviet society:

> Here the discrimination against women is terrible ... with regard to women, this country probably has the most barbaric attitude among other European countries, so that a woman ... well, even during socialist times there was this two fold attitude toward women ... on the one hand, the woman was required to be a leading worker, to work non-stop, forgetting about her family ... on the other hand, she was required to constantly have children and be married ... so that if a girl didn't get married by the age of 25, everyone would start pointing at her saying that she is abnormal, that she is not married ... so women are only given low-paid jobs ... they can't get ahead in business, because she is constantly pushed to the background, it is emphasized that she is not a complete human being ... even to see how men treat women, and women-parliament-deputies: they are looked down upon ... we understand that we will need many, many years before a woman can take an appropriate place here ... (E, 37, former librarian, unemployed)

The larger critical theme that unifies Russian and Ukrainian women's narratives is not simply a criticism of the quality and pace of modern change, rather it is an ongoing contestation of gendered social practices of post-Soviet society and a reflection on their own positions in it:

> [These changes] turned out to be rather sad, because I didn't manage to fit in into this life, I don't fit in academically, and psychologically I don't fully fit in either, it must be my age too ... (K, 49, scientist turned patent consultant)

All of the participants in the study remarked on the difficulty of fitting in, tying together the concepts of gender, identity, financial status and employment:

> No, I didn't find a space for myself in our society. I tried, very hard, wasted a lot of time and energy and health to change my profession somehow, to find some niche in our new business. I understood that I won't be a businesswoman ... I also knew very well that I could be an office worker, a secretary, I had the necessary background. I went to a special school, studied languages, but then I understood that no one values my efforts, my work ... I understand that the society is pushing me out ... (E, 37, former librarian, unemployed)
>
> So, I am thinking now, it is time to go back to work [the informant had a child and stayed home with him for a while], but I have a gap ... not only some things are forgotten, but now everything is computerized ... go somewhere, offer myself, you see, I have some acquaintances, connections ... well, not really connections ... but I wouldn't be able to beg someone, please help me find a job ... it is embarrassing, I am thirty five ... open the newspaper, the jobs are offered to twenty five year olds, cute, with legs all the way to the neck, you see ... (I, 35, a homemaker, a wife of a successful businessman)

The gendered futures of their children don't seem any more promising than their own:

> [I want my daughter] to be able to get education, have a child, raise him, live a regular life ... here it's impossible... here [young people] can't study, can't find jobs ... for girls it's prostitution ... [for men] racketeering or something like that, black market business ... (L, 47, a clerical worker in a Russian–American mission)

This generation of women, clearly at the crossroads, is forced to employ contradictory discourses to make sense of what is happening in their society and to them personally. While unable to support the new hegemonic constructions of gender, these women cannot afford to remain on the margins of the society, thus, they continue to negotiate their own positioning, carefully balancing their act between assimilation and resistance. But then, it is nothing new for them: their lives have always been a 'balancing act' or, as Gray (1989) stated in the title of her study of Soviet women, they have been forever 'walking the tightrope'.

Conclusion

Based on the evidence presented in the chapter and on the previous work carried out by Western and post-Soviet feminist scholars (Edmondson, 1992; Marsh, 1996a; Pilkington, 1996; Posadskaya, 1994a), I have argued that an understanding of sociopolitical and socioeconomic conditions is critical for capturing the range of subjectivities available to women prior to and following the collapse of the Soviet Union. I demonstrated that the changes taking place in post-Soviet countries led to marginalization and objectification of women under the ideology of the 'purely womanly mission', which, in turn, was influenced by the demands and pressures of the free market. An analysis of the media discourses demonstrates that while many subjectivities pertinent to the Soviet era are currently questioned and dismantled, new identities – such as a happy homemaker, a hard-currency prostitute, a beauty queen, a shuttle, successful businesswoman or a wife of a New Russian businessman – are constructed and adopted, and moreover 'invested with merit and meaning' (Ries, 1997, p. 175). This analysis also demonstrated that historic and political changes in the country led to the current reconsideration and renarrativization of gender equality and women's role in the Soviet Union by the media together with other aspects of Soviet history. Most importantly, the study documented a shift as well as implicit continuity between pre-1990 and post-1990 subjectivities available to Russian and Ukrainian women. The shift is linked to radical historical, political and especially socioeconomic changes in the former Soviet Union, while the continuity was explained by the predominant patriarchal ideologies reinforced by the masculinization of the market place. The analysis of life story interviews with Russian and Ukrainian women suggests that although targets of the new ideological campaign for 'return to the eternal womanly mission', post-Soviet women, do not uncritically assume new identities and positions, their attitude is both that of assimilation and of resistance, just like they always assimilated to and resisted official discourses of the Communist ideology.

Note

1. I am greatly indebted to Charlotte Linde and Mihaela Kelemen, and to my Russian girlfriends Tatyana Pyntikova, Viorica Marian, Lena Baltiiskaia, Irina Zhiman, Lida Dolinskaia and Luba for their invaluable emotional support, assistance, inspiration and encouragement throughout the various stages of this project.

6

Control: Accounting for the Lost Innocence

Monika Kostera

Making sense of control

Control is one of the key terms in management; it is the foundation for accounting. With the intensive dissemination of Western management models and ideas after 1989, it is also one of the most commonly used words in management education and consulting. Most of the existing courses and textbooks in Poland can be classified as mainstream messages, where the reflexivity about the sense words carry is minimal, and the consideration of moral and emotional effects that ideas have on the Polish cultural context is not overwhelming. As I became interested in the word 'control' the meaning it carries, its emotional side and the context it is embedded in, I decided to collect stories people tell about 'control'.

The narrative approach in organization studies

Having said this, I owe the reader an explanation of how I see the role of stories within contemporary science and organization studies. Jean-François Lyotard (1979/1984) wrote about narrative knowledge as opposed the logo-scientific knowledge. The former is a pre- and post-modern concept, the later a modern invention. In organization studies, the narrative approach in organization studies is increasingly gaining popularity (for example, Czarniawska, 1997). The interest concerns both the academic text as a genre (Kociatkiewicz and Kostera, 1999) and the themes typically being studied by the management scientists (such as organization (Philips, 1995); institutional identity (Czarniawska, 1997); and gender (Czarniawska and Calás, 1998)).

In 'Narration or science? Collapsing the division in organization studies' Barbara Czarniawska-Joerges (1995) explores the links between science and story telling (narration). She argues for the reintroduction of narrative knowledge into social sciences and humanities, and particularly, into organization studies. This approach to knowledge is related to research methods frequently used in organizational research such as ethnography, qualitative case studies, discourse analysis and various other interpretive methods. If scientific ethos which assumes that 'good scientific writing is true writing' is to be abandoned, then we are left with questions of beauty and use. Representation of relational truth comes to mean political representation: 'Theories do not "represent" reality; theoreticians take upon themselves to represent other people and even nature' (p. 27). Barbara Czarniawska-Joerges argues for a conscious and reflective creation of a specific genre, which recognizes tradition without being paralyzed by it, which seeks inspiration in other genres without imitating them, which derives confidence from the importance of its topic and from its own growing skills (p. 28).

Guillet de Monthoux and Czarniawska-Joerges (1994) emphasize that studying literature is valuable for management learning and for the enhancement of people's understanding of organizations and organizing. Philips (1995, p. 626) claims that 'the barriers between fiction and fact, and art and science, have become increasingly difficult to defend.' In fact, 'social scientists often do what writers do: they create rather than discover, they focus on the unique and individual, they use illustration and rhetoric in an effort to make their case' (p. 626). Kostera *et al.* (1995) follow through this argument, suggesting that science is art and can be both conceived of metaphorically and evaluated aesthetically as a way of artistic creation. Umberto Eco (1973, pp. 27–8) said the following about the openness of texts:

> The poetics of an 'open' text aims ... to inspire the interpreter to 'acts of conscious freedom', to make him an active centre for an unlimited net of relationships, whom he is to give an own shape, not being limited by a *compulsion* implied by the given rules of organization of a given text.

In the earlier decades, science aimed at closure and precision. Currently, academic texts tend to be more open, authors take up the issue of writing, exploring the potential for good writing in management and organization studies (Czarniawska, 1999) and examining how they can become better writers (Golden-Biddle and Locke, 1997). Thus, we approach a more narrative genre of writing, and also more and more often use narrative methods for the exploration of reality.

Czarniawska and Calás (1996) use a narrative method to explore cultural differences in gender construction. Their study was designed around a collection of short stories with a female heroine. These stories were purposefully imprecise and vague. They were distributed to participants of 6 different cultures to be filled in with details and interpreted. Similarly, Glinka and Ludwicki (1997) used short stories to see how people construct the institution of marriage.

In this chapter, I use the method of collecting short stories, following the idea of Barbara Czarniawska and Marta Calás. However, I did not sketch any narratives myself but asked my informants to author them themselves. Also, I use the narrative mode of writing in the concluding part of the chapter, where I switch genres, from the academic to narrative fiction. It remains to be stated that my paradigmatic position within this text is radical humanist (Burrell and Morgan, 1979). In this I differ from most of the authors quoted above, whom I read as social constructivists and representatives for the interpretive paradigm in Burrell and Morgan's typology. I do not analyse field material in order just to understand social reality better, but to show the socially constructed limits to organizing, the contextual boundaries that people find oppressive. I wish to give voice to the fears, dreams and struggles of people who entrusted me with stories about them, composed in short narratives.

Dimensions of accounting

My interest in the moral and cultural side of issues of management accounting is rooted within a relatively recent but vital tradition. In order to make the reader conscious of which foundations I invoke as my frame of reference, I would like to briefly present my reading of this tradition here.

Gareth Morgan wrote in 1983 that 'accounting researchers [we]re obliged to face the dilemma that they [we]re really social scientists in disguise' (p. 385). In another text, co-authored with Stanley Davis and Krishnagopal Menon (1982), he emphasizes that accounting theory elaborates imagery. Numbers are signs, and they are made to depict an organizational reality. If so, why should numbers be regarded as the only legitimate language to *account* for organizations? Indeed, since the early eighties, many authors have explored other narrative modes with that purpose.

Gareth Morgan (1987) lists the various metaphors that have exerted impact on recent accounting theory. The list contains the following images of accounting: history, economics, information, language, rhetoric, politics, mythology, magic, disciplined control, ideology and domination and exploitation. Even though the myth of objectivity is still strong, it is no longer as predominant a view as it once used to be. Gareth Morgan advocates the need for 'recognizing and accepting the basic subjectivity of accounting' (p. 7) and acknowledging accounting as an interpretive act. The book edited by Polesie and Johansson (1992) entitled *Responsibility and Accounting* contains various historical, cultural and other contextual reflections on accounting, the enterprise and organization theory. The book can be read as a celebration of the new possibilities opening up before accounting theory. Czarniawska-Joerges writes the following: '[n]ow ... when social sciences in general are freeing themselves from the (self-imposed) slavery of natural sciences, the time for encounters has come' (1992a, p. 74). Thus, accounting may meet with other disciplines, such as anthropology. Arrington and Francis (1993a) depict accounting as cultural practice and consider the hermeneutical implications of the structure of the economic account. Nelson (1993) reflects on the postmodern modes of accountability, the role of narratives and representation and, consequently, the communicational aspect of accounting. The author addresses the rhetorical dimension, pointing out that linguistic conventions should be analysed, and that their role in shaping meanings should be taken into consideration. Shearer and Arrington (1993) adopt a feminist perspective to look at accounting and depict some of the consequences of the use of language within mainstream accounting for women and the imagery of the gendered society. In this chapter, I will follow the linguistic convention, exploring imagery and language in context.

'[A]ccounants need to be sensitive to the many dimensions of the realities which they are attempting to "account for"' (Morgan, 1987, p. 10). There are many such dimensions that should, in my opinion, be accounted for more extensively: from the cultural to the moral. Arrington and Francis (1993b) remind us that accounting is permeated with moral involvement. 'Its vocabulary is one of values, of evaluation, of welfare, of rights, of expectations, of obligation, of equity, of contracts, of punishments and rewards, of utility, satisfaction, responsibility and accountability. The moral force of accounting needs to be questioned in the light of the values that it promotes and the values that it implies' (p. 305). The cultural dimensions are extensively taken up by Corvellec in his 1997 book *Stories of Achievements*. The book is based on a sports metaphor of performance, as explicitly and implicitly used in organizational accounts, and the consequences of this extensive use for reality construction.

In this chapter I explore a key accounting term in its moral and cultural context. It is my conviction that this may enhance the communicational aspects of accounting, and that it may be a starting point for an international dialog around the term, instead of the now all too common unidirectional managerial crusade from the West to the East (I write more on this crusade in Kostera, 1995b).

Control: The story of lost innocence

Viktor Suvorov, the well-known Russian writer of spy novels and an ex-spy himself, wrote a book about the Stalinist system of totalitarian rule, entitled *Kontrola'* (1995). The heroine, Nastia, is an ex-master parachutist and an employee of the special group created to control the controllers – that is, the highest KGB and Party officials. The book depicts the paranoia and the utter inhumanity of the system, as well as Nastia's fight for dignity, while whole heartedly participating in that system. The Stalinist system was based on endless suspicion and intensive supervision of everyone by everyone. No one, except for Stalin himself, was free from mistrust, and there were no human rights to invoke in the face of the system. 'Traitors', and indeed, everyone could be considered 'traitor', were not even given trial, but shot on the spot, and even the trials that were performed were, without exception, schemed and devised to suit the aims of the system. The individual was helpless and devoid of any right to justice and fairness. Various organizations were active with the sole aim of 'unmasking' 'betrayers of the people' and detecting intrigues (or inventing them, when needed), of which the globally most famous was the KGB. Nonetheless, these organizations were far from trusted themselves. The system produced superorganizations, and even within them, no person was beyond supervision. Nastia, a member of the top elite of supervision, falls foul, in the end, of the same scheme which she was herself actively pursuing. I will not reveal all the plots in the book, as it would spoil the fun of reading it. My point is that the title and the contents of the book depict a reality that is, thank God, past and gone, but nevertheless may – in my opinion – be a valuable metaphor for the understanding of the historical roots of how people in the ex-Eastern Bloc may associate the term 'control'.

To begin with, I should point out the difference in meaning of the word 'control' and *'kontrola.'* According to the *Oxford Concise Dictionary,* the term 'control' signifies:

as a noun:

1 the power of directing, command (under the control of);
2 the power of restraining, esp. self-restraint;
3 a means of restraint; a check;
4 (usu. in pl.) a means of regulating prices and so on;
5 (usu. in pl.) switches and other devices by which a machine, esp. an aircraft or vehicle, is controlled (also attrib.: control panel; control room);
6(a) a place where something is controlled or verified, (b) a person or group that controls something; and
7 a standard of comparison for checking the results of a survey or experiment.

as a transitive verb (controlled, controlling):

1 have control or command of; dominate;
2 exert control over; regulate;
3 hold in check; restrain (told him to control himself);
4 serve as control to; and
5 check, verify.

Leksykonia, the multimedia English-Polish dictionary[1] defines control as 'kontrola', 'sprawdzanie' (checking) and 'nadzór' (supervision). Only one of the three meanings of the English word is, thus, conveyed by the Polish 'kontrola'. Nonetheless, the term 'kontrola' is used as an equivalent of 'control' in management contexts, among them in standard management textbooks, such as the bestselling *Zarzadzanie: Teoria i praktyka* (1994/ 1997).

My endeavour is to explore the current associations of 'control' among the Polish future management theorists and practitioners. I used a narrative device to see how students of Warsaw University make sense (see Weick, 1995a) of the term. The students attended the 4th year of studies at the Faculty of Management (Warsaw University) at a paid study programme,[2] and took a course in organizational sociology lead by myself. Among them were 39 women, 15 men, and 6 persons who failed to mark their gender. At the first encounter I asked them to write short stories or poems about 'control', without any further explanation of the aim or of any understanding of the term. They have come across the word many times in their earlier studies, which I can affirm, after having read the programmes of their studies.

'Managerial control' and 'controlling' have been taught to them during classes in accounting, organization theory, and the economics of production. Most of the students (except for one person) are young enough not to have experienced the communist system as adults, and no one (including myself) remembered the totalitarian period of communist rule in Poland, which ended with Stalin's death.

The majority of the responses were written as some kind of personal definitions, sometimes including examples. A few authors wrote short poems (protest songs and ironic poems), and some wrote short stories, among them realist stories and a moral parable. Generally, the picture of control the students depict is gloomy and dark. Among the answers I received, there is perhaps one positive image of control, and even that one is ambiguous.

Most people associated control with '*kontrola biletów*', that is, the checking of tickets. However, most typically they did not just refer to the understanding of the word, but use the particular understanding as a metaphor. One author says that the carrying out of *kontrola* in public transportation is connected with stress and is generally unpleasant. Another says that it is only superficially the question of checking tickets – [the controller] checks honesty and loyalty. One of the stories is about young persons behaving loudly and having fun but far from doing any harm. They were subject of *kontrola* exerted by a police patrol: five armed men, with angry and bitter faces. They demanded to see the documents and hit some of the young persons to stress their own authority. A little child was observing this – as the police dispersed the youths and drove away, she was left alone, very much afraid. One of the stories about the checking of tickets reads as follows:

> Caught. With a malicious glimmer in his eye, he approached the door of the tram and demanded that I leave the vehicle. Never mind that I was on my way to an exam, that I had a ticket but forgot to take it with me. He couldn't hide his joy that he'd managed to catch me. What an abomination, my hands tremble with anger. I experienced a strong desire to smash his horrid face with a pickaxe, and yet he was just doing his duty. I hate such situations, I can't handle them. I suppose that if he'd looked differently, I wouldn't have reacted like this. I told him that I'd give him a bribe if he didn't order me to leave.

A story about an encounter with *kanars* is concluded by an ironic 'happy end' – a group of young women were asked to leave the bus but as they left they were offered to either pay the fine or to drink coffee with the *kanars*. They chose the latter. Another account, similar in its tone, contains the following lines:

> When they [officials checking tickets] catch a delinquent, who ceases to remember his own name in the process, it awakens the most primitive instincts in them. They submit him to the most nosy inquisition, repeating the same question over and over again: 'why didn't you punch the ticket?' And he just hadn't remembered to do it that day. Every control is to me a *kanar*,[3] drenched in sweat, with bloody eyes and a malicious smile: YOU CANNOT EVADE ME.

An ironic poem depicts the *kanar* as greatly enjoying his or her duties. A story features a person among the passengers, suddenly showing his ID to the others, shouting: 'Tickets please!' Once a person not willing to participate in the game of authority and submission was shackled with handcuffs to a handrail in the train. The story ends with the question: 'Who is responsible for this?'

One person gives the example of *kontrola* performed by the police: 'A small mistake of the driver grows to the level of something gigantic.' The police person often fails to perform his or her duty according to the rules. Therefore he or she would need someone to supervise him or her, and so on. It's a vicious circle. The tax office is another example of *kontrola*. The author questions the necessity of being rude and aggressive – and the officials act that way until they are given a bribe.

Another typical association was the one with family and parents. 'Control starts in the family. As children we are under *kontrola* of parents, and this continues when we grow up.' Some believe it's natural and understandable that parents (mothers) control their children. One person writes:

> I look for associations in my head and I go back to my childhood. *Kontrola* was something at the same time intangible and permanent in my life, at home and outside of it. Unconsciously I imagined how I would behave, how I would perform the tasks I was assigned ... all would be evaluated by some *kontrola*. Apparently, I didn't care – however, I constantly referred to it mentally. Becoming an adult meant, among other things, the liberation from *kontrola*, at least the weakening of it. I think that I'm still working at it and I rather don't like the feeling of being submitted to *kontrola*.

In one text, the *kontrola* performed by the parents is depicted as excessive inquisitiveness. It is only natural that parents care for their children but there must be some reasonable limit to it. They restrict, perhaps unknowingly, their children's autonomy. I particularly like a story written by one of the students:

> As I woke up at seven in the morning, I saw that it was still night outside. Even though I dislike getting up when it's dark, I felt happy. At least, I was free! Yesterday I broke up with my boyfriend. I've had enough of him. He was checking on me [*kontrolowal mnie*] all the time. Ceaselessly, he asked: 'What are you doing? Where are you going? With whom?' I got up and went to the bathroom. 'What are you doing there such a long time?' – my mother asked, as usual. I threw a scrutinizing [*kontrolne*] look into the mirror, and went out. I left home late, as usual. At the bus a rather unpleasant surprise awaited me. The routinely checking [*kontrola*] of tickets. The official was unyielding. At school it turned out that we had a test assignment [*praca kontrolna*] in mathematics. Even though my pal assured me that everything was under control [*pod kontrola*], the assignment didn't go too well. I returned home in a bad mood. It turned out that during my absence my mother checked [*skontrolowac*] the degree of ordering of things in my room. In a gloomy mood I went to the dentist for a control visit [*wizyta kontrolna*]. As I was sitting by my desk in the evening, I heard my mother's voice: 'What are you doing there that it's so quiet?'

Surprisingly few relate the term to management practice. One noted that the term refers to the relationship between the boss and the subordinate, and to the supervision of the production process. Another one adds that such a control is partly positive, because 'too much is not healthy'. A person writes:

> My enterprise can serve as an example. I associate the word with work in the first place. It awakens panic and fear. *Kontrola* – people from the central unit, whose aim is to find some mistake. They write gigantic protocols about it. They never give advice what to do in order to avoid them. These people are never liked, but they awake respect and sometimes fawning, submissiveness.

A person tells the story of sitting by the desk, while her boss comes by, looks over her shoulder and starts asking numerous questions. 'He doesn't give me a chance to work independently, to do things my way.' Another person writes a short narrative about a workday – phones ringing incessantly, people asking questions. 'It takes so much time, hours pass, days, weeks.' The narrator feels exhausted and drained of energy and cannot use the procedures according to their aim.

One student writes that she associates the term with the control of one's feelings and needs, a repressive and often unconscious act. Another student thinks of the oppressive control of gestures and looks. However, she adds that self-control leads to interesting reflections about oneself and one's feelings. The issue of self-control is recurrent, and valued positively in most cases. However, in some texts it is added that self-control limits spontaneity and self-expression, for example: 'limiting originality, [one's] passionate [aspects] – thinking how others see me, what they will think if I behave in a way deviating from accepted standards.' She concludes that artistic expression is, in a sense, the rejection of self-control. One student associates control with mountain climbing (she is a climber herself). This kind of control gives her satisfaction and the feeling of liberation. Nevertheless, she 'hates to be controlled'. It invokes in her an urge to spite the other person, to do the opposite of what is expected of her. *Kontrola* limits initiative and creativity, says another of the students.

Some people elaborate on associations with distrust. One person thinks about jealousy, about phoning, checking, asking questions. Another answer reads:

> *Kontrola* is to me:
> - interfering with someone else's business;
> - curiosity;
> - lack of trust;
> - aversion; and
> - suspicion.

One person notes that *kontrola* makes her behave unnaturally. Another has similar observations, and emphasizes the paranoid dimension of her feelings: 'I'm afraid even though I haven't done anything wrong, I get scared that the controller will end up finding something wrong anyway, to hurt me.' A person believes that *kontrola* is carried out with the purpose to find things that are not right. It sneaks into a person's privacy and most often surprises him or her. The author of this note explains that she is an honest person, but when someone is trying to submit her to *kontrola*, she becomes afraid of beguilement. The paranoid dimension is emphasized in other accounts as well.

The students fear control and speak of it in critical words. However, the criticism is not only addressed to others. One person, after having noted how damaging excessive control could be, added, that it also is true about oneself, that is, that it is equally wrong 'when I am the controller'. However, one author admits that as much as he hates being the subject of *kontrola*, he likes to control others. He says in a rather Foucauldian manner: 'To know is to have power, to control is to know.' '*Kontrola* is the opposite of trust' – according to another person, 'it is the limitation of freedom, not only physically but psychically as well.' She goes on to state the following: 'Control between people who love each other is oppressive, embarrassing. It produces the attitude of rebellion, a feeling of limitation of freedom.'

The issue of the limiting of freedom appears in many texts. A student admits to having rather negative associations with *kontrola*, and sees it as pertaining to people, things, documents:

> It means a way of interfering with what some one else does. The aim of *kontrola* may be 'enlightened' but it is always connected to the activity of interfering, inquiring, 'looking at someone's hands'.

The awareness of varying objects of control is recurrent throughout the texts collected by me. 'The first thing that comes to my mind when I think of *kontrola* is power, and hierarchy' – writes a student, who then equates the term with evaluation. Another person believes that control serves to give the feeling of security and 'the control over the situation'. A person controlling something may feel free. But the giving up of control may be a wonderful experience.

One author plays with the word and comes up with the term *kontrarola,* counter-role, and elaborates on the image: it is a role that is against somebody else, that is at the same time repellent and tempting. A good life awaits the person who falls for the temptation. The author says that she is trying to resist it, repeating to herself: 'be yourself, be yourself'.

A great deal of people stress the omnipresence of *kontrola*. 'Maybe it's impossible to live without *kontrola*?' They emphasize that the word is used in all possible circumstances and that the phenomenon is present everywhere in everyday life, even though, they often add that they do not approve of it. Typically they admit to fearing it. 'I am trying to avoid *kontrola* as much as possible. I am capable of controlling myself and setting my own limits of acceptable actions.' Nonetheless, typically, they also admit that *kontrola* can be useful, 'when I can use someone, the knowledge of someone wiser than myself'. One writes the following:

> something that:
> - exists everywhere;
> - is necessary;
> - can be bribed;
> - can be 'bent'; and
> - can be fair or unfair.

One student believes that *kontrola* is characteristic of modern civilization. Another person writes the following:

> *Kontrola*. We are subject to it all our lives and in different ways. We are subject to *kontrola* when we are born – how much we weigh? How long we are? Do we have the appropriate reactions or not? Then we are controlled by our parents, the lady in the nursery, the lady in the kindergarden, in school, finally at work. We are controlled at home and on the bus, in the train, and whatever else. Really, if it weren't for control, a lot of people wouldn't have anything to do. Finally, we control ourselves, all the time and this is perhaps the least pleasant but unfortunately necessary. I think that *kontrola* is unpleasant for the controller and especially for the controlled. Because, in the end, what do we care what someone else does?

Some authors stress the relationship to punishment: 'if I do something wrong, I can expect punishment.' But the punishment may also be a pure manifestation of someone's power, and then it becomes morally questionable.

One of the authors of the poems says that *kontrola* actually makes it difficult to control oneself, the feeling of being constantly observed gets at one's nerves and makes her or him (the author failed to mark her or his gender) scream: 'Down with *kontrola*, may people respect my opinion.' One of my favourites is a diagram, containing three overlapping circles (see Figure 6.1): Koniecznosc (Necessity), Konsekwencje (Consequences), Konwulsje (Convulsions). At the base of the drawing on the right hand it is written Koniec (The End).

One student wrote a very short poem, ending with a rolling *rrrrrrrrrrrrrrr*. Another wrote three poems, in the convention of

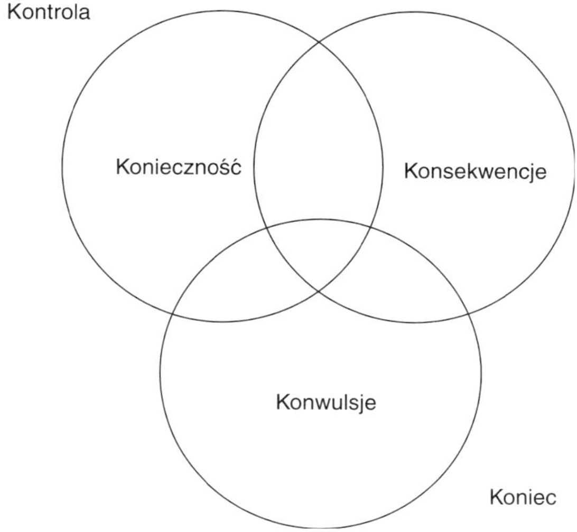

Figure 6.1 'Kontrola' according to students

protest songs. The first is about a strong person, who looks down on others, and feels free, because he doesn't care about what they think. The second is about a moral citizen who will never end up in jail but may go mad. The third is a kind of a declaration of dislike to a person whose world fails to change.

The authors typically state explicitly and emphatically that they don't like *kontrola*, and that it is unpleasant, oppressive and omnipresent. One states that it doesn't evoke any emotions in him. One states that *kontrola* is necessary, but he'd rather control things than people. A few admit that it has both positive and negative sides to it. The one account that is a positive impression, is a moral parable:

> There once was a tired and thirsty pilgrim, who met a woman and asked her for some water. She offers him water in a bowl, but throws some bran into it. The pilgrim must, every time he lifts the bowl to his lips, breathe away the millet from its surface. The pilgrim may be dissatisfied and impatient, because he would like to swallow lots of water at once. The woman had foreseen this and kept him from too rapid and greedy drinking of the cold water. This was a good *kontrola*.

Another response ends with the sentence: 'God, thank you that you observe me but that you do not *kontrol* me.'

Kontrola – a coda

Nastia is dead. So is the Stalinist system she was supporting through her work in *Kontrola*. If she were still alive, what would she say about the current practice of disseminating Western management models that are called 'kontrola'? Maybe she would say: 'Be careful.'

I would like to emphasize that I do not consider the group of students whose short texts I quote here as statistically representative. They are a critical and perhaps rather unique group of people. However, I think that the texts they wrote are important, not only in the Polish context, but for other people as well. I think that the inhabitants of the ex-Eastern bloc have lost their innocence – the totalitarian system has taught them to be careful with words, with meanings and not to take things by their face value. On the other hand, it has also encouraged people to do the opposite, to read without thinking and accept without reflection. I believe that both attitudes coexist in the Polish society. Typically, they are represented by different groups of people. Sometimes they coincide within the same group. The clash of the tendencies: to believe and to doubt, is, in my opinion, a paradox of the contemporary Polish society. On the other hand, I do not claim it is specific to Poland – there may be other societies where this paradox is manifest. I do not believe that the peoples from 'behind the fallen Wall' are so specific that they should be treated as a case for themselves. I do believe, however, that they may have something to say about the social construction of their reality from a perspective that may give their voices a particular strength that is, perhaps, too often disregarded or left unheard for many reasons: because it is *ex ante* considered to be 'too idiosyncratic' or 'identical' and, therefore, uninteresting.

Having said this, I will go further to suggest that the students' texts carry such a universal message about modern organizing. *Control* does indeed contain the meaning that can be translated as *kontrola*, as numerous critical ethnographies show, for example, Van Maanen and Kunda (1989) talk about the control of feelings at Disneyland, Kunda (1992) talks about the totalizing corporate culture of a large computer company called Tech, Leidner (1993) talks about the control of behaviour at McDonald's and the control of minds and emotions at Combined Insurance. The issue of subjecting employees to *kontrola* is present in Western 'humane' corporate cultures. George Ritzer (1996/1997) shows how both employees and consumers are exposed to this kind of influence. In the Western world, *kontrola* was (is) concealed and disguised as something else, as the Free Market, something that people want and accept. The Eastern totalitarian system, usually hypocrite beyond measure, sometimes managed to name things in a surprisingly direct manner. The word *kontrola* used in the context described by Suvorov, also signifying censorship and direct meddling of various authorities with what people did and thought,[4] is an example of a rather surprising directness.

It should also be noted that the part of the meaning of 'control' that I, having spent an important part of my life in a Western country, associate with a very practical everyday functioning of the social systems (someone sees that things are okay, such as that cars are parked where they should be parked, that citizens are not treated unfairly by the authorities, that clients are not cheated by the advertisers, and so on), is absent in the students' stories. Most of them express, in my reading, a desire to resist *kontrola*, to question the right of some people to use it as a display of power. Few noticed responsibility (it is only present in the parable about the woman and the pilgrim).

The following is my own story about control.

Kontrola

> There once was a person who was walking in a tunnel. She had been walking there all her life and she couldn't remember ever having been outside. Maybe some glimpse of another reality? Not enough to form a memory, just the substance to make up a dream. She walked all alone, in darkness, carrying a small lantern whose permanent light, although pale, lit up the grey walls around her. She stopped to eat mushrooms and snails that she found in the cave. She stopped to sleep whenever she felt tired. She knew nothing about the day or about the night, as she was immersed in endless darkness. But she had those dreams that made her wake up with a feeling of intense longing. Somewhere, out there, there was light, much more bright than anything she has ever experienced, light of an unimaginable magnitude, and she was walking towards it. The tunnel had an exit: freedom was beyond. On the days that followed the dreams she walked more energetically, not entirely allowing herself to have hope that such fantastic dreams may come true, but nonetheless, the dreams were stronger perhaps than the reality. If not for them, she would not have the strength to go on. She would have stayed in some stony niche a long time ago, spending her time in blissful immobility, but then probably she would have died. To accept is to wither.

But finally there came a time when she was close to giving up. She walked slowly, dragging her feet, not even having the strength to look up, she walked and stared at her tired despairing feet. Suddenly, something changed, something like a premonition, which made her lift her eyes. And she saw a light. It was far away, but clear enough. The exit! She started to run towards it, forgetting her tiredness, forgetting her caution never to part with doubt. There it was! Within the distance of moments, within her reach, small but bright. Fifty steps, thirty, twenty ...

But as she approached, she saw: it was no exit, not the end of the tunnel, but a man, walking, like her, carrying a lantern in his hand. He looked at her, she looked at him, they passed each other, without saying a word.

She continued to walk, automatically, like a machine, without a thought, darkness all around, nothing mattered any more, nothing would ever change. The dreams ceased, she didn't care. She walked on, days passed without her calling them days, weeks, months, years. Sometimes she would stop for some time, ready to die, but something would always make her get up and continue her march. Usually it was hunger. But at some point the dreams began again. She would not admit it, but the hope still lived somewhere. There had to be an exit, and outside there was infinite light.

Years and years passed. Nothing much changed. The walls around her were as grey and immobile as usual. Darkness was of the same impenetrable shade. She walked, and walked. More mechanical with every day, almost accepting. And then, one day – she saw a light. It was far away still, a tiny flame, a clear dot within the dark. She hurried her steps, first hesitant, but then delirious with hope, she ran.

As she came closer, she saw that it was no end of the tunnel, but a man, walking, carrying a lantern in his hand.

They were just a few steps away from each other.

They looked into each other's eyes, without a word. Then, she saw: it was the same man.

In my story, the two people did not even exchange a greeting. What would happen if they started to talk with each other? What would the man say? Maybe he would tell a joke. As the history of Eastern Europe shows, as do the quoted critical ethnographies, it is impossible to control people. When control gets oppressive, people seek some escape not just in open rebellion, but in togetherness and in irony. I remember very well myself the custom of telling political jokes from before

1989, among friends and family, but in Poland also among people who accidentally met each other, such as at the hairdresser's, or even at a bus-stop. So maybe the people in the tunnel would exchange jokes, such as the following ones, known as 'Radio Eryvan answers'. The legendary radio station supposedly answered listeners' questions, in a highly ambivalent and ironic manner, 'explaining' the ideals of communism and the system, while in reality ridiculing them. I have an underground Polish booklet, entitled *Radio Eryvan Answers*, containing jokes collected by Adam Rosenbusch (1980). I have chosen a few from the collection:

Q. Is it true that comrade Brezniev collects the jokes that people tell about him?
A. In principle, yes, however, not jokes, but people who tell them, and he doesn't collect them, but locks them up.
Q. Wouldn't it be good for the sake of the peace in our country to lock up all opponents of the system?
A. In principle, yes, but who would then work in the factories and in the fields?
Q. What is an old joke?
A. It's a joke that you got locked up for in three years in the old times and currently only for three.

But they are wrong if they think that they can make us stop dreaming about the light.

Notes

1. *Leksykonia, multimedialny slownik angielsko-polski* (1996) Wydawnictwo Naukowo Techniczne: LexLand.
2. At the Faculty, there are mainly two kinds of study programmes: non-paid studies, access to which is limited by admission exams, and paid studies leading to various degrees. The students participating in this study are those aspiring for a Master's degree, generally employed, and generally about the age of 24–25.
3. Polish slang word for official checking tickets in public transportation means [MK].
4. Glówny Urzad Kontroli Prasy i Widowisk (The Central Bureau for Control of the Press and Spectacles) was the official name for the state censorship institution; 'rozmowa kontrolowana' (controlled conversation) said a recorded voice in the phone receiver at the beginning of the 1980s, during the Martial Law, which signalled that someone was listening to phone calls (also private calls) – most likely calls very subjected to such *kontrola* even before, and so on.

7
Powerful Accounts: Identities, Principals and Agents

Karin Svedberg Nilsson

The analysis of a cross-border acquisition in the former German Democratic Republic supports the notion that accounting practices have constitutive as well as regulatory powers. In this case, project accounting was instrumental in promoting company reform. It helped increase the powers of the acquirer over the acquiree. It also affected internal power relationships, and furthered a transformation of individual and organizational identities.

This chapter looks into the powers of accounting in organizational settings. It describes some of the ways in which new accounting practices affected the power relationships between two organizations, thereby furthering organizational reconstruction. The empirical basis of the chapter is a study of a cross-border acquisition in the former German Democratic Republic. In this case, a Swedish construction 'combine' introduced decentralized and project-based accounting in an acquired German firm as part of an overall reform programme aiming to increase competitiveness and identification with the acquirer.

One conclusion is that the new accounting practices affected organizational boundaries in the German firm. It facilitated change in internal power-relationships and lead to the transformation of individual and organizational identities. Another conclusion is that that project accounting helped establish a principal-agent relationship between the acquirer and the acquiree, that is, a relationship where organizational members considered it natural for the German firm to be governed by the Swedish one.

As the cross-border acquisition theme implies, the chapter can also be read as tale of an encounter between the 'East' and the 'West'. Here, the East/West divide is used mainly as a signifier denoting differences in knowledge claims and relative power when discussing the relationship between the two organizational parties.

Accounting: regulating and constituting

Accounting can now be seen as a set of practices that affect the type of world we live in, the type of social reality we inhabit, the way in which we understand the choices open to business undertakings and individuals, the way in which we manage and organize activities and processes of diverse types, and the way in which we administer the lives of others and ourselves (Miller, 1994, p. 1).

Accounting is woven into wider systems of management control and power within organizations and between organizations and other actors. However, when regarding organizations primarily as economic entities striving for effectiveness and efficiency, accounting is traditionally often defined as fulfilling a limited number of regulating functions. Danielsson (1989) states that accounting has three main regulatory roles: to enable the market control of firms, to help principals control agents, and, to keep track of information about products, processes and activities in order to keep management well informed. It follows that accounting practices enable a form of controlling and explaining actions at a distance (see Latour, 1988). Principals need not be present in order to govern agents, accounting does it for them.

Most students of business and practitioners tend to be familiar with the economic perspective on accounting. The regulatory roles of accounting it delineates are fundamental from an economic viewpoint, but as all perspectives, it is a perspective with limitations and blind spots. One type of critique is that this type of perspective takes too little notice of differences between organizations and settings, for example, in how accounting systems and other control systems function across various market economies (Whitley, 1999). Accounting practices have wider power implications than the ones made evident from a narrow economic standpoint. Importantly, governing through accounting is no neutral, exogenous practice, reporting on events and actors already in place. Accounting affects our ideas of individual identities or personhood; for accounting supports a view of individuals as being manageable and efficient entities (Miller and O'Leary, 1987). The focus on costs and calculus inherent in accounting practices makes them active parties in the rationalization, or 'McDonaldization' (Ritzer, 1993), of individual members of society. This renders another role of accounting visible. In addition to being a regulatory practice, accounting has constitutive capacities. Or rather, because it is a regulatory practice, accounting has constitutive capacities. It is a language of power, constraining the men and women of organizations to speak within the realm of, and act on behalf of, the world as constituted by accounting:

> Accounting imposes a certain understanding and definition of reality; the individual must explain his or her action in terms of this imposed understanding; individuals' own understandings are in principle irrelevant to this process. (Roberts, 1991, p. 361)

The constitutive capacities of accounting are not limited to affecting individuals. The construction of organizational identities is another issue where accounting is important. As organizational boundaries are neither self-evident nor reproduced without an effort, we need an aid in order to be able to identify them. Accounting can serve that purpose. It has a role of 'boundary maintenance' (Llewellyn, 1994), of creating and maintaining organizational boundaries. Thanks to accounting, we can know what to count as part of a specific organization – for example, what resources, cash, buildings, products being processed – and what not to. From this perspective, it is not surprising that accounting has been found to be instrumental in attempts of strategic organizational reform (Dent, 1990).

Accounting is also involved in shaping new forms of society. Societal and more explicitly political aspects of accounting are evident in Power's (1994) conception of the 'audit' society. His argumentation suggests that auditing has evolved to become a 'rationalized myth' (Meyer and Rowan, 1977) in society:

> The idea of the 'audit' society, which describes systematic potentials as much as identifiable practices, draws attention to the function of audit as a 'rational norm' which is greater than the apparently diverse technical practices which are conducted in its name. (Power, 1994, p. 313)

So far, I have discussed some powerful consequences of accounting on the individual, organizational and societal level respectively. In the following, I will concentrate mainly on the organizational level. Individual and societal aspects are not explicitly excluded from the discussion, for they inform and are informed by what goes on in the organization.

The next section describes the empirical background of the discussion. The chapter moves on to briefly look at the influence of societal transformation on the relationship between the organizations studied. It then outlines the aims and measures of accounting reform as part of a wider reform programme initiated by the acquirer. In the concluding section, I come back to the 'powers' of accounting in connection with regulatory and constitutive issues.

Fieldwork

Northcon and Sibco are the main organizational actors in this study. Their names are fictitious, as their real life counterparts have been promised anonymity concerning their names.

I conducted the fieldwork between 1990 and 1993. The study of the relationship between Sibco and Northcon is part of a research project focusing on the social construction and reconstruction of privatized organizations in different settings (Svedberg Nilsson, 1999). The fieldwork consists mainly of interviews. At the head office and sites of Sibco, 26 formal interviews were conducted. German interviewees belonged to different hierarchical levels ranging from manual workers to top-management. At Northcon, eight interviews were conducted with Swedish Northcon personnel in Stockholm, Berlin, and, eventually, at Sibco. These interviewees also covered different hierarchical levels, but the main selection criteria was that they were engaged in, and/or responsible for the reconstruction process. At Sibco as well as Northcon, the interviews were complemented by informal discussions with interviewees and other organizational members.

Apart from interviews and discussions, various internal documents have been analysed. Among those most pertinent for the present discussion are the project accounting forms, reform and training plans, and the firm magazine which were all involved in, and thought likely to be instrumental for, the attempts of Northcon to reconstruct Sibco.

Organizational actors

Northcon, the Swedish construction 'combine', is the organization deemed relatively more powerful in this study due to it being not only the acquirer but also Western. However, Northcon's position in the ex-German Democratic Republic of the early nineties was by no means unproblematic, if not as complex as Sibco's, the GDR construction firm it acquired and strove to reform.

Traditionally, Northcon supplied building materials, and was engaged in building projects for the East German State. Northcon had been present in East Germany for more than two decades by 1990 and had a subsidiary in East Berlin.

The fall of the Berlin Wall affected Northcon in a more direct way than it did many other foreign firms which had no historical ties with the GDR. Consequently, Northcon suffered a severe blow and lost its main customer as the political and economical system of East Germany crumbled. The prospect of a reunited Germany further complicated Northcon's situation, as it was not present in the Federal Republic of Germany.

The acquisition of Sibco was an important element in Northcon's strategy to handle the ongoing societal change in East Germany. The acquisition was intended to help establish Northcon on the construction market of a re-united Germany, a market Northcon expected soon to be booming.

Sibco, the Small-town Industrial Building Company, was originally a GDR *Kombinat*. It was then turned into a *GmbH*, a change of organizational form that was a compulsory part of the preparation for the upcoming monetary union between the two German states in the summer of 1990.

Sibco's main production area was industrial construction. It was also engaged in housing and other forms of so called community construction projects. The number of employees amounted to 1900. Sibco was thus close to the average size of a GDR construction *Kombinat*, which was of about 2000 employees (Grabher, 1992).

During the spring of 1990, Sibco faced financial and other difficulties as the economic system of East Germany was falling apart. Hence, it had to reduce the number of employees by some 20 per cent, through outright lay-offs and by a kind of outsourcing. The survival of the company was no longer to be taken for granted.

It was at this problematic stage in the history of Sibco that the Northcon combine appeared. Northcon put its initial bid on Sibco in June 1990. Following several months of negotiations between Northcon and the seller, the *Treuhandanstalt*, the acquisition was finalized in March 1991.

Setting the stage for accounting reform

Before turning to the aims and contents of the accounting reform, a few remarks need to be made about the societal setting in which the reform took place. The ongoing transformation limited the views of actors regarding the reasons for reform. It also affected the form of relationship between Sibco and Northcon thought possible and desirable.

The planned economy was deemed irrelevant for the present situation by the Germans, a finding in accordance with Rottenburg's (1991) study of another *Kombinat*, at that time. The members of Sibco, and of Northcon for that matter, had concluded that what was fitting for a firm in a planned economy was not likely to be appropriate for a firm in a market economy. Similarly, they agreed that experience and knowledge from the planned economy were not likely to be of much significance in the market economy.

In the eyes of the Germans, Sibco suffered from a problem of environmental misfit. The surrounding environment was expected to adhere increasingly to the principles of a competitive market. Sibco had to evolve into an actor in such a market, it was argued. It had to turn into an autonomous and competitive firm. The Swedes did not disagree.

The Swedes of Northcon had several reasons for wanting to reform Sibco, not all of which were evident to the Germans. Importantly, there was a strong need for Northcon to adapt to the ongoing East German transformation. This need of Northcon's was downplayed, however. Both parties concluded that Northcon, being a Western firm, was a carrier of knowledge and practices that Sibco did not have, or indeed could not have yet due to its limited experience of the market economic system. The knowledge gap between the parties induced a relationship where Northcon was the teacher and role model whereas Sibco was a student and follower. The idea that Northcon could have something to learn from Sibco was not expressed at the time. It surfaced later in the relationship, as discussed in Nilsson (1996).

It would be incorrect to regard the reformist–teacher–student relationship as entirely of Sibco's and Northcon's own making, though. The relationship was supported by dominant ideas in the wider societal setting. What has been termed the 'transition perspective' (Grabher, 1995) dominated the debates and analyses of East and Central Europe in the early nineties. Within such a perspective, the planned economic system was proven wrong. It was considered wholly different compared to the market economy. Consequently, it was hard to claim that organizations previously intertwined with, and adapted to, the planned economy could function without major changes in the evolving market economy. It was difficult to argue that experiences and knowledge grounded primarily in the old planned system would be of immediate use in the new market one. It was, therefore, reasonable to view Eastern firms as in need of reform, and legitimate to claim that Western ideals were to be followed. Western firms were supposedly market-driven firms able to provide experiences and knowledge suitable for actors new to a market economic system (see Kostera (1995b) for a discussion of the unidirectional character of communication in the Polish setting). In conclusion, by recognizing the need for reform of Sibco with Northcon as the role model, the members of Sibco and Northcon acted in accordance with predominant myths as represented by the transition perspective. In so doing, they portrayed both organizations as legitimate, or at least as acceptable, actors in the new economy.

To sum up, there was surface agreement concerning the reasons for and aims of reform between the people of Northcon and Sibco. This common frame of reference was supported by the wider societal context. The stage was set for Northcon's reconstruction programme – where the practices of project accounting were an integral part.

Project accounting as part of reform

Integrative efforts and change attempts are commonly assumed to be necessary in order for mergers and acquisitions to be successful (Shrivastava, 1986). Diverging organizational cultures, and clashes between these, are among the recurring problems to be worked out (Buono *et al.* 1985). Thus, one does not usually ask if post-merger integration is needed, but rather what integrative instruments are best suited for the particular complexities of the situation at hand (Strandgaard Pedersen, 1998). Northcon followed this script. It was self-evident for Northcon that Sibco needed to be more integrated in Northcon for the acquisition to be a success.

Accounting has been put forward as one integrative instrument promoting identification with the acquirer (Jones, 1985). In the following, Northcon's use of accounting as a reform instrument is portrayed, focusing on project accounting issues. To understand what Northcon set out to do, what it strove to change, and why project accounting mattered, it is necessary to describe some of the main characteristics of Sibco at the time of the take-over. This is the topic of the first of the following sections. Then I turn to the issue of reform and its consequences.

Pre-reform problems and reform aims

In 1990, Sibco was infused with values and structures of the old system. In the planned economy period, the external control of Sibco was formalized in the plan. Central plan production targets stated how many, of what type, where and for whom Sibco was to erect houses and other buildings. Accounting procedures at Sibco were adapted to the targets set out in the plan. A main task was to transform the central plan targets into targets for the various production sites and 'collectives', as the work groups were called. Sibco's department for planning, a department within the accounting area was in charge of these proceedings. As a symbol of the old order, it was among the first to be abolished in the spring of 1990.

The planned order worked as a main internal structuring device in several respects. The hierarchical order of the plan was reproduced within Sibco. There was a large degree of centralization of accountability and responsibility to top managers. Departments and areas were labelled and numbered in accordance with plan standards. The range of activities was wide, as prescribed, including holiday arrangements and ideological schooling.

The functionally oriented organizational structure of Sibco, which included the areas of accounting, production, personnel and technology, also followed the plan. Administrative personnel were based at headquarters and where thus separated from manual workers producing on the sites; this separation had a gender subtext. Women worked at the head office but were a rare sight on the sites. In addition to this overall separation between areas and groups (and sexes), there was a wide range of specialized functions further subdividing the members of Sibco and their tasks. By way of illustration, manual workers at the sites could be specialized carpenters, roof-builders, concrete- or iron-workers and so on.

In many respects, Northcon was totally different from Sibco in terms of internal structure and control. The structure of Northcon was centered around production and in particular, around single construction projects. The project, usually construction projects, was the major accountable entity and project accounting was an integral part of building at Northcon. Project accounting practices involved explicitly designating resources to single construction projects and the allocation of costs accordingly. For this, there was computerized support. Project accounting also meant following and accounting for construction project across years, that is, not only following the calendar year principle in accounting reports as had been the case at Sibco.

Another feature of the organization of Northcon was that administrative personnel and productive personnel were mixed. The cross-functional team was an important building block. There were teams at the head office as well as on the construction sites. As people with accounting competence were included in teams on lower managerial levels, it was possible to decentralize accountability for cost to the single team.

The main features of Sibco and Northcon as presented here are summarized in Table 7.1. It can be noted that I have not explicitly mentioned the issue of internal versus external accountability present in the table. What I would like to stress with the help of this dimension is that accounting at Northcon, not least project accounting, was an integral part of the internal governance system. In contrast, accounting at Sibco was focused primarily on external accountability, on producing accounts satisfying central authorities.

Reform measures and results

Simply put, the overall aim of Northcon's reform measures was to transform Sibco into an image of Northcon. The primacy of production was promoted through a new internal structure centred on production. Accounting, the so-called technical area, and personnel were deemed secondary support functions. The CEO duo at Sibco, consisting of the personnel manager and the accounting manager, was replaced by a Northcon man. The accounting manager returned to her previous position, but now with the support of a controller recruited from West Germany. The other management positions were not changed. However, what was called a 'support structure' of Swedes was set up at all managerial levels.

Project accounting was promoted already before the take-over. A small group of Swedes worked closely with some of the economic-administrative staff. The staff candidates chosen were the ones considered especially change prone and open-minded. This excluded the

Table 7.1 Pre-reform at Sibco

Sibco	Northcon
Centralized accounting	Decentralized accounting
Accounting for the organisation	Accounting for projects
External accountability	Internal accountability, and external
Wide range of activities	Narrow range of activities
Wide range of specialities	Narrow range of specialties
Functional brigades and work groups	Cross functional teams
Four peer areas	Production centre area

head of accounting. She was repeatedly referred to as being adverse to change, and as a source of trouble, by the Swedes.

In the early stages, Sibco spread the ideas of, and reasons for, project accounting. Attempts were also made to account for production on the limited number of construction sites still under way. After the take over, the early work was followed up by educational efforts teaching accounting principles and techniques, to staff and production managers. A computerization task was also undertaken. The computerization was also needed to enable an overall modernization of other administrative routines. Here, it can be noted that modernization, in terms of new technology within production and administration, was what many of the Germans at Sibco had longed for, and had associated with the West. Thus, computerization met with little resistance in this case.

Project accounting supported the idea of the team as an important building block in the organization – and vice versa. They were both expressions of the idea of decentralized accountability favoured by Northcon. Teamwork was also encouraged through training programmes for managers – ranging from top-management to onsite managers. Lower level employees were then supposed to learn from managers on the next level. The training programmes underlined the importance of shared marketing responsibilities; that is, managers within production were co-responsible for the marketing of Northcon's construction services. They could not expect to be given work. Being accountable for projects did not only include accounting for projects under way, it was argued. Planning ahead and being able to account for prospective projects in tendering situations was equally important. It was stated that a *Northconite*, was somebody who was an 'accountable marketer'; an individual who was accountable for costs and responsible for the marketing of a specific task, project or the company as a whole, apart from being well skilled at his, or her, other work tasks.

The personnel manager was involved in the implementation of several of these training programmes. Personnel still appeared to be an area with functions related to its previous ones. The technical area, however, lost its core to the growing production area. The technical area was soon reduced to a couple of people only. It was then somewhat revived by being turned into a teamworking environment with the acquisition of properties for development.

The accounting area shrunk as well. The activity range of central accounting was limited by the shift to project accounting. People within central accounting were moved closer to production. Moving to the area of production included a relocation of offices, making the restructuring very visible. The main responsibility left for the accounting manager was the external accounting on which tax payments were based. Project accounting staff kept track of costs and revenues in the projects and they were involved in the cross-functional teams. The controller surveyed the activities, costs and revenues of projects, and reported to the Swedes.

The production area increased its importance, but was not untouched by the reorientation. Notably, construction activities considered peripheral by the Swedes, such as carpentry, were outsourced, thereby reducing the range of specialties and number of onsite workers employed by Sibco.

Summary traits of the reformed Sibco are presented in Table 7.2, together with a reproduction of the portrayal of Northcon from Table 7.1. In the post-reform phase, Sibco had decentralized accounting, worked with accounting for projects and emphasized internal accounting. Structurally, production was at the centre. The range of activities was narrow, as was the range of specialties.

Identities and boundaries

A comparison between Tables 7.1 and 7.2 makes the overall impact of reform more clearly visible: Sibco had grown increasingly similar to Northcon. This result indicates that an overall identification of Sibco with Northcon had been achieved, as intended by the Swedes. This identification, or reconstruction of Sibco, was made possible by a large amount of 'boundary maintenance' (Llewellyn, 1994).

Maintaining boundaries involves not only delineating them in the first place, but every-day maintenance as well as major efforts every

Table 7.2 Sibco as reformed

Sibco	**Northcon**
Decentralized accounting	Decentralized accounting
Accounting for projects	Accounting for projects
Internal accountability, and external	Internal accountability, and external
Narrow range of activities	Narrow range of activities
Narrow range of specialties	Narrow range of specialties
Cross functional teams	Cross functional teams
Production centre area	Production centre area

once in a while. Northcon's accounting reform measures included all of these. The introduction of project accounting was a major effort. It moved the boundaries of a centrepiece of organizational reality, that is, 'construction'. Before, construction was an activity. It was carried out by specialized workers and resulted in houses, factories and other buildings. Now, construction was 'a project'. It was set out in figures and, hopefully, eventually it resulted in profits. Constructing a building of some sort was only a means to achieve this profit aim.

Not only were project accounting practices introduced, a large number of organizational members were trained in the language of project accounting. Being fluent in that language, they were then part of maintaining the new entity in their everyday work.

In addition, project accounting, and accounting as a whole, helped define what was part of the company, and what was not. For instance, in all prospective plans and budgets for new projects organizational members were constantly reminded that carpenters and roof-builders were no longer part of the organization. They were outsiders, and were brought in when necessary. The territory within the organizational boundaries had shrunk.

This illustrates quite clearly the effects of accounting reform on the content of work identities. Previously, the plan order prescribed a wide range of activities and specialty functions. In so doing, it fostered work identities that were narrow in scope, but many and diverse although to a varying extent united by an ideological building block. Workers were identified not primarily with the company but with their work tasks. They were professional persons. In contrast, the accounting practices and structures implemented by Northcon fostered fewer work identities as broad construction tasks and competencies, not specialized tasks and competencies, were required. Northcon norms emphasized that a main building block in all identities should be the image of 'the accountable marketer'. Organizational members were not only accountable for themselves, they had better be aware that they were accountable for the organization at all times. As a result, work identities were based more on accountability – for themselves, projects, and the organization as a whole – than on specialized skills. Another conclusion is that the content of the main building blocks of the new work identities were hard to distinguish from the new organizational identity of Sibco. It was not only workers that were accountable marketers, so was the organization. The identities of the human persons and the identity of the organizational 'super person' (Czarniawska-Joerges, 1994b) had merged.

Out of count

Another effect of the project accounting was that it made the maintaining of old boundaries around central accounting difficult. The head of accounts had lost most of her power base. Having previously been a central figure, responsible for contacts with major actors in the environment, she was now reduced to being a taxpayer. Project accounting was not her responsibility, it was part of the internal control system supervised by the new controller. It was thus he who was the manager in charge of the role of accounting as an information system – not the head of central accounting. As a result, central accounting was largely cut off from internal control and accounting practices in other parts of Sibco. The maintenance of central accounting as a separate entity was hit hard by the fall of the plan system. Moreover, the new organizational structure placed central accounting together with other so called support functions, making its boundaries and importance even less noticeable.

This development implies that the head of accounts need not have been adverse to change, as the Swedes argued, just adverse to changes being entirely to her own disadvantage. The CEO, the controller and the other top managers at Sibco were all male. The head of central accounts was female. This position as a 'token woman' (Kanter, 1977) is not likely to have helped her case, especially as she was marginalized by the top managers at Northcon.

Principals and agents

To deemphasize central control by decentralizing accountability, as done by Northcon, could be interpreted as reform measures increasing the powers of individuals on lower levels as well as the powers of the organization. Such an interpretation of the development at Sibco is supported by interviewees claiming to have larger freedom to act than before the take-over and before the transformation. Most members felt more powerful, and for a reason. They were free of the many rules that had governed their work- and private lives. However, as we have learned from studies of deregulation, abandoning central regulations does not automatically imply that all rules disappear. Rather, what can be expected is a re-regulation involving a change in the form and content of rules governing the system, actors and activities in question (Majone, 1996). In turn, this indicates that deregulation does not necessarily make it possible for actors to act in accordance with their own free individual wills and preferences. A case in point is the abandonment of central rules regarding compulsory components in the structure of Swedish municipal authorities. This deregulation did not result in a diversity of locally adapted structures, as hoped for initially; it resulted in a widespread implementation of fashionable purchaser–provider structures (Fernler, 1996). Similar structures enforced by compulsory central rules were thus exchanged for a new set of similar structures enforced by common norms.

In the case of Sibco, centralized accounting, plan targets and communist ideology were indeed abolished. The consequence was not that individuals were free to act according to their personal preferences, however. The empty margins in the regulatory space were soon filled with decentralized accounting, budget targets and Northcon ideology.

In addition to this, it can be noted that bureaucratic control, such as centralized directives, need not be abandoned in order for norms and other versions of self-imposed control to arise. One does not exclude the other. Implicit governing by norms, for example, in the form of a strong national or corporate culture, does not exclude explicit governing by more bureaucratic means. Bureaucratic control can be overlayered and supported by self-imposed control in a company, as studies of corporate cultures have shown (Kunda, 1992). In the GDR, bureaucratic control in the form of plans used to be meshed with self-imposed control in the form of ideology. Similarly, Northcon introduced formalized, and centrally produced rules such as project accounting at Sibco, in addition to new norms of conduct and other less visible means of control. One was not exchanged for the other. They reinforced one another. The form and content of rules had changed but Sibco was still very much an agent governed by a principal.

Summary conclusions

The chapter aimed to analyse some of the powers of accounting by focusing on a relationship between two organizations where one strove to reform the other using project accounting, and complementary practices. One main conclusion of the analysis is that project accounting had a regulatory impact. It was instrumental in re-establishing a principal–agent relationship with the acquirer as the new principal, thereby fulfilling one of the traditional economic functions of accounting. In short, accounting reform helped establish the hegemony of Northcon over Sibco and prohibited alternative paths of development. What was defined as support and modernization was also about control and domination. On the other hand, if Northcon had not taken over Sibco, and if Northcon had not made an effort, monetary and otherwise, to reform it, it is doubtful whether Sibco would have continued to exist at all.

The second main conclusion is that accounting had constitutive powers in this case. It furthered a transformation of boundaries and identities. On the organizational level, accounting promoted a shrinking of organizational boundaries. A number of activities and actors fell outside company accounts. Some actors no longer had access to organizational membership. A redrawing of internal boundaries complemented this change. Production was the implied new ruler and the remaining parts of the organization were followers. Furthermore, the meaning of the main task of production, construction, was transformed from being an activity into being a 'project'. A focus on producing things was thus turned into a focus on producing profits. And accountability – for projects, costs, profits and more – turned into a main building block in the identity of the organization.

On the individual or personal level, it is concluded that the redrawing of boundaries and shaping of a new organizational identity was intertwined with changes in the relative positions, powers and identities of organizational members. Notably, the head of production had increased his relative powers whereas the head of central accounting had lost a major part of her power base. Being the only female top-manager, her fall from grace also implied a setback for women as a group at Sibco. Also, there were no other female top managers at Northcon to serve as alternative role models. Turning to the issue of identity, a standardization was noticeable. Having previously been manifold and individual, work identities had turned increasingly similar and accountability oriented. In other words, work identities merged with the new accountable identity of the organization as a whole.

8

Reinventing the Past: Stories about Communism and the Transition to a Market Economy in Romania

Mihaela Kelemen

'... who controls the past controls the future: who controls the present controls the past.'

(George Orwell, *Nineteen Eighty-four*)

Introduction

In recent years, the transition to a market economy in Central and Eastern Europe has received increased attention from researchers, particularly in terms of government democratization and economic reforms (Clark and Soulsby, 1995; Whitley *et al.*, 1997). However less attention has been paid to the 'private' face of the transition in terms of how individuals make sense of these reforms and what may be its impact upon subjective experience. This chapter attempts to redress the balance by engaging with some of the processes by which individuals attempt to understand and cope with the day-to-day complexities of the transition in one Eastern European country that has received less attention in the literature, namely Romania. The central argument of the chapter is that the construction of the present is interwoven with the ways in which the immediate past, that is, the history of the communist regime, is rendered meaningful[1]. The argument is resonant of Ricoeur's (1978) position (quoted in Alonso, 1988) that meaningfulness is neither fully linked to present nor totally contained in the present time but inextricably interwoven with representations of the past and present.

Hertzfeld (1987) argues that there are two types of histories: those produced by the state, that is, official histories, and those produced by the people themselves, that is, popular histories. Popular histories are seen to be less endurable than the official ones, being the outcome of bricoleurs' work rather than of the 'experts'. They are seen to be disjunctive, fragmented and less trustworthy (Bond, 1976). Official history on the other hand is given a privileged epistemological status due to the perceived ability of the experts to represent the truth in an unmediated, factual way.[2] The relationship between popular and official histories is not fixed but constantly negotiated. Official histories are not monolithically installed nor everywhere believed in (Bommes and Wright, 1982, p. 207). Despite the fact that they attempt to appropriate, translate and transform popular interpretations of the past via a number of techniques (Alonso, 1988), their domination can only be partial. For example, a potential gap between the official representations and the meanings embedded in lived experience makes possible the emergence of popular counter-histories. Thus, official representations may be open to popular contestation as they are to affirmation. They are not neutral value-free assessments but constructions whose object is to advance a claim, to levy praise, blame, justify and/or condemn the existing state of affairs (Scott, 1985, p. 178).

In order to liberate the past from the tight mould of official history, one needs to look at alternative interpretations of the past, the way they come about and the purposes they may serve. The chapter attempts to orchestrate various voices, which contribute in one way or another to the making of the past. In so doing, it subscribes to the idea that there can be no closure either empirically or theoretically on the way in which the past is manufactured and that the people studied have the capacity of constructing their own version of the past and of imagining their own version of the future. The chapter is thus sympathetic to the qualitative approach of asking people about their experiences of the past and present. For the purpose of the chapter the past is taken to refer to the years of the communist regime in Romania (1945 to 1989), while the present is taken to refer to the period of the transition to a market economy (1989 to date). The construction of such boundaries around past and present is arbitrary, serving solely heuristic purposes. The relationship between the two needs in fact to be problematised and any fixed categorization unsettled, as past and present live and speak through one another. In Alonso's words (1988, p. 51), 'histories are not about a past that is dead, which is finished and behind us but instead about a past which lives in and has significance and consequences for the present.'

Although obviously intended to report 'authentic' experience, the way experiences acquire meaning depends upon the already existing acceptable vocabularies for describing subjective experiences (Peltonen, 1998). Language intervenes in the process of making experience known: thus the language for describing the past can be found in discourses laying the foundation for present relations. The chapter is based on 15 in-depth interviews with a wide range of individuals: four entrepreneurs, two retirees, two unemployed, five public sector employees and two students. The interviews were semi-structured conversations and the focus was both on work and non-work experiences associated with past and present. About 100 pages of transcribed material were analysed using discourse analysis (Potter and Wetherell, 1987; Silverman, 1993).

There is little doubt that the ontological realities surrounding the Romanian individual have changed dramatically in the last ten years. More importantly, however, the 'official' and personal ways of interpreting and instantiating the past and the present have changed as well. Talking about 'how it used to be' and 'what it is like now' has become a national pastime. Individuals all over the country irrespective of gender, age, ethnicity or education are more than keen to express their views on the communist regime and the transition to a market economy. While the majority of such talking is spontaneous, taking place on the streets and in the home, institutional means have also been created in order to capture the mood *(zeitgeist)* of the people. For example, numerous newspaper columns are specially dedicated to such subjects and public debates are being organized by radio and television stations.

However, the construction of the past, or indeed the present, by such individuals is not entirely the result of human agency. Various discourses from the economic and political fields condition this process (Bond and Gilliam, 1994). Indeed, the discourse of transition to a market economy and the wealth of practices surrounding it has provided the means for a dramatic reinterpretation of the communist past, shaping to a higher or lesser degree popular, personal interpretations of the past. Furthermore, the newly constructed official history of the past also appears to influence, to some extent, individuals' views of the past. Jenkins (1991) argues that the ways in which (official and popular) history comes to be expressed, the choices made to single out certain events at the expense of others, are shaped by prevailing societal power relations and their associated ideologies. Representing the past is, therefore, an expression and a source of power; and therefore not all representations are equally successful: some of them are elevated at the expense of the others. The representation that wins out on a temporary basis and gets to replace the multifaceted past becomes the official history of the past. This official past is not static; rather it is being continuously re-crafted, reflecting changes in power relations taking place in the present (Cooke, 1999).

The past: a flexible resource?

The official rendering of the past may serve a number of functions. Bond and Gilliam (1994) for example stress some of the positive aspects of such renderings, namely poetic, social and national efficacy. Poetic efficacy refers to that situation were past provides the individuals with the tools to understand themselves and others, while social efficacy refers to the past playing a role in ensuring social harmony. National efficacy occurs when interpretations of the past are rehearsed and marshalled towards the creation of collective and individual identity. Jenkins (1991) argues that the continuously re-worked and re-presented renderings of the past may also serve to legitimize the present and particular versions of the future. However, under certain circumstances, the official past may become the focus for intellectual debates, political struggles and popular revolts (Bond and Gilliam, 1994). Indeed, the official interpretation of the communist regime is a highly contested terrain which has led on many occasions to intellectual debates as to whether one should move completely away from the planned economy and the welfare state or one should still build around some of these values. On other occasions it has led to political struggles between the left and right-wing parties and to strikes and popular manifestation (see for example the miners' strike from January 1999 and their march to Bucharest in which they were demanding job security and salaries pegged to the inflation rate).

The chapter argues that the past is always in the making and in a dialectical relation with the present which writes it. The past is a flexible resource to be drawn upon, being amenable to different interpretations and interests. Collingwood highlights the complexities of constructing the past when he observes that: 'the object of present thought is past thought, the gap between the present and the past being bridged not only by the power of present thought to think of the past, but also by the power of the past thought to reawaken itself in the present' (Collingwood, 1961, p. 294). Indeed, one of the main functions of the past is to socially construct the present (Shack, 1994). Thus, the recreated past can be used to legitimate various claims for resources or status and accommodate the hegemonic practices of the present. The impulse to preserve the past in a particular format is closely linked with the impulse to preserve a certain version of the present.

The invented traditions of the present

Romanian society has undertaken social transformations that have challenged, weakened and destroyed the social patterns formed during the communist regime. Given that communist 'traditions' and their institutional carriers did no longer prove suitable and flexible enough to be reinterpreted and adapted to the new social arrangements, new traditions had to be invented. 'Invented traditions' refer to practices normally governed by overtly or tacitly accepted rules of symbolic nature, which seek to inculcate certain values and norms of behaviour by repetition, and which rely on some form of continuity with the past (Hobsbawm, 1984). They are usually responses to novel situations and tend to establish their own past by quasi-obligatory repetition.

The overthrow of Nicolae Ceausescu in December 1989 made the communist form of ruling impracticable. This required new methods for establishing a sense of loyalty and togetherness for the Romanian people. Some of these methods were conscious efforts by the government and its institutions and had political purposes in mind. However, such deliberate efforts were only effective to the extent they were in tune with genuine popular beliefs and drew on a common past shared by most people. Rather than adopting the view of communist governments that social progress is the result of centrally planned and controlled action, the transitional governments recognized and attempted to magnify the importance of the spontaneous, of the so-called 'Romanian spirituality', in ensuring social coherence and progress.

In so doing, traditions were (re)invented to solve a dual dilemma: first, there was the dilemma of how to prove historical legitimacy for the transition period and, second there was an issue of how to deal with a large part of the population that would have preferred the communist regime not to change. One way of dealing with this was to construct a universal benchmark against which all Romanian people could define their identity. Such a benchmark was provided by the concept of freedom, a concept also drawn upon by the communist regime. In fact, freedom appears to occupy a central position in the official accounts of various pasts: history books from past and present tell us that freedom is what Romanians have pursued relentlessly for two thousand years. The struggle for freedom from foreign occupation was always played up by the communists in their own attempt to strike a chord with the masses. However, the institutions of the transition downplay this interpretation, redefining freedom as the successful struggle against the tentacles of communist ideology. Another way of dealing with this dual dilemma was to point to the standard of living of developed countries and to their market economies as the cause. If only such a market economy model could be emulated, the Romanian people would enjoy a similar standard of living and thus political and spiritual freedom could be joined by material freedom.

A number of traditions were thus (re)invented with a view to construct and convey the importance of political and economic freedom in the constitution of a so-called Romanian identity. First, the role of the church in private and public life was elevated to a central place. Drawing on the survival of the church and of religious beliefs throughout the communist years, the institutions of transition (re)positioned the Church at the core of Romanian spirituality and social harmony. Interestingly, however, there is no mention of the fact that the Church in its various guises (other than, perhaps, the Reformed Church which openly resisted communist ruling in 1989) has aligned itself to communist propaganda in order to survive it.

Second, public gatherings and debates were encouraged (as long as they were lawful) and recast into 'normal' features of social life. Romanians were told that it is OK to express one's view in public, that it is OK to organize and take part in meetings, marches, strikes and so on. Third, one could see a rush to destroy public monuments which paid tribute to the communist regime. In an attempt to wipe communism off people's memory, durable images associated with the regime had, more or less, been silenced: monuments and statues were removed, paintings and sculptures were hidden from public view, books were burnt or placed in archives away from the public gaze. However, ten years after the collapse of communism one can see a resurgence of interest in such memorabilia. One of the most sought after books about the communist regime is *Omagiu* (Homage), an illustrated biography of Nicolae Ceausescu. The book now sells at auctions and fetches more than £1,000 per copy (its original price was approximately £10).

Such invented traditions serve significant social and political functions[3] (Hobsbawm, 1984). Invented traditions fulfil their functions, that is, are effective, to the extent they are able to objectify individual experience and meet felt needs among particular collectivities (Bond and Gilliam, 1994). Thus, the effectiveness and continuity of traditions is achieved in the process of transforming individuals into objects by furnishing them a limited choice of identities and opportunities. In so doing, invented traditions are manifestations of a particular type of essentialism in that that they reduce complex and intricate past social relationships to a few prominent cultural images and ideas that have the power to evoke a certain version of the past in ways that upheld or challenge the present.

These traditions must also meet the felt need of various social groupings. Such needs could be quite diverse but an important question to ask is why such needs come to be felt at various points in time and not at others. The need for political and economic freedom felt by Romanian people in the late 1980s has to be understood within the broader political and economic context of that time. In the next section I attempt to take some steps toward reconstructing the contours of that time, remaining aware of my paradoxical in-betweeness and the inescapable gaze of the (my) present that may order, explain and impose a logic hardly evident at the time of the original events.

Taking steps towards the reconstruction of the past

According to Zernbavel (1996), the first step toward the reconstruction of the past is the realization that our own social environment affects the way we remember and interpret the past, as well as the ways in which we draw upon these interpretations to make sense of the present and imagine the future. Mannheim (1936, pp. 84–5) quoted in Schwartz (1996a) argues 'that every point of view (including points of view about the past) is particular to a social situation'. Thus, the construction of the past and present takes place within particular social surroundings. This is not to say that the individual cannot break away from social discourses at least on a temporary basic to pursue interpretations of his/her own which may contradict the official version(s). Lilley and Platt (1994) argue that individuals' interpretations of a social phenomenon depend on their cultural baggage and their immediate circumstances and aspirations. However, culture is not an individual achievement, and similarly, immediate circumstances are not entirely private to the individual, but are constituted via language and social interaction.

The communists grabbed power in Romania as soon as World War II ended and immediately installed the 'dictatorship of the proletariat' (Harsanyi, 1993). A new ideology of egalitarianism, which sought to establish equality between people and eliminate patriarchy was espoused. Collective property replaced private property: all firms were nationalized and private farms were confiscated by the government. Everything became state property or in the words of the regime 'the property of the people'. Forced industrialization also took place, changing the profile of an agrarian country and forcing thousands of people to move to towns. Everybody was expected to work, women included, since one of the central communist values posited that the individual has the right and the obligation to work and the society must provide the necessary resources for that to take place. In order to ensure that everybody could work, community services were developed, free of charge to all. Highly praised at the time by Ceausescu's acolytes, the achievements of the regime have been under ferocious criticisms more recently (during the transition period).

Critics such as Hausleitner (1993) and Harsanyi (1993) present a bleak picture of the communist years. The former (p. 53) says: 'over the last twenty years all of Romanian society was terrorized by party ideologists and the Securitate, but above all through hunger and cold.' Hausleitner argues that the cause of rationed foodstuffs and energy for the population was the result of mistaken policies of forced industrialization leading to enormous external debts which Ceausescu decided to re-pay at the beginning of the 1980s. She also argues that the communist discourse and its associated material practices colonized the individual's experiences and thoughts to the extent that there was no space for the individual to articulate an identity away from the tentacles of the regime. The official discourse constructed the ideal Romanian as a citizen proud of his/her national identity and whose life and work is dedicated to the construction of communism. According to the authors above, to escape this discourse would have been equivalent with escaping the country, without the possibility of ever returning, since one would have been branded as a country traitor.

The chapter challenges the accounts held by both the proponents and the critics of the communist regime as extreme forms of analysis which essentialize and fix the past along some indisputable lines. While it is accepted that some people complied with the system because they were indoctrinated with communist propaganda, it is also suggested that other people might have complied selectively in order to derive personal gains while others might have simply performed some empty rituals without necessarily changing their personal beliefs. Furthermore, there were those (a minority, of course) who openly rejected the values and the goals of the system. It is fair to say that in this latter case repercussions typically followed. But despite repercussions, spaces of resistance inside the communist discourse were possible and indeed constructed. Without such spaces of resistance, it would have been impossible to overthrow the regime in December 1989. Furthermore, the deterioration of the standard of living was only characteristic of the last decade of communism, prior to that, Romania enjoyed one of the highest standards of living in Eastern Europe and had an open door policy to Western ideas and discourses.

I would also like to challenge the taken-for-granted view that in the communist regime, the public space (work place) offered no opportunity for individuals to construct their own identity. It is typically argued that at work people could only be what it was safe to be rather than what they wanted to be and that only the family provided the so much needed space where one could work at being oneself. Only in this trusted environment, one could carry out identity work (Scheppele, 1999). The chapter takes issue with this deterministic view and argues that identity work was being performed, in some cases, both at work and at home while in other cases, it was performed only in one of the two places or in neither. Indeed, there were families which did not provide a trusted environment in the same way in which there were groups within organizations that could be trusted and where one could pursue one's job without playing the ideology game. This depended on the individuals' responses to the communist discourse, responses which could not be predicted and monitored in totality however much efforts and resources were being committed to this project.

These varied responses seem to be in open contradiction with the view proclaimed by both proponents and critics that the communist regime achieved cultural and material homogeneity. In the following section, the chapter turns to some of these individual responses to the communist discourse as they are being remembered and told by the interviewees at present. It is argued that their interpretations of the past shape the way in which the present is constructed and acted upon.

Going back to small stories: reinventing the present

This section explores individual stories regarding the transition to a market economy in Romania. Fifteen interviewees were asked questions about their public (work) and private (non-work) experiences. According to Ezzy (1997), individuals' evaluation of their experiences as worthwhile or meaningless are related to the nature of the narrative they tell about their present. Although the focus of the conversation was 'the present', most interviewees made repeated references to past experiences and oriented some of their thoughts towards the future. Thus, the transition period is described via three types of narratives, all of which make references to past events and hint to possible futures. Drawing on a framework developed by Wolfram Cox (1997), I have coined these narratives as narratives of regret, narratives of relief and narratives of uncertainty. Indeed, some individuals appear to miss or regret the past, wanting to have it revisited and returned to. Others appear to be keen on leaving it behind in relief. While for some the past carries both positive and negative connotations; nevertheless, they are happy to leave it behind in order to be able to move forward.

Work and non-work experiences are juxtaposed to various degrees in individuals' narratives regarding the transition to a market economy. Some individuals, particularly the self-employed and entrepreneurs construct narratives in which work is experienced as worthwhile and meaningful, counting more than non-work experiences. Other individuals, particularly those employed by the state are more sceptical as to whether their work is indeed fulfilling. Despite being experienced as meaningless, such work experiences appear to still count in that they order the private life of the individuals in powerful ways. The unemployed and the retired are more concerned with private (non-work) experiences in their narratives. Whether work is experienced as worthwhile or not depends on the social and cultural context in which interpretative processes take place (Weil, 1978). The cultural and social framing of entrepreneurial work as central to the success of the market economy may explain why entrepreneurs find their work more meaningful than other categories of people. Furthermore, the financial rewards accompanying this type of work place the entrepreneurs in a privileged material position. Thus, the challenge is to identify the economic, social and cultural resources that could enable more categories of individuals to find meaning in their work, rather than only a selected minority as in the case of self-employed and entrepreneurs.

There is an interesting interconnectedness between the physicality of past work and non-work experiences and the emotions and imagination it engenders. The connection between the physical and the emotional may lead to either confirming or rejecting the past. For example, some may remember the long queues and the poor diets on offer particularly in the last five years of the communist regime, which may trigger negative emotions about the past. Others may remember the physical comfort of having a safe job and free social assistance, in which case their emotions concerning the past are confirmatory. This physical embodiment triggers not only emotions towards the past but also stimulates imagination regarding the future.

Some individuals imagine that the past will return, that it will be recreated if and when the Communists seize power again, while other individuals imagine the future in ways that have little in common with the past. But past experiences are always interpreted in the context of present experiences and aspirations (Schwartz, 1996b). Present experiences could trigger emotions which confirm or reject past experiences while present aspirations may dictate versions of the future which are in tune with or a far cry from what was perceived to have gone on in the past.

The following analysis subscribes to the view that current events and social relationships are capable of being invested with multiple meanings by individuals and therefore the past and future can also be interpreted and imagined in infinite ways. The stories told during the interviews have been grouped for the purpose of the chapter in three categories: narratives of regret, of relief and of uncertainty. This categorization serves heuristical purposes, rather than reflecting the intentionalities of the subjects.

Narratives of regret emphasize the concept of loss. Fiol (1991) argues that people assign meaning to loss, to that which resides in the 'empty spaces' and that this meaning becomes visible through repeated patterns of the manifest. Narratives of regret herald the past as a 'golden era' where everybody had a secure job, social security was all-pervasive and individuals did not fear the future. However, most of these things have now been lost. In the words of retired 1:

> The socialist regime guaranteed a job for everybody and obliged people to work: if you did not work you were arrested. It guaranteed housing for people ... It gave you the possibility to spend your holidays in spas and resorts, however poor you were. There was only a small percentage of people living in poverty; the majority was represented by people with a reasonable standard of living.

Such narratives endorse the view that the past was built on humanistic principles, as the state cared for the people and made sure that inequalities were absent. According to such narratives, the communist regime promoted people mainly on merit whereas now:

> political parties promote incompetent people now more than ever. You get ahead only if you have the right political colour. The minis-

> ter of agriculture is an expert in electronics while the minister of health is a lawyer (retired 2).

The transition to a market economy is described in terms of failures of government and political parties to build upon the successes of the past in areas such as the provision of jobs, housing and free education:

> The new regime did nothing to build houses. What was unfinished at the revolution was left in that state and people stole everything they could. Nowadays people drop out of schools because they do not have adequate resources. A student scholarship barely covers one's accommodation and a meal per day (unemployed 1).

The political class is typically blamed for the failures of the present in that it is putting its interests first and it lacks patriotism and communal spirit:

> The political class has looked after itself first and then after the country. Every government has passed laws advantageous to its members. Instead of working together the political parties are fighting and spitting on each other. They all say the same thing: if we were in power, we would do this and that. But when they are in power they do nothing for the country. They all promise to take the country out of crisis but these are just empty words (unemployed 2)

Other narratives construct the blame on different lines: rather than externalizing blame, these accounts internalize it referring to the so-called Romanian 'gene':

> which is totally different from the peoples of the neighbouring countries in the sense that the Romanian is too adaptable and too quick to find a way under any circumstances. However bad it is, we adapt ourselves and say it is fine. We are not at all perfectionists, we do not strive for better (Self-employed 1).

According to narratives of regret, the transition economy has dehumanized people, transforming them into individualistic subjects and has lead to the destruction of a sense of community and sharedness. It is suggested that most of those who have become rich have done so by exploiting the rest of the community and by stealing from the state:

> Corruption is the name of the game. It's a disease that has infiltrated very quickly in the Romanian texture. We were very quick to learn how to steal from the state and each other. I am totally sick of it (retired 1).

Narratives of regret result from failure by some individuals to appropriate the present or to project a future story (Polkinghorne, 1988). For most of the retired, unemployed and some state employees, the appropriation of the present has not taken place and indeed cannot take place given their marginal position in the society and the limited material or indeed political freedom they have. They appear to be dissatisfied with the present, long for the good old days of communism and find it difficult to imagine a meaningful future for themselves and for the country.

Narratives of relief focus on the present and the future and on the progress made possible by the move away from communist ideas and practices. Such narratives describe the past as a political and economic prison where one could not express one's thoughts freely or pursue innovative business ideas. Some narratives go as far as to describe the last years of the communist regime resembling a

> period of war: there was food rationing, all newspapers were censored, there was only one national TV channel with limited programmes on which there were mainly patriotic songs, political teaching and party news (private company employee).

The communist regime is depicted as

> totalitarian without any democratic liberties but one, lack of responsibility; because everything was given to you, your job was being allocated to you, you were sent to a work place where you stayed for ever, you were given your portion of food. Your life was planned for you until your last day (state employee 1).

The idea of excess planning and control is a central theme:

> Our life was pre-established: we did not go astray from the line. I have an acquaintance who did not work in his life, which is quite an achievement because those who did not obey the party line were usually disciplined in one way or another and made to conform ... You knew roughly how much you could ask for from the system. If

> you were a Party leader you ate in the restaurant. If you were a foreman in a company you could obtain your food portion more easily. I have learnt since my childhood what it is like to queue for food. By the time I was 18, I was well trained. I wanted to write for the local newspaper, but did not have anything to write about. They told you what to write. These were the two things that got at me in the worst way: the queues and the lack of freedom of speech. However, there were other things which I valued enormously: the books, the plays and the music (state employee 2).

'The books, the plays and the music' is a narrative fragment played back at me on a number of occasions, suggesting perhaps that despite the pervasiveness of the dictatorship one could not control the thoughts and sensibilities of all individuals. Unlike the Chinese Cultural Revolution which imposed a monolithic approach to thinking, most of the poetry, prose and plays written in Romanian at the time was free of communist slogans and dealt with subjects far removed from the building of a 'multifaceted and multideveloped communist society'. There were also numerous translations of foreign philosophical and literary oeuvres and most of the plays were about classic subjects rather than contemporary ones. Most rock and pop Romanian music also appeared not to be contaminated by communist terminology. One of the most popular rock songs of the 1980s by Iris (A Romanian rock band) starting with the lines:

> One day soon
> You will discover the rest of the world
> Which is different from yours

Of course such narrative could be interpreted as, 'one day soon, you'll grow up and understand better what goes on around you' but also as 'one day soon, the communist system will collapse and you will be able to travel and meet other people, see other countries'. The latter interpretation was typically associated with the song given the context of the song whereby someone was travelling by train but did not have a ticket.

Narratives of relief suggest that freedom is the most important achievement of the Revolution. Freedom, however, is a problematic social relation which requires some unpacking (Bauman, 1988): first, freedom does not guarantee that what one does reaches the purposes, or that what one says will be accepted. Second, freedom has more to it than lack of restrictions: to do things one needs resources. Third, it takes for granted that the human individual is the source and master of his/her thoughts and actions. In so doing, it overlooks the connection between our beliefs/assumptions and the features of our society. In the communist regime, the will of the individuals as subjects was replaced by the will of the communist leaders. The displacement of individual will however led to temporary stability in that the society was characterized by regularity, steadiness and predictability. Indeed nothing was left to chance. Individuals knew that as long as their conduct was not at odds with the demands of the regime, they could think the way they wanted to. At present, however, political freedom appears to be ubiquitous as long as it is not problematical in a Baumanian fashion.

But the present is also depicted as offering individuals a real opportunity to win in economic and cultural terms by taking responsibility for their thoughts and actions. In the words of one of the entrepreneurs:

> 1989 was a new start for me, it meant everything. I started my own run. I started to go up the career and professional ladder. I became director of the mining company and then started my own business. As far as my standard of living is concerned, the increase was more than significant (entrepreneur 2).

An employee in a private company also emphasizes the flexibility of the new system:

> there is now the possibility to move from a job to another one, if you are not happy with what you are doing. There is also the possibility to negotiate your salary and to be appreciated for your performance. Other things have changed too: the fact that the mass media is free, that you can travel freely and can express yourself freely. Now, possibilities for work and non-work achievement are more diversified (private company employee).

Other narratives of relief, while discrediting the past and valuing some of the political achievements of the present, question the economic and cultural achievements of the transition and the way they affected the work and non-work experiences of a great number of people.

> For most people, living conditions have gone from unpleasant to unbearable because the economy is crumbling and we now pay for the mistakes of both the past and the present. The sins of the past

are still with us, for example the forced industrialization of the country but we also pay for the sins of the present, namely the country's leadership in the last nine years (state employee 1).

Nevertheless, all narratives of relief are optimistic regarding the future. The future is portrayed in terms of political and material achievements. For some, it is interwoven with the hope that private businesses will flourish in Romania and that more individuals will have a (bigger) stake in this success, for others, with the hope that the young generation will come to power and resolve the political crisis that is sweeping the country at the moment:

I am an optimist because the young generation is competent and correct. I am sure that once they get the power, they'll know what to do with it (student 1).

Narratives of uncertainty debate whether the path of change from socialism to free-market economy has brought people back to where they were before. These narratives tend to bring together past, present and future, highlighting the ambiguities and paradoxes of each of these timeframes. Indeed the past and the present are seen to encompass both meaningful and meaningless experiences. One of the interviewees said for example that

the working conditions have been relatively good in the past. But the living conditions were inhumane: there was no hot water and heating and the food was portioned and was of poor quality. However, the education system was of good quality and the social security system functioned very well (unemployed 1).

Another interviewee gives the following detailed account of the socialist regime from the point of view of working conditions and overall standard of living:

There has been a certain period when socialism offered a decent standard of living in Romania: in the 1960s and the 1970s. After nationalization in the 1950s, the country started to develop its industry: heavy industry, machine tools, energy and electronics. In that period a lot of towns were built and the village population started to migrate towards towns. The demand for work force was high and it was relatively well paid. This was accompanied by adequate housing policies and social assistance. After the 1980s, one could start noticing that the idea of a multideveloped socialist society and the communist slogan that accompanied it, 'to everybody based on needs', is a utopia and that Romanian society cannot sustain it in practice. The idea that the Romanian industry can and has to produce everything without any international cooperation or support was being enforced from the very top of the society. This has led to visible signs of an economic crisis after 1980. After 1985 we stopped reporting the reality: there was a gap between what was real and what was reported as real. But this is what the system was asking us to do. It was evident to me that the economy would collapse sooner or later. Even if the political system did not collapse, the economic system would have collapsed anyway. One of the causes of this economic collapse was the ambition of the leaders of the country to repay the external debt by stopping all imports from the West from around 1982 and exporting at a loss only to be able to gather some more hard currency. From a social point of view, everybody had a work place and those who did not want to work were caught by the state and forced to work. All people were on waiting lists to obtain housing and in the end they all obtained a flat. Companies had their own technical high-schools and had the obligation to hire the graduates of these schools. There was a system of social security which ensured sick pay, accident compensations, cheaper holiday and spa tickets. Trade unions had their own network of hotels and spas which offered free and cheaper accommodation to the employees. The system had however a great disadvantage: it was populist, it did not encourage the very best. The opportunists and those who were connected to the right people could enjoy benefits at the expense, sometimes, of those people who were in real need (state employee 2).

Some narratives suggest that the same opportunists have carved a privileged space for themselves; like chameleons they have changed their political colour in order to benefit from the new system:

at least 50 per cent of the people who were at the top politically and economically in 1989 are still in a position of power (retired 2).

the old hierarchies in towns and organizations have been replaced by the same sort of hierarchies. People did not really changed: they stayed the same. Corruption has replaced totalitarianism (student 1).

Given that in transitional economies 'the influence and guidance of an effective leader becomes crucial to present and future economic and social success' (Hewett, 1988, p. 187), more and more individuals appear to blame the leaders for the failures of the economy and their own failures. Indeed, the 'dark side' of leadership (Conger, 1990), that situation where leaders use charismatic qualities for personal gains and abusively turn against what is good for their followers is seen to be a chronic disease of the Romanian political and economic system. In the words of one the interviewees:

> Nothing has been done other than those things from which political leaders could profit for themselves. I always thought that a leader is like a ship captain, someone who first has responsibilities towards those below him and who remembers about his own rights only from time to time. But this did not happen with any of our political leaders. More than that it has become clearer and clearer that Romanian people unlike other people do not know how to live in democracy and that we have to be forced to work (state employee 2).

In these narratives, uncertainty is what characterizes the present:

> We have to learn how to live in the uncertainty that did not existed before, to take decisions on our own. Before you had a clear pallet of alternatives. Now these alternatives are more problematic and this gives way to tensions in the society (student 1).

One of the entrepreneurs interviewed also said that

> We live in very uncertain time and this gives me no peace. One cannot have a plan, a strategy, you have to live and think for the moment.

This perceived uncertainty has both positive and negative connotations. Some narratives welcome the 'freedom' brought about by such uncertain times, others regard it as a mere necessary evil, while others go as far as to suggest that uncertainty could mean the death of their private businesses.

These narratives question what would have happened if another course of action had been taken immediately after the collapse of communism.

> In nine years if we had an intelligent national strategy, we would have got somewhere different. But instead, we continued with the state monopoly and the old mentality. In 1989 I did not think that there would be so much inertia in the system. It could have been better if we had restructured state owned companies, closed down firms which were energy intensive and given a real support to the SME sector in term of a fiscal relaxation, better credit mechanisms, consulting and managerial support (entrepreneur 3).

All the entrepreneurs interviewed complained that the state does not give real support to the SME sector:

> The state could have given a real support to the SMEs in terms of taxes and liberalism but SMEs were instead being destroyed, intentionally or not. Many SMEs have disappeared in the last 2 years: there are too many obstacles ahead of them. Taxes are too high: if you pay them, you are left with no resources and die, if you don't pay them the newspapers talk about you and the financial penalties are even higher. However you approach the situation, you can't win (entrepreneur 2).

The crafting of the future

> Time present and time past
> Are both perhaps present in time future
> And time future contained in time past
>
> (T. S. Eliot, quoted in Colville *et al.*, 1999)

In the three types of narratives presented above, the past appears to be constantly fabricated so that individuals could make sense of the present and project some sort of future. This future may be contained within 'the past' or may be a far cry from past experiences. This future may be mediated by the present or may be undermined by it. In narratives of regret, for example, the present is depicted as unable to mediate the move from past to future. The only version of future imagined here is deeply rooted in a sense of past. Thus, it is hoped that the past will return, if not in its wholeness at least in terms of those things that provided meaning for these individuals. A more humane version of communism could thus be recreated, which would offer individuals job security, social-assistance and overall material freedom.

In narratives of relief, the future is depicted away from a past that had now been buried and never to be returned to. The language of the present is drawn upon in order to substantiate such a future. The future brings with it the achievements of the promises the present cannot fulfil. The present writes itself in the future. It is suggested that it is only a matter of time and the young generation will seize the power and will take the country out of its political crisis. It is only a matter of time and small businesses will flourish, inward investment will provide new jobs for the people and thus material freedom will join political freedom.

Narratives of uncertainty challenge altogether the distinction between past, present and future viewing them contained within each other. Thus, there cannot be a dystopian future as imagined in narratives of regret or a utopian future depicted by narratives of relief. The future seems to be as messy as the present and the past. Perhaps this scenario is the most realistic one in that it does not essentialize either the communist regime or the transition to a market economy but views them as inter-linked and characterized by both achievements and failures. One cannot, thus escape past and present in the future as 'they are both perhaps present in it'.

Conclusions

This chapter explores the 'private face' of the transition to a market economy in Romania through the eyes of various individuals. The position of some of these individuals is central to the constitution and functioning of the market economy, others are marginalized and therefore lack the necessary resources to make themselves heard. The chapter orchestrates their voices in such a way that each is given equal credit and status. Indeed, all individuals are thought to have the capacity of interpreting their present and thus must be given an equal chance to express it. In expressing their views regarding the present, individuals tell stories about the past and make value-judgments about the present based on comparing what it is like now with what it used to be like.

The past appears to be a (slippery) resource drawn upon by individuals in order to explain what is happening at present. Both work and non-work experiences are corroborated in their descriptions of past and present. While official history attempts to fix the past along clear and rigid lines (via, for example, the 'invention of traditions'), individual stories of the past are more malleable, fluid and diverse than that. This is not to say that such stories are private to the individuals, reflecting entirely their peculiarities: rather, such stories are mediated by existing discourses and material practices which are collective achievements. The official representation of the past may thus influence to a certain extent individual attempts of narrating the present and re-constructing the past. However, despite 'invented traditions' and the functions they play in producing some sense of social meaning, individuals interpret the period of transition in a multitude of ways that cannot be controlled or managed entirely from the top.

Their rendering of the past plays also a significant part in imagining possibilities for the future. In some narratives the future is severed from the past, in others it is written within the language of the past. The past, thus, provides the language or the counter-language to imagine dystopias or utopias. The chapter is critical of the boundaries it constructs between past, present and future and concludes that they are contained in each other and should only be separated for heuristical purposes. Past, present, future is a sequence that may need to be challenged and re-written. Thus, in the case of narratives of regret it becomes past-future, in the case of narratives of relief it becomes future-present and in the case of narratives of return it becomes futurepresentpast (as one word). Future research in the area of transitional change in Eastern Europe may need to address this sequencing and the displacement of past, present and future with the hope to learn more about how individuals make meaning about themselves and what is important to them at various points in time.

Notes

1. Jenkins (1991) argues for a distinction between past and history. The past comprises an infinity of events which can never be fully known: not even the people who were part of it have a complete window into the past. History, or our knowing of the past is constructed by elevating some events and downplaying others. Although, I fully submit to this distinction, I shall be using past and history of the communist regime in an interchangeable way.
2. Alonso (1988) challenges this claim by suggesting that in fact, official history may only succeed better at hiding its own hermeneutics and that is what makes it look more factual and objective than popular history. However, just like the former it is 'infected' by broader social projects and relations of domination.
3. Hobsbawm (1992) talks about three particular functions:
   - to establish social cohesion;
   - to serve purposes of socialization; and
   - to legitimize institutions and relations of authority.

9

The Impact of Societal Transformation on Czech Managers: A Study of Post-Communist Careers[1]

Anna Soulsby

Introduction

It has been more than ten years since the Velvet Revolution and new or 'reconstructed' managers have started to replace the generation of senior managers (already in their fifties or coming up to retirement) who were active before 1989. The purpose of this chapter is to explore the views of Czech enterprise directors and managers regarding the course of their careers as they reflect on the decisions and choices they made within the context of communist and postcommunist times.

Until the Revolution in 1989, the possibility of access to conduct field research at the level of the enterprise was practically impossible for Western researchers. After the invasion of 1968 the decision of the Communist Party to re-establish a 'normalization' (Renner, 1989; Simecka, 1984) of life in Czechoslovakia meant a return to a 1950s style strict control of social, economic and political life, which continued up to the late 1980s and restricted the possibilities for empirical research. The purpose of this research project is to contribute to filling in some of these micro-level research gaps. The chapter is structured in the following way: the next section is a review of the literature on careers, the third section discusses how the particular historical development of Czech society has affected the development of management careers. The fourth section outlines the research project and gives some more details about the respondents, the fifth section consists of three brief career histories; and this is followed by a concluding discussion.

Concepts of career, choice and life stages

While there is an extensive literature on the concept of a career and its relationship to managers and organizations, the study of careers is fragmented and confused (Gunz and Jalland, 1996). A particular problem is the cross-disciplinary nature of the subject which has meant that researchers from different disciplines, in particular, developmental psychology, and organizational sociology, have often been unaware of each others' work (see Arthur *et al.*, 1989). Dyer (1994), for example, argues that, while there has been a long tradition of research into careers, these have usually been studies done in parallel. Gunz and Jalland (1996) also observe that another problem is caused by the multiplicity of levels of analysis from which the subject of careers has been studied.

Careers have been studied at the level of the individual, where the object of research is the subjective perception and experience of a career (Collin, 1986; Hughes, 1958); careers have also been considered as part of the research into life stages and adult development (for example, Levinson, 1978; Schein, 1978; Setterson and Mayer, 1997; Smart and Peterson, 1997). Researchers have also focused upon issues of family (Edgar and Glezer, 1994) and gender (Cox and Harquail, 1991; Kvande and Rassmussen, 1995). The individual and her/his career have also been studied by social scientists interested in social class and occupations, for example, Pahl and Pahl (1971). The study of professionals and professional work (Bloom, 1997; Goode, 1957; Leicht and Fennell, 1997; Orzack, 1959) has been extensive; as has been the study of industrial and clerical workers (Dubin, 1956; Dubin *et al.*, 1975). Careers have also been studied as the objective, observable progress of an individual's flow of positions in or through organizations, including at times his or her education and training (Schein, 1974, 1978) or job satisfaction in relation to career stages (Mount, 1984).

At the organizational level of analysis, the focus of the study of careers is on the flows of people through and between organizations, rather than upon the individual's experience. The patterns of these flows are termed 'career streams' by Gunz and Jalland (1996, p. 721) who prefer this term to that of Sonnenfeld and Peiperl's (1988) 'career systems'. Gunz and Jalland (1996, p. 721) regard 'career systems' as a much broader concept. They tend to encompass the human resource practices that that drive the flows (for example, the ways people are recruited, compensated, chosen for advancement, developed by lateral moves or sidelined).

Organizations can have many 'career streams'; the discernible pattern of the flows can be straightforward or complex, vertical as well as lateral. Identified career streams in research include 'fast track', 'plateaued managers' and the pattern flows of technical or specialist managers (Katz *et al.*, 1995; Lynn *et al.*, 1996). A particular feature of this type of research has been the interest in the consequences of radical organizational restructuring in the 1990s (Evans *et al.*, 1997; Newell and Dopson, 1996; Stroh and Reilly, 1997). Managers in different 'career streams' can have very different rewards and very different access to power structures (Gunz and Jalland, 1996).

Schein (1974, pp. 401–2) developed a conceptual framework that connected the individual and organizational levels of analysis. This framework articulates:

> the relationship between (a) the career as a set of attributes and experiences of the *individual* who joins, moves through and finally leaves an organization and (b) the career as defined by the organization – a set of expectations held by individuals inside the organization which guide their decisions about whom to move, when, how, and at what '*speed*'.

Inkson (1995, p. 183) argues that the idea of 'career' is strongly embedded in modern Western culture. A career is usually conceived of as representing a meaningful sequence of positions, occupied by a person over long period of time, often a whole working-life. Common ideas underlying this conception include psychological commitment, educational investment and life-long development. Inkson (1995, p. 183) draws out the individual and social aspects of the concept of 'career'. He argues that:

> the idea of 'career' provides a coherence and stability to individuals as they consider such matters as choice of job and occupation, economic security and prosperity, self identity and esteem, status in the community and the establishment of a base on which to plan one's life. Careers are also social constructions, establishing within the community and its institutions expected patterns of long term individual aspiration and action which organizations may utilize in the planning and implementation of their own objectives and structures.

Inkson (1995, p. 183) considers that the concept of 'career' has clearly identifiable characteristics. First, a career should be integrated around a single theme, for example loyalty to a specific occupation or organization; second, it is accepted and expected that there will be a continuity of orderly progression from position to position. Third, the progression will be a hierarchical one, as success is implied in moving up the 'career ladder' and 'getting to the top'. Fourth, it is assumed that the individual has a proactive approach to the management and control of his/her career, with the intention of satisfying personal goals and values.

In short, the normative image, which dominated academic thinking until recently, is one where the individual is assumed to have a rational approach, laying 'his or her pattern of choice on the mosaic of organizations in which he or she builds a career' (Inkson, 1995, p. 184). However, as he notes, this view does not take into account how careers are constrained by influences that are external to the individual, for example labour supply and demand, organization structure, gender and family issues. The development of a career is partly shaped through the planning and skills of the individual and partly shaped through the influence of social structures, the institutions of society and events.

The inter-relationship between the individual and society is discussed by Rose (1989, p. 226) who extends the concept of career by exploring the idea of the individual self-consciously designing and managing his or her life, especially in the area of work:

> Individuals are to become, as it were, entrepreneurs of themselves, shaping their own lives through the choices they make among the forms of life open to them.

Giddens (1991, p. 75) argues that

> the self is seen as a reflexive project, for which the individual is responsible. We are not what we are, but what we make of ourselves ... The self forms a trajectory of development from the past to the anticipated future. The individual appropriates his [sic] past by sifting through it in the light of what is anticipated for an (organized) future. The trajectory of the self has a coherence that derives from a cognitive awareness of the various phases of the lifespan.

The personal concept of career provides a powerful vehicle for the project of developing the self because individuals can interpret the subjective nature of the development of their working lives. Grey (1994, pp. 481–2) notes that:

> Career links the present, past and future through a series of stages, steps or progressions. Career offers a vehicle for the self to 'become' ... in societies where work, and especially hierarchically organized work, is important, career can offer one of the most obvious sites for realizing the project of the self.

Choice and managerial careers in the Czech context

The concept of a career as discussed above is essentially a Western and capitalist one, predicated on having a wide range of possible choices. As Kalleberg and Stark (1993, p. 182) argue:

> Individuals' work values – 'their conception of the desirable' regarding work – are rooted in, and largely shaped by, the work structures and social institutions in which workers participated and are embedded ... Structures operating at macroscopic levels (such as the state) and mezzoscopic levels (industries and organizations) affect the kind of interests that motivate workers and the types of incentives and benefits that motivate their work activity.

While there were a number of variables that affected the development of careers under the Czechoslovak state socialist system (for example: education, housing and labour mobility), the most important was the stance the individual took with regard to the Communist Party. Western writers have found it difficult to appreciate the all pervasive nature and influence of the Communist Party on every aspect of daily life; it was embedded at macroscopic and mezzoscopic level of Czechoslovak society. If an individual's 'conception of desirable work' was to develop into a management career, then one had to either support the values of the Czechoslovak state socialist system, or compromise one's values, or give the formal appearance of compliance. After the invasion in 1968 by the Warsaw Pact forces and the imposition of 'normalization', the choice was made absolutely clear (see for example, Kušin, 1978; Šimečka, 1984). 'Normalization' was like a 'heavy mantle descending on the country'(Jeffries, 1993, p. 253), and the 'principal weapon ... was carefully controlled repression' (Myant, 1989, p. 182). The 'normalization' process had profound effects that went beyond the political subservience of Prague to Moscow, the rigidifying of its economic institutions and the stultification of the economy. The autocratic enforcement of the neo-Stalinist political reality and its social consequences defined the critical dimensions of Czechoslovak society, in which context the management of industrial enterprises took place between 1970 and 1989 (Clark and Soulsby, 1999).

'Normalization' exacted a moral price, in that most citizens renounced political activity and withdrew from the public and civic spheres of society. But in economic terms, the price to pay was possibly much higher and more far-reaching (Paul, 1979). The sociopolitical repercussions of the events of 1968 had major consequences for enterprise managers both as individuals and as a group of *nomenklatura*. The widespread purges of reformist communists that followed the normalization policy led to the loss of a whole generation of talented managers. Many managers or potential managers had their careers truncated because their conduct and attachments during the Prague Spring were deemed contrary to the priorities of the Communist Party. As such, their names were not approved in connection with *nomenklatura* posts. The managers who replaced them owed their promotion mainly to their loyalty to the Party, and there was the expectation of at least the formal appearance of compliance and loyalty. As Wong (1996, p. 62) observed:

> Except for the brief period of the Prague Spring, political reliability on top of proletarian class origin was consistently a prerequisite not only for most responsible jobs, but also for promotion in a wide range of jobs ... Thus, in conjunction with a widespread patronage within the party, political criteria often took precedence over expertise and professional qualification in personnel selection under the socialist system

Siklová (1996, p. 60) took a different, more cynical, view she argued that:

> In Czechoslovakia, with some 15.5 million inhabitants, there were, before November 1989, 1.7 million members of the Communist party, which comes to about nine per cent of the total population. Since the party was clearly a ladder facilitating career mobility, many of its members were competent, ambitious, flexible, opportunistic, adaptable, and full of aspirations. That is why they became party members in the first place. Young people, not yet 'invited,' and people who would have liked to have joined but could not ... were placed on a waiting list. Such people are now among those who take credit for never having been members of the Communist Party.

In a way that probably cannot be appreciated in Western societies, the nature of Czechoslovak society under state socialism inevitably led to a situation where the chance to realize the 'project of the self' (Grey, 1994) and the development of a career was directly a consequence of the personal moral and political choices one made within these constraints. The consequences of these choices came back to haunt many of these managers after the Revolution, particularly when the Lustration (Screening) Act was passed in 1991 in order to check the political backgrounds of individuals in positions of political or economic influence (see Janyska, 1992; Kavan, 1992; Siklová, 1996).

Apart from the political context, the development of a managerial career was also affected by other structural variables such as education, labour mobility, and the shortage of housing. Education, especially higher education, was intentionally biased towards engineering (see for example, Krejci, 1972) because of the emphasis on developing heavy industry after World War II. In any case, access to courses in the social sciences was politically controlled, entrance depended on one's political record and family background as well as qualifications. There was no labour market in the sense that it is understood in the West (see for example, Altmann, 1987; Knight, 1967). Students usually knew where they would work after graduating as they were usually allocated a job in the enterprises where they had done their placement research for their undergraduate studies.

Another important structural variable was the shortage of housing that still affects the development of the post-1989 Czech economy. Many of the managers who took part in this research project were pleased to join their enterprises because the enterprises were prestigious enough to obtain the resources needed to get workers' flats built. Even if a worker or manager wished to move to another enterprise, they would not usually do so unless they were certain of obtaining accommodation.

Labour mobility was also affected by the traditional preference of Czechs to stay close to their families which reinforced the tendency to find a position in one's home town. The cumulative effect was that there was little incentive for workers and managers to change jobs unless they were directed to do so by the Party. Even now, ten years after the Revolution, it is not unusual to find workers and managers who have spent their entire working lives in the same enterprise. The development of their careers was and is bound by their original choices.

The research project

The author has been studying changes in management and organization in three privatized engineering enterprises in Moravia (these have been re-named as Vols, Jesenicke Strojirny, and Montaze Jesenice) since early 1990s. The research for this project is primarily based on 32 intensive biographical interviews conducted over six weeks in 1996 in the Czech Republic. The sample of managers is not random nor designed to be representative. Within the constraints of everyday fieldwork, the sample was originally intended to include managers who had managerial careers during the period from 1968 to 1996. It also had to cover as many levels of management as possible. However, where an opportunity arose to interview some retired directors and general directors who had become legendary figures within the enterprises, it could not be refused. This research is grounded in an interpretivist paradigm which assumes that individuals negotiate and enact meaning depending on their immediate circumstances and needs as well as cultural backgrounds. The story is not necessarily generalizable to other settings: rather it provides insights into the career choices made by a few Czech managers who under the pressure of events made political decisions which affected the course of their managerial careers.

The overall sample consisted of general directors, directors and heads of departments. The 'retired' sample includes four men (there is only one woman in the sample) who started their managerial careers after World War II and were in positions of influence by the 1950s. The directors and managers in this study have all had different personal management experiences in the pre- and post-communist period which have inevitably shaped their perceptions of their careers. Table 9.1 indicates the positions of the respondents at the time of the research.

The overwhelming majority of the respondents in this research project either held *nomenklatura* positions or aspired to them before 1989. Table 9.2 gives details of those who joined the Communist Party, those who later left, and those who were dissidents.

Of the respondents, 17 were local people who had returned to their hometown after finishing their education. The majority of the group was highly educated with graduate qualification, and not suprisingly over half were qualified engineers. Only four of the group had not been educated beyond secondary level, and this was because World War II had interrupted their education. Table 9.3 outlines their educational qualifications.

Table 9.1 Organizational positions of the management sample

Position	Vols	Jesenicke Strojirny*	Montaze Jesenice	Total
General Directors	2 (1-left enterprise, 1-retired 1989)	*9	1	12
Directors	3	0	3	6
Senior Managers	5 (2 retired)	3	6 (1 retired)	14

Note: *only includes daughter companies of the holding company.

Table 9.2 Details of Communist Party membership

Party membership	**Vols**	**Jesenicke Strojirny**	**Montaze Jesenice**	**Total**
Party member	4	7	4	15
Left the party after events of 1968	1	0	0	1
Never joined	1	1	3	5
Never joined (including members of Civic Forum)	0	2*	2	4
Left the party before the Revolution	0	2	1 (then joined Civic Forum)	3
Not clear	4#	0	0	4

Note: * includes a director who was active in Civic Forum at another enterprise.
includes three young respondents who joined the enterprises in the late 1980s.

Table 9.3 Educational qualifications

Qualifications	**Vols**	**Jesenicke Strojirny**	**Montaze Jesenice**	**Total**
Graduate Engineer	5	8	7	20
Secondary Education (Engineering)	2	1	1	4
Graduate Economist	3	2	1	6
Graduate Social Scientist	0	1	1	2
Total	10	12	10	32

The managers' careers: Support, compromise, compliance and dissent

As argued above, in order to understand the choice of career path that a manager made it is necessary to understand how their careers related to wider societal structures and events in Czechoslovakia (and later the Czech Republic). The managers in this study can be classified under four group headings: those who shared the values of the previous regime, the 'supporters'; those who compromised with the system in order to advance their careers, the 'compromisers'; those who, usually after resisting or dissenting, complied with the expectations of the previous regime, the 'compliers'; and those who withheld their consent, the 'dissenters'. The 'dissenters' group consisted of those whose pre-1989 careers had been hindered or terminated either because they refused to join the Communist Party or because of their actions after 1968. For some members of this group, the post-communist period has been one of personal vindication because their careers have been unexpectedly revived through promotion, a belated recognition of their skills and competence as managers.

In order to explore the different types of responses the author will focus on the careers of three respondents in more detail. Since there are only three examples of 'supporters' in the sample and as they all retired before the Revolution, the three cases discussed in this chapter are examples of compromise, compliance and dissent. It is important to note that these classifications are working categories, and in fact, some of the respondents moved between them at different points in their lives. For example, after the events of 1968 some of the respondents moved from support to compromise and others moved from dissent to compliance or compromise. For the majority of the respondents in the sample the two critical decision points in their careers were first, how they responded to the events of 1968, and second, whether or not they joined the Communist Party. The younger managers in the sample who joined the enterprises in the late 1980s were obviously not put under the same pressure to conform. These classifications are intended as a key for opening up our understanding of the respondents' careers.

Mr Grulich's career (the names of the respondents have been changed to preserve anonymity) is an example of how it was possible to advance in an organization through compromise. At the time of the interview he was the Director of Finance at Vols. He joined Vols in 1976; it was his first position. He joined the Research and Development section which was part of the Technology Department. His career proceeded very quickly within the organization. In 1981, he became the deputy assistant of the Technical Director. In July 1982, he was promoted again to become assistant to the General Director. In March 1983, he became head of information technology and in 1985, he replaced the previous Director of Economy (Finance). Mr Grulich took the view that before 1989 membership of the Communist Party was a precondition for top management:

> The Communist Party affected almost everyone in the country; everyone was scrutinized by the Communist Party, for example,

> membership. When I started as the Director of Economy, I was not a member but it did not make any difference, I had to listen to their views. Communist Party control over the workplace lasted until 1989, and did not diminish before. Those who protested were a few in Prague, and then there was an overnight revolution. It was shock for some in Vols, but not for me. Many people left top positions after 1989. They voted, in some sense, on heads of department and those who were not trusted left their position.

Mr Grulich stayed in his position after the Revolution. Although he was known to have been a member of the Communist Party, his financial skills meant that he was thought to be indispensable during the immediate post-revolutionary period when the survival of the enterprise was uncertain. Other respondents commented on the high reputation he still had within the enterprise; he was called by his colleagues 'the financial magician' because of his ability to find the money to pay the enterprise's bills.

Mr Grulich regarded it as an advantage for his career that he had been promoted steadily, 'one degree at a time'. His personal development was not in a single area because he was shifted to different departments:

> It was also a very great advantage to have started in the Technology Department and learn the deep parts of the organization as an assistant of production director, and as an assistant to the general director. I had a chance to learn about running the organization.

He was used to staying two to three years in each post and then moving on, but he had been in the current position for a long time and now he felt 'a little bored'. He had been motivated in his career by change and the realization of new ideas. He was comfortable with change and could not have moved on otherwise. He felt the current system was more favourable to him, compared to the central planning system because he had many more ideas and the freedom to apply them. Under the communist regime, they were forced to fulfil the plans of the ministry and he had felt himself to be a 'technical expert rather than an economic one'.

As far as his future career was concerned, he saw two alternatives: he would either become the General Director or join another enterprise and start from zero. He felt that it 'would be just a matter of a few days or a week to get used to losing my friends, to overcome the painful reaction and start somewhere else'. He believed that he would be able to get used to the change because he 'can do new things and overcome problems, and after years [here] it would be something new'. However, when he was asked how he felt about the enterprise he gave a very passionate reply that seemed to contradict the pragmatic tone of his earlier reply:

> [I feel] too much, because I started my career in Vols; without Vols the infrastructure of this region would not exist. We are paying half a milliard crowns per year to employees and they spend it in shops and on services; so without Vols the small firms could not exist. Vols is the most dominant enterprise in the region and has had the dominant role in the development of this region. I have had a chance in Vols, because of Vols.

The second case study is an example of a career where dissent evolved into compliance before the Revolution and promotion after it. The course of Ing. Novak's life and career was irrevocably affected by the decisions he made in 1968–9. He joined the engineering department at Vols in 1959. He originally came to work at Vols because he was from the region, and at the time, there was a central worker allocation system. He has always lived in Volna. After a few months he started his military service which lasted two years because he was a non-graduate. When he returned he worked from 1962 until 1968 in an ordinary job. He studied part-time for his degree in engineering from 1963 until 1969. He regarded this as one of the positive experiences of his life, although several times he had thought of 'quitting the course. Studying was a different experience for part-time students because of pressures of work – it was a prestigious thing to finish the course'.

He joined the Communist Party in January 1968 and had left it in April 1969. He received his first promotion in 1968, which lasted until 1973 when he had stepped down from his position and became an ordinary worker because of his political activities. Until that time his career had looked full of promise and he had won an important design award. He described the period 1973 until 1977 as the low point of his career.

> In 1973, I seriously thought of leaving Vols. It was serious. My wife's family was in Staremesto but she didn't want to go [back there]. The children were against leaving; they were seven and

> eight years old at the time. I thought about becoming a teacher but that was too difficult because of my political punishment. It was very depressing.

He did not get involved in the development of the *Charta 77*[2] political movement. He believed that it would have been too difficult for him to sign the Charter because of the personal consequences for his children who already had experienced problems at school because of their attendance on religious courses. His daughter had been interested in studying for teacher training at college, but she did not bother to apply because she knew she could not gain a place because of her family's political background.

In 1977, his career situation seemed to improve because he was asked to take part in a project in the Far East, working on the building of a new factory. They needed someone with his technical knowledge, and he was allowed to travel – his director guaranteed his return. His wife was permitted to join him later but his children were kept behind so that he would have to return. 1977 was a year of change. It was a regarded as success to have been sent abroad. That was a recognition of his skills and abilities; he had been working in a developing country and fulfilling difficult tasks. He also had the possibility of travel for he had saved most of his money before his wife arrived and so they could travel to the Himalayas. In terms of personal satisfaction in his career. He was happier during this period but not as happy as he had been in 1968–9. After this project finished in 1978, his career went flat again until 1987. 1978 to 1987 was not a very good period for his career. He could only do his best in a given situation – it was a very difficult economic and political time. In 1981, he and some of his colleagues introduced the idea of an information technology system to top management, but the idea was refused several times. It was difficult to get computers but eventually the general director agreed to the proposal. In 1987, he became part of a team that had to set up a new information technology system in the plant, which was a very satisfying experience for him.

After the Revolution, everything changed, the events of 1989 were very positive for him. In 1991, he was invited by the general director to become the director of development. Between 1991 and 1996 he managed to create a successful new department which he built up according to his own ideas; his responsibilities included developing the enterprise's strategy and preparation for privatization. At the beginning of 1996, the General Director offered him the position of head of the machine division which was very prestigious, with over fifteen hundred people reporting to him. The offer came at a good time because there was no personal challenge left in his current position of Head of Development and so he was glad to move. He commented that the suggestion of the general director was a surprise for him. He was frightened at first, and had to think very hard whether to accept it or not. The results of the machine division were worse than expected in 1995, and he felt he must live up to high expectations. He designed a three-year programme plan – to overturn the negative character of the results. He wanted to stay on to help the machine division; also by then he would be close to retirement age.

His new position was very time-consuming. There were high expectations placed on him and he was aware that there were people who did not want him in this position. He observed that there were three groups of people in life when it comes to responding to change: those who have high expectations; those who have negative expectations; and those who don't say anything, but are never surprised.

He believed that he was motivated in his career 'by an inborn need to try new things and manage new things, never money. It was never my ambition to be at the top for social position.' When he was asked whether he would have done things differently if he could map out his career again, he replied 'everything!'. He was not sure whether he would have studied the same subject for his degree, but he would have learned a foreign language. If he could, he would have not done army service, they were 'lost years'. He felt that what he could have done was 'limited in influence by the Czech situation at the time'. If he could start now he felt he would have gone up to the top of the organization much more quickly. His parents had brought him up in the 1950s and they advised him not to be active, and keep his head down:

> this was not a very good start to your education. In US films, you can see it clearly, the children are very self-confident, but we were brought up to be very self-conscious. The middle way is better.

He believed that if the political events of 1968 had not happened his career would have been completely different. He would not have been replaced in 1973 and received more promotion more quickly.

In the third case study, Ing. Holub's life also reached a turning point in 1968 and the rest of his life was affected by the decisions he made then. His decision not to accept the legitimacy of the invasion made him a 'dissenter', but unlike many, he did not conceal his dissent with formal compliance. He graduated in 1964 in mechanical engineering from a regional technical university. Unusually he did not start his working life at the enterprise where he had carried out his placement studies but instead he found a position in the technical division of Jesenické Strojirny where he stayed until 1989. He commented that 'my career was influenced by my politics.' His political activities prevented him from having a managerial career until after the Revolution. He had started work on his PhD but in 1970 he was prevented from completing it 'the saying was "a qualified enemy is a dangerous enemy".' The Communist Party punished him and his family: he had a low salary and was prevented from travelling abroad.

Although formally he was in a low position within the enterprise, in time, because of his technical expertise, he managed to develop a career of sorts:

> Informally I had a respectable position and I was responsible for big research projects. I reported to the head of research who reported to the head of Technical Department.

However, he had remained politically active:

> I did not sign the *Charta 77* because I had no opportunity to do so. I was active in politics before 1989 because I had nothing to lose. The Civic Forum[3] started in November, beginning on the evening of the 17th in Prague. It was not an organized movement; people just had to express the wish to become members. Slowly and quickly, it changed, so it is difficult to characterize the movement. I was active, but I cannot say I was a leader, because it was a democratic movement – anyone who wanted could join, and from the beginning there were individuals, and then it grew into hundreds of people. Communist Party members said nothing locally, because they did not get any instructions about what to do. It seems crazy, they were so devastated, and they were unable to do anything without instructions. It was very exciting; some of the current top management was very active then as Communist Party members. There were spontaneous meetings and it was not prepared as an organized event – everything was spontaneous.

After the Revolution Ing. Holub was unexpectedly promoted to director of human resources in 1990 (the reformed cadre and personnel function) by the new general director. He believed that he was given this politically sensitive position as he was known as 'clean' because of his dissident activities. The General Director (a member of the Communist Party) needed him in top management as a symbol of anti-communism (Soulsby and Clark, 1998). He consulted other people because he did not believe it was a proper job for him. He was:

> oriented towards a technical profession, and it was a question of technical specialism and conscience. I felt it as a conflict of conscience all the time. I had some time to think about the decision, and then accepted it.

Although initially he had qualms about accepting the position, as time moved on, he settled into the new position for which he had been completely unprepared and he found that he grew to like it:

> I had to replace people. It is difficult to evaluate my role – it is a question of time. Gradually I became more and more involved, and I considered the work very interesting. There was a barrier between me and the members of senior management, who had a past – they did not believe me, and I could not believe them. There was a barrier between me and [the general director], emotional and intellectual. Our contacts were not very frequent, but I considered them sufficient.

However, in 1994, after major changes in Jesenické Strojirny's structure, which he had opposed, he was removed from his post. He is now back in a middle-ranking technical position as a project manager. He is quite phlegmatic about his career:

> Could be worse. Getting the children into school [grammar school or gymnazium] was a problem, the only way was bribing people. All the time I was keeping some independence, it was more important than status and so on.

When asked whether he had ever wished to leave the enterprise he replied:

> Of course, but I did not. It was a question of age. Gradually work is everything that remains. I like physical work, such as building my cottage in the mountains. Pleasure comes from creating something

> new. Before 1989, it was rather difficult to leave because of my bad reputation and party records. Now it is the problem of age again. Jesenické Strojirny is my destiny.
>
> I have not much time [now] for [for my career]. If you are over 50, you see things differently; you have a limit, regardless of whether or not you are willing to accept it. I believe I will stay in the same position – it depends on younger colleagues. But there is not much competition. It would make no sense [to think about having done things differently in the past]: I am the type of person who lives in the present rather than in history.

His career had had negative and positive consequences for his family:

> Negative first: not much, except that we did not have much money. We overcame the problem of educating our children; it was a temporary problem. Positive: probably it made the family stronger – if you have to put effort in, it makes it stronger. The problems make the family closer.

He believed that 1968 and 1989 were two most important years in his country's history and the key events of his career lay in those years. The most positive value in his view was his self-belief:

> In myself and my own power; to have some standard in the work you produce because it is difficult for powerful people to move you if you have achieved some high standard.
>
> Probably, I am a bit ambitious; probably I strive for some results of my work. As I told you before, I believe I am a creative man. I produced some new machines. Of course, if you see your product through, it is very exhausting.

Although he was qualified as an engineer, he believed that, overall, when he looked back over his career, in terms of personal satisfaction in his career he had been happiest when in the position of director of human resources. Ironically, a role he had been given because of his personal political history, not because of his career history as an engineer.

Concluding discussion

The careers of the three respondents share some characteristics; they were all graduates (two engineers, one economist) who worked in engineering enterprises. However, the differences in the development of their careers lie in how they responded to the historical conditions of the particular Czech situation from the 1970s up until the Revolution, the personal choices they made determined the course of their careers before and after the events of 1989.

After the Revolution two of the respondents, Ing. Novak and Mr Grulich had very successful careers. Ing. Holub's was initially successful but later he was demoted to a middle management position. Mr Grulich, whose career has been one of steady promotion, was confirmed in his position as Director of Finance after the privatization was completed in 1993. Ing. Novak was initially promoted to the position of head of development and then became a director of the machine division, a position he took evident pride in achieving after the travails of the 1970s and 1980s.

Mr Grulich, who pragmatically accepted the reality of the Czech situation, compromised and thereby managed to develop and sustain a successful career which was not interrupted by the events of 1989 and the Lustration (Screening) Act of 1992. Arguably, a major reason for his success lies in his undoubted ability in financial matters – during the period before privatization the enterprise needed him to find the money on a weekly basis in order for wages and bills to be settled.

When he started his career in 1976, 'normalization' was fully in place and a career in management could only be pursued by recognizing and accepting those conditions. However, one could also argue that because 'normalization' had been established and the purges completed, the time for open dissent was past and there was little point in resisting 'real existing socialism'. By an accident of history, he was not called on to make the same personal choice that directly confronted Ing. Novak and Ing. Holub. They had to decide after the invasion in 1968 where they stood with regard to the Communist Party and the regime. Their decisions at that time changed the course of their lives, and in particular, their managerial careers.

In the purges that followed the invasion in 1968 Ing. Novak was punished for his activities and lost a potentially very promising career. He had to become an ordinary worker not only because of his actions in 1968, but also because of his views regarding the invasion, he would not sign to approve the actions of the new regime. Eventually, however, pressure led him to comply with the system, which by the mid-1970s, must have seemed as though it would be in place forever. Compliance was the only way he would have the opportunity to pursue more interesting projects and travel abroad. He seemed to regret the choices he had made in 1968–9 because of the consequences it had for him and his family. He could see how his life would have been different if the events had not happened. However, rapid promotion after the Revolution appeared to have re-invigorated him and revived his optimism; his managerial expertise and technical competence had been recognized within the enterprise and he had unexpectedly developed a successful career after all.

Ing. Holub identified the events in the years 1968 and 1989 as the critical points in his life. The choices he made in 1968 changed his life but it does not appear that he regrets them. He always remained a dissident, playing an active role within the enterprise as a member of the Civic Forum in 1989. He had a strong degree of individualism and possibly stubbornness that had sustained him during the years of 'normalization'. His concept of self seemed less tied up with having a successful career in the sense of achieving formal recognition via promotion, but rather more in succeeding in the technical and creative aspects of his work. Even in the 1970s and 1980s when he was kept in low position within the enterprise and not permitted to travel, his technical expertise enabled him to develop an informal career that satisfied his individualism and pride.

Overall, his career since 1989 has not been completely successful in that he was demoted in 1994 from the prestigious position of director of human resources after a major reorganization. He regretted the loss of that position which he had unexpectedly come to enjoy for he had found the nature of the work more interesting and challenging than he had thought it would be. Even so, he appeared to have come to terms with the situation. In the middle-ranking position of project management he has been able to return to designing complex technical machines for which he was originally qualified and which he found so satisfying before the Revolution.

The career histories of the three respondents demonstrate that even within the tightly determined and controlled circumstances of Czechoslovakia after 1968, it was still possible to develop a managerial career but only if one was prepared to compromise or comply with the system. Qualifications and competence were not enough to achieve promotion and progression within enterprises. The respondents in this research made different choices, two of them Ing. Novak and Ing. Holub, in the context of deciding how to personally respond to a crisis in history, a period which brought Czech patriotism to the fore and forced them to decide whether to confront the system or submit. The third respondent, Mr Grulich, made his choice under less dramatic conditions, but arguably when the consequences of choosing to dissent were clearer.

Notes

1. The author would like to acknowledge the help of Milos Kerkovsky, Milos Drdla and Subodh Kumar (Faculty of Business and Management, Technical University of Brno) in conducting the research. I would also like to thank my research colleague, Ed Clark, who has collaborated on the other projects that have contributed some of the materials for this chapter.
2. *Charta 77* a text published in January 1977 in Prague by a group of Czechoslovak dissidents denouncing the government of the Czechoslovak Socialist Republic for using the powers of the Party-state apparatus to hold its citizens hostage. The Charter's signatories called on the Czechoslovak Socialist Republic to abide by the conventions of the International Covenant on Civil and Political Rights and the International Covenant on Economic, Social and Cultural Rights signed in Helsinki in 1975 (Keane, 1999, p. 244).
3. 'Civic Forum' (*Obcanske forum*) the anti-communist coalition forged by Vaclav Havel and others. The movement was instrumental in organizing the 'Velvet Revolution' of 1989.

Part III

Managing the Transition: Crossovers in Practice and Representation

10
Local Problems and Foreign Solutions: Issues of Management Training in Russia and NIS

*Bruno Grancelli**

Management training in transitional societies: some preliminary remarks

How much can foreign assistance help in forming the cultural capital needed for the transition to the market economy in the former USSR? The evaluation exercise described below suggests it can do a great deal, even if a lot of problems may emerge (see research on organizational change in the former Soviet-type societies, Boisot 1994; Eberwein and Tholen, 1997; Grancelli, 1995a; 1998a; 1998b; Kozminski, 1993; 1995; Puffer, 1992; van Zon, 1996; Warner and Cambell, 1994). It is also possible to think that a dialectic relationship between the West and the East could ensure that Western management orthodoxy is itself challenged, adapted and reformed in line with the changes taking place in contemporary Europe. In this chapter I suggest that it may be quite misleading to think that this process could be framed within critical theory, constructivist and postmodern approaches (Grancelli, 1995b). Let us take, for instance, one of the main directions of the critical analysis proposed in this volume: the problematization of Western management models and their mechanistic application to Eastern European organizations. Generally speaking our editors are right, of course, when they state that economic policy should be formulated in the light of economic concerns but also be commensurable with societal and cultural values. But here one should be more specific. Which values? Whose values? The values of (the many) rent-seekers or those of (the not many) innovators? Who are the social actors we refer to, the *Homo Sovieticus* or the people who believe in democracy without descriptive adjectives? Local culture is certainly to be approached with respect. But one should not forget that it has been moulded by 40 to

70 years of Soviet socialism. Thus Eastern Europeans have to practice 'the fine art of learning and forgetting' because the long exposure to the mechanisms of the old system has left behind it a substantial amount of 'residual communism' (Ploszajski, 1995). As for the beneficiaries of the training programmes referred to here, they did not seem to perceive (if they perceive it at all) 'critical management' as the antidote to the noxious effects of that long exposure. A general reason may be that they are not so eager to jump out of the modernity train because they have long been riding the one of 'fake modernity'.[1] That is why the majority prefers to learn about more or less 'orthodox' western management tools with the view to adapt them to their problems, that is, to a crisis management of an unprecedented gravity.

So what kind of theoretical sources must we tap in order to think about the issues of East–West collaboration in management training projects? I think the current debate on social capital can yield many useful insights.

One recent research study on social capital in the Russian context concluded that, under certain structural conditions, transitional or crisis situations can engender cooperative relationships between key political and economic actors. In the short term, cooperation between political and economic elites may promote governability under the auspices of proto-democratic and proto-market institutions. In the longer term, however, these relationships may in fact prove problematic for the further development of democracies and markets (Stoner-Weiss, 1997, p. 26). This is an important conclusion because it points to the necessity of focusing on the action of local organizational and institutional elites, and on distinguishing between the short- and long-term effects of the social capital possessed by these two kinds of elite. In other words, the question is that of clarifying the twofold potential of Soviet legacies: how much can they hamper or facilitate organizational and institutional transformation? How much can one build *on* – or *with* – the ruins of communism?

Those advocating an approach in terms of *network capital* are a case in point for their aim is to demonstrate that the collapse of the Soviet model has not left a tabula rasa in terms of human and social capital (Grabher and Stark, 1997). This approach has the merit of accurately describing the ways networks of firms, banks, local governments and parts of the public administration single out the enterprises to be rescued, prepare strategies of restructuring, negotiate the allocation of resources and recombine property. But here one gets the impression that *all* the actors are only engaged in an endless process of 'recombinant property' guided by the principles of risk avoiding and risk sharing. Thus the questions which arise are: Is there some risk taker around? Are there actors who prefer to invest more in linkages with external actors, organizations and networks? Why should we focus only on the capital of networks and not on the individual differences in terms of cultural capital?

The network capital approach shows what the result of all those property recombinations is: the privatization of assets and the socialization of liabilities that has brought about an institutional deadlock already seen in countries such as Italy, for instance, where a huge public sector only recently began to be touched by the privatization drive.

The point is that the authors quoted above focus on social capital only in a relational perspective, which looks a bit claustrophobic because the linkages with external actors are either removed (Baglione and Clark, 1997, Stoner-Weiss, 1997) or considered as a way to impose from outside a kind of *designer capitalism* (Stark, 1994). On the contrary, the basic lesson taught by the programmes of technical assistance is that these programmes, despite their shortcomings, are one of the few ways for extricating local actors from the current institutional deadlocks. Of course, some of them may apply to foreign resource providers the same techniques of deception they applied to higher authorities in the recent past. But the art of window dressing is becoming increasingly difficult to apply as the experience of foreign actors in the field is growing. As a matter of fact, the best programmes have already shown how the take off may begin to be propelled. In other words, we are witnessing the creation of standard-setting institutions where the social capital (know who) of local leaders act in synergy with the cultural capital (know how) of consultants, teachers and administrators who benefited from the training programmes. Consequently, the transfer of knowledge to enterprises has started to take place, even though quite slowly given the current state of deep economic crisis. We are witnessing the emergence of a transformational leadership.[2]

What we should watch carefully, then, is the ways this transformational leadership express itself, the way it combines (and recombines) social and cultural capital, technical and cultural rationality. This implies an evaluation of the ways the cultural (human) capital introduced from outside is going to impinge on the existing social capital for it is probably true that the basic problem of transition lies in the potential of social capital to adapt the Soviet legacy to the needs of a modern market society. But when we look for analytical tools we see that the approaches to social capital as a property of social aggregates overwhelm those which see it as a property of individuals (Portes, 1998). And this does not favour the research on organizational and institutional change in the countries under examination.

As Elster *et al.* (1998) remind us, the key variables are everywhere the same: Soviet legacies, institutions and decisions. The results of transition processes are different though. To catch the reasons one should realize that the post-communist world is not made only of legacies, networks and institutions. One should bring the rational (or reasonable) actors back in, even if sometimes this is very difficult to do. The definition of rational actors borrows from Elster (1991) who distinguishes between cultural action, as oriented by the precedent, and rational action, as the one oriented to the future. It is not easy to orient its action to the future in societies which were 'without present' because they were supposed, until recently, to have only a bright future. It is not easy in societies which do not express 'transformative interests' even if their legal and constitutional framework has been defined (Elster *et al.*, 1998). It is not easy when the bulk of economic organizations have to survive in a sort of no-man's land between the end of the command economy and the beginning of the market.

Rational action exists, and rational choices can be made even in the 'chaos of transition'. Western assistance can do a great deal to help create a less hostile environment for them.

This chapter addresses some issues raised by Western programmes of management training (MT) in the former Soviet Union, starting from an independent evaluation of 20 projects supported by TACIS and carried out by a team of experts for the European Training Foundation (ETF) in the period 1991 to 1997. The first section sketches the main features of TACIS policy in the field, along with those of other Western institutions. Then, after a short description of the data gathering techniques, the achievements and failures of different kind of projects are highlighted according to the criteria of relevance, impact, effectiveness and self-sustainability of beneficiary institutions.

The following section refers to the main conclusions and recommendations of the evaluation team for the running of future projects. Specifically, the issues dealt with are the following: training of local trainers; role of Western administrators, teachers and managers; attitudes and behaviour of beneficiaries and local decision makers; and difficulties in transferring knowledge to enterprises.

The final section refers to some lessons learned on possible ways to improve cooperation between Western consultants and local beneficiaries; a cooperation which should increase cross-cultural sensitivity and the local knowledge of donors and increase the number of 'standard-setting institutions' in the local environment.

An outline of TACIS policies in the field of management training in the NIS

TACIS is a programme of the European Community initiated in 1990 whose main aims are to provide financial assistance to the countries of the former USSR in the areas of training and education. Other sectors are also covered such as privatization and enterprise restructuring, SME development, transport and energy, food production and distribution. The initial assumption of this programme was that building a style of management different from that of the command economy was a basic precondition for the success of political and economic reforms. An assumption shared by the local partners, and clearly expressed by one of them: 'It is impossible to build a market economy with managers who do not know what the market is.'[3] Thus MT programs were conceived of both as means to foster a sustainable entrepreneurial environment, and as the necessary condition for the achievement of the more general aims of the transition to a market society.

In the subsequent years two other major strategies emerged: the reform of public administration and social protection, two issues clearly linked with the process of privatization and marketization of the economy, as one can see in the TACIS Action Programmes for 1992, 1993, and 1994. These documents call for a coherent regulatory framework for MT, decentralization in economic management in relation to the need of finding new resources because of the rapid fall of federal funding.

At the beginning, TACIS projects were concentrated mainly in the Moscow area and carried out by private business schools. This was due to the fact that the ministries of education were then unable to devise new strategies consistent with the process of economic reform. Consequently these early projects were aimed at strengthening the capacity of local institutions to deliver training courses for young students rather than managers and officials. In other words, the main objective of MT in the early 1990s was that of institution building, which included: development of business plans for the institutes, definition of curricula, training of local trainers and administrative staff, dissemination of teaching materials. On the basis of the first round of projects, the possible areas of improvement included the preparation of standard teaching packages, the advice to administrations in the field of certification of diplomas and accreditation of schools.

In 1994, a total of 40 projects were financed for a total budget of more than ECU 100 millions.[4] This first wave of training projects was discussed in a workshop in Brussels with a focus on four major themes: project identification and preparation; development of local staff and training programmes, and self-sustainability of institutes initially supported by TACIS technical assistance. The conclusions and recommendations of this workshop concern the improvement of the Project Cycle Management (PCM) through the involvement of beneficiaries in all the stages of the project starting with the draft of the Terms of Reference (ToR). There also was a call for more flexibility in project implementation and improvement in monitoring procedures. Moreover, the workshop called for improvement of the evaluation criteria applied later on in the evaluation programme and discussed in the following section.[5]

The evaluation method

The starting methodological issue of this *ex-post* evaluation exercise was the elaboration of an operational definition of impact. As stated in the Final Report (1998, p. 6),

> impact can be defined as the wider change brought about by a set of actions, which in the case of a project are organised in the framework of an intervention logic. It is important to stress that project activities might have brought about an unexpected change, even if they were not originally aiming at attaining that precise kind of change.

In this evaluation – which occurred shortly after projects' completion – the definition of impact included both the direct and indirect effect of management training, and the wider impact of projects on the local environment. In other words, it was decided to use individual project histories as instruments for policy evaluation relating the fulfilment of declared aims to the wider policies for management training designed by TACIS in agreement with NIS authorities. The evaluation tools to be used in the field were previously outlined in two basic documents: a paper of the ETF (1996) whose methodological approach was in line with the second document which outlined the recommendations given by the OECD/Development Assistance Committee on Aid Evaluation

(1993). These documents were the basic reference for an operational definition of five evaluation criteria (Final Report, 1998, pp. 7–8). The first one was *Relevance* used for assessing whether a project or a policy has been actually focused on the removal of constraints hampering the fulfilment of the project aims. In practical terms this was a criteria for checking whether the activities and results of a projects were consistent with its mandate and whether any significant outcome should therefore be realistically expected from a project, also taking into account the sectorial policies supported by other agencies in the same area. This was the preliminary criteria, which helped to test different hypothesis made at the beginning by the planners in the Logical Framework or other documents in which the planning choices were expounded.

The second criterion was *Effectiveness* used to verify the degree of achievement of the objectives set forth in the ToR by comparing them with the end results as reported by the consultants who carried out the project, and the monitoring teams who evaluated them along the project cycle. Effectiveness was assessed by taking into account the many intervening variables that had a direct or indirect impact on the final results.

The evaluation of *Efficiency* was made by comparing the resources earmarked in the planning stage and those actually made available, the actual resources and the actual results, the expected results and those actually achieved. The concern here was to verify whether a project used efficiently the human, material and financial resources engaged in it and the factors which impinged on the level of efficiency such as means, costs, organization, management, monitoring and intervention techniques.[6]

The criterion of *Impact* was applied to verify whether project execution brought about noticeable changes in the local environment with special reference to enterprise managers and entrepreneurs. Particular attention was devoted to multiplier effects on the local demand for management training and the capacity to meet it by the existing institutions. Finally, *Sustainability* was the criterion used to assess the benefits yielded by the project to the expected beneficiaries. The aim here was to verify the extent to which the project aims will continue to be met after the end of TACIS assistance. Both internal and external factors affecting the degree of self-sustainability were considered, that is, financial, environmental, technological, institutional and social/cultural factors.

This set of criteria was then used by an evaluation team whose composition reflected the need to combine specific expertise in the field of management training (both in the West and the East) and in the evaluation skills.[7] After the methodological framework was completed, a desk review began with the aim of examining all the available documentation of TACIS activities in the area of management training in order to classify the projects in these broad categories: strengthening of MT institutions, delivery of MT services to specified groups, and MT components of sectorial projects. Seven questionnaires were designed to address the different categories of participants in the projects: teachers, trainees, local companies which took (or did not take) part in the training activities, actors operating in the political and economic environment, and other donors among those indicated above.[8]

Achievements and failures

The 20 projects of the sample examined were distributed as follows: 11 in the 'Strengthening of MT institutions' category; four in that of 'Delivery of MT services'; and five were those in which MT was a component of sectorial projects. The minimum value of the projects was around ECU 2,500,000 and the maximum around ECU 3,350,000. The duration was between 31 and 39 months.[9] The percentage of sampled projects rated 'very good/excellent' or 'good/satisfactory' was as follows: about one-third according to the criteria of effectiveness and efficiency; around half on sustainability and impact, and more than two-thirds on relevance. Specifically, against the five criteria, the results were the following.

Effectiveness

Of the total of 20, seven projects scored well or very well with four of them being of the 'institution strengthening' type. The best related to two management institutes, in St Petersburg (IMISP) and Kiev (IMI), where the faculty members' MT was effectively upgraded so that they became much more competent in teaching modern management and really felt to be part of the school's corporate culture. The international contacts were well established, the equipment up-graded, and the schools' libraries were the most complete in the sample examined.

Two projects (out of four) of the 'MT delivery' type which scored well or very well did produce the expected quantitative and qualitative outputs, and achieved the objective set forth in the ToR. In practice this meant that they were able to reach the group of managers for which the programme has been designed, that the selection of participants was carried out professionally and on the basis of objective criteria. Effectiveness was also improved by an action-learning approach, which combined training, consultancy and on-the-job experience. A good case in point was the Samara project.

Among the five projects of the 'MT component of a sectorial programme', only one proved effective. This was an interstate project of technical training relating mostly to the banking sector which was a good example of how training can be combined with other forms of technical assistance such as consultancy, institution building and investments in infrastructure, in a framework of cooperation among various donors. The best results were obtained in Uzbekistan, where the bulk of activities was carried out, as compared to the other two countries involved (Tadjikistan and Kyrgystan).

The less satisfactory results in the 'Institution strengthening' type projects stemmed from two problems. The first concerned the limited capacity of schools to acquire a real autonomy from the parent institutions, as the latter showed very conservative attitudes. The second expressed itself in the difficulty of targeting managers – and not just young graduates – as was the case at the High Commercial Management School (HCMS) and The International Business School (IBS) in Moscow, and the Kazakhstan Institute of Management (KIMEP). On the one hand, it was not easy to prepare classes which would be relevant for these practically oriented people; on the other hand, managers' demand itself was not clearly defined because, in the huge industrial sector, it is not restructuring that has prevailed but the mere survival of factories. Also important is the competition among business schools, especially in the Moscow and St Petersburg areas.

On the 'MT delivery' type projects, the less satisfactory results appeared, for instance, in a selection of participants made more on the basis of language skills than previous management experience (that is, 'Training Courses in International Trade') or in courses' organization not suited to the participants. It was also difficult to find EU firms willing to offer internship to NIS trainees. There was also a case in which the group of small entrepreneurs which should have been the main target group was not reached by the project activities.[10]

Among the 'MT component of a sectorial programme,' the reasons why projects' activities were only partly implemented were that the prospective attendants were not available or were simply uninterested in implementing the organizational changes suggested by the Western contractors. This was what happened in projects aimed at assisting the institutions dealing with privatization (Assistance to the State Committee for Property and Investment Funds) or in cases in which an attempt was made to turn a former Soviet enterprise into a 'learning organization.' (The Volosovo Sovkhoz, and KAMAZ in Naberezhnye Chelny, Tatarstan).

The main factors which have contributed to the negative achievement singled out in the Main Report were: choice of the beneficiary based on political grounds rather than on potential for future development; training of trainees (ToT) based on theoretical assumptions rather than actual demand of participants; selection of teachers based on non-objective criteria, lack of analysis of the potential market for the School; lack of flexibility in the Project Cycle Management to adapt it to the changing conditions, and insufficient involvement of beneficiary institution in the PCM.

Efficiency

This criterion was not included in the initial remit of this evaluation programme, thus there was not a systematic review of budgets and accounting procedures. Nonetheless, a good deal of data have been gathered during the desk review and the research 'missions'. On this basis, the overall conclusion was that in seven of the projects efficiency was satisfactory or good, and these were projects which scored well also on the other criteria. In this case there was evidence of appropriateness and good quality of purchased equipment,[11] provision of suitable premises and capable local management. In one case, very good results have been achieved with administrative costs unusually low, that is, the 'Productivity Initiative Programmes' (PIP). On the efficiency issue, the Main Report contains two caveats. First, it is difficult to expect a high level of efficiency in this first generation of projects and, second, in periods of rapid and turbulent changes, the task to be undertaken at the time when ToR were drafted may have become obsolete by the time the projects begins. That is why the analysis of efficiency has been restricted to the identification of the extreme cases.

Sustainability

Among the projects with the aim of institution strengthening, five scored 'good' or 'very good'. Again IMISP, IBS and IMI were judged as those with the best chances of self-sustainability, in that the programmes they offered were attractive to customers, their faculties continued to upgrade the teaching material, and the existing contacts with the West were also improved. In the category of 'MT delivery' the best project was the 'Productivity initiative' which provided training and internships abroad to many managers of various countries of the former Soviet Union. An indirect indicator of sustainability here was the formation of a network of programme alumni and the continuing relation with many companies which provided internships. Where MT was a component of a branch project, a good measure of self-sustainability was the willingness of clients to pay for the training as it happened, for instance, with the 'Regional Bank Training in Central Asia' (RBT-CA).

In the other six cases in which sustainability was low, the reason may have been that the strategic development of the beneficiary organization met the opposition of the parent institution as already mentioned in relation to the effectiveness criterion. In other cases, the project focused more on the individuals (many of whom left later on) than on the institution. When MT was delivered directly to managers, a basic issue emerged concerning the knowledge transfer to the enterprise: 'One, sometimes two or three employees from a company cannot be considered as a critical mass able to give impulse to lasting changes' (Final Report, 1998, p. 26).

Impact

The three projects which scored best in relation to the previous criteria had, of course, the highest impact on their environment and the MT market. These institutes have been able to define a development strategy and their teachers have been able to upgrade their skills and improve their careers. The 'MT delivery' type of projects were considered successful in terms of impact when the programme was able to affect the outlook of managers, that is, when a precondition was created for actual changes in their parent enterprises. Here the best indicator has been considered the capacity to involve the CEOs of the firms from whom the initiation of organizational change may more likely be expected. Indeed this was what happened in the PIP project and in the 'Human Resource Development, Samara Oblast.' As for the third type of projects, four out of five scored well or very well. The RBT-CA acquired a leading position in the MT market for the banking sector. The same happened to the curriculum produced under the 'Development of Volosovo Sovkhoz Technikum of Besseda,' which was then introduced by the State authorities into similar educational institutions. The impact was quite low, however, for the project for the support to the privatization process: in this case the final recommendations had no or little impact on the way the state property has been dealt with.

Relevance

This criterion may serve as a foreword of sort for the final discussion. All respondents were in no doubt that management training can have a high relevance to their enterprises and the whole economy, but the way they conceived of the matter varied widely. On the other hand, this kind of training is not a homogeneous commodity, thus a programme may be relevant in a set of circumstances but not in others. What can make the difference in this respect are factors such as: real knowledge of the market on the part of enterprise managers, the pace of economic reforms in a given country, the extent to which the legal and institutional framework has been designed, the degree of power of industrial elites and local governments in the present circumstance. Sometimes the running of projects has shown a tendency to overlook these environmental factors, and certain mismatches between intentions and achievements became evident. Thus, for instance,

> the idea of launching a program for young entrepreneurs in Kazakhstan was probably inspired by the success of small business in Western countries as employment creators and sources of dynamism. Transported to a profoundly different cultural context, and without careful prior groundwork, the training fell flat. (Final Report, 1998, p. 29)

Or, as it happened with KAMAZ, respondents suggested that the relevance of the training activities would have been much greater if the contractor had been given the opportunity to seek out openings where Western systems might be accepted and might demonstrate their usefulness. In other words, instead of delivering pre-determined training packages, the contractor could have been given the task of first identifying critical problems to be dealt with. In this case, the individual report concludes that

> little or no account had been taken of the residual habits of Soviet mentality and culture ... For example, the contractor had been asked to provide instructions on 'organisational restructuring' as that is understood in a large Western firm. The training was not directed at identifying and dealing with the many intervening factors which for a firm in the NIS impose constraints at each stage in a restructuring plan. (Grancelli, 1997, p. 10)

Lessons learned

Among the respondents there was a general agreement on the needs for training. First, the projects should continue to be targeted to two basic groups: middle managers and young graduates or specialists at the beginning of their career. Second, training should be sustained beyond the period of Western support both in sector-specific institutes and in business schools. Third, the endorsement of top management would be critical to the success of the knowledge transfer to enterprises.

Beyond these points of agreement, local circumstances dictated different replies. Where the local economy was relatively well developed and differentiated (such as in the Moscow and St Petersburg areas) the demand is for all kind of programmes, from vocational training to MBA courses. On the contrary, where the local economy is not differentiated (and usually declining, such as in areas where the military industry prevails) the basic need was seen to be for short, practical programmes for middle managers and for the creation or strengthening of local training institutes. Managers did not want lectures on Western methods and practices, be they in the areas of 'orthodox' or 'critical' management.

Deans and Directors of local institutes were preoccupied with the difficult issue of retaining their teaching staff formed through the Western training programmes. The reasons were simple: these people can usually find a better salary in business than in schools. Another important problem was seen in the administrative backup for establishing fruitful links with enterprises whose people are attending courses. Also felt was the issue of establishing procedures and structures for targeting of possible trainees, the revenue to be earned and the salaries to be paid. Finally, Deans and Directors put a high priority on establishing and maintaining contacts with business schools in the West beyond the period of technical assistance

Local trainers recognized that they needed to acquire new capacities in the teaching methodology such as, for instance, business games. They also felt the need for more exposure to the practical problems of the firms in the local environment, and acknowledged that their internship in Western firms and study tours helped them to appreciate what questions they should ask.

The conclusion one may draw from the interviews with the people involved in the projects is that the problem lies in the matching of a project with the local stage of development. Indeed, rapid changes took place in all the countries involved with TACIS projects, but the nature and pace of change varied widely from country to country and from region to region. Sometimes there was political change with little economic change, in others the opposite was the case. More often than not the changes within training institutions failed to keep up with changes in the economic environment. On the whole, there were two scenarios: (a) environments where there already was a commitment to reform, and (b) environments where there were some reform-minded individuals but where Soviet-style institutional arrangements still prevailed. In the 'chaos of transition' it was difficult to 'know' for certain at the start of and throughout a project just what type of training was suitable to which local context. In many cases, there has been an overestimation of the readiness of local markets for anything beyond the most basic training (Final Report, 1998, p. 46). Consequently, among the recommendations proposed in the Main Report, the following are worth recalling.

Regarding the *forms of training*, the first suggestion concerns the necessity for a finer discrimination to recognize the wide differences in the kind of training appropriate to different locations and circumstances. This means that clearly differentiated packages should be offered to different categories of potential recipients. In settings where old style administrators still prevail, the first task should be to identify people able to carry out reforms in the beneficiary institution be they schools, enterprises or governmental agencies. In other, more advanced settings, it is possible to build up some institutional flagships that acquired the capacity to set high standards and develop new forms of training for which enterprises would be prepared to pay realistic fees. Thus the choice to assist flagship institutions and initiate programmes that deal directly with managers should be further developed because this would give a competitive edge to institutions already operating in a real market. In the future more resources should be applied during a project's preparatory stages in order to provide for a fully informed choice of beneficiary and an adequate understanding of local environments (Final Report, 1998, p. 64).

The right choice of the beneficiary and its involvement in the various stages of the PCM is then very important for the success of future projects. In performing the selection, these factors should be given particular attention: the way the recipient organization is managed; the degree of its cultural openness and flexibility, the real capabilities of local programme managers; and the environment's receptivity to the proposed assistance. But this should go along with a more proactive role of the donors in negotiating conditionalities and major changes if they appear necessary during the implementation stages. There should be a kind of 'forum' where the contractor, the monitor, the beneficiary and the donor(s) can align the project more closely with developmental objectives and demonstrate sensitivity to the changes in the local environment. Future projects should be characterized both by a 'flexibility of blueprint' allowing for changes in design prior to implementation, and 'flexibility of process', that is, the capacity to adapt to the evolving needs of its beneficiaries (Final Report, 1998, p. 67).

Notes

* The evidence provided in this chapter is drawn from the Final Report prepared by the evaluation group for the European Training Foundation in Torino. However, the ideas expressed are those of the author, and do not involve the responsibility neither of TACIS and the ETF, nor of the other members of the group. The Final Report may be consulted on the Internet site: http://europa.eu.int/comm/scr/evaluation/reports/tacis/951467.pdf

1. That is a social reality in which elements of modernity coexisted with vestiges of the pre-modern social order and with ornaments created for the imitation of democracy (Sztompka, 1996).
2. The reference here is to the way this concept is used by A. Kozminski (1993, 1995), who takes into account both the 'hard' and the 'soft' (cultural) aspects of management.
3. This statement is contained in the Terms of Reference of the KIMEP Project in Alma Aty, Kazakhstan.
4. Of these projects, 15 were in Russia, 3 in Ukraine, 3 in Kazakhstan and the remaining in other NIS and Mongolia. Five projects covered more than one state.
5. There are of course other donor agencies in the NIS whose programmes complement those of TACIS at many points. The first is the World Bank which is operating in the field through the three centres of the National Training Foundation in Moscow, Nizhny Novgorod and St Petersburg with the cooperation of the Russian government and various private institutions. The second is the EBRD whose training activities are financed by the Technical Cooperation funds established by a certain number of national donors. Much of the EBRD support has been channelled to many training centres in the countries, 35 of which operate in collaboration with the Russian Morozov projects. All these projects have been carried out in partnership with TACIS, USAID and various other donors. Besides, EBRD has been among the founders of the Joint Vienna Institute, which conducts teaching activities in the management of financial institutions.
   Another important donor is the German Agency for Technical Cooperation, which operates in many countries, and whose expertise is aimed at improving organizational structures, management systems and inter-institutional coordination. The UK Know How Fund has chosen instead to concentrate the bulk of its activities in five Russian regions, and here too management training is a component of sectorial programmes such as industrial restructuring, food marketing and financial services.
   Finally, among the major provider of Western technical assistance one has to mention USAID (United States Agency for International Development) whose programmes are focused on three strategic areas:

economic transformation, democratic transition and social stabilization. As for management training, the main activities concern the organization of short-term courses in the USA for senior and mid-level Russian professionals. Also various US private groups and institutions are active in the field, with the Harvard Business School playing a prominent role.

6. The evaluation activities were focused more on effectiveness than efficiency in that the latter was verified in global terms, that is, referring to the whole sample and taking into account the degree of correspondence between the results indicated in the project mandate and those achieved in the end.
7. The team leader was a senior management training specialist, the other core team members were: one evaluation specialist, one management training specialist, one expert in technical assistance in the NIS, and one sociologist with research experience in Soviet and post-Soviet management. Each core team members carried out fieldwork activities and drafted two to four evaluation reports. They were: David Chambers (team leader), Annie Cordet, Liudmila Derevjagina, Bruno Grancelli and Massimo Tommasoli.

   The need to gather data in the field for a wide range of projects required the integration of the core group with other evaluation and management training specialists, one of them charged specifically with the surveys of other donors' activities. The other experts were: Ken Charman, Bruno Dufour, Carsten H. Laugesen, Anna Lysenko, Jan Michel Netter and Gustavo Rinaldi.

   The ETF and TACIS team composed Livio Pescia (Deputy Director), Siria Taurelli (Task Manager), Elena Carrero Perez, Paola Gosparini, Margit Ostman and Angela Trisoglio. The administrative support was provided by Stefano Tirone and Simonetta Cozzi, Scuola di Amministrazione Aziendale, Universita di Torino.
8. These questionnaires were not designed for a quantitative analysis of data; rather, they aimed at gaining qualitative insights on the project according to the established evaluation criteria.
9. A notable exception was a sector-specific project that involved the big car factory KAMAZ (Kamski Avtomobilny Zavod) in Tatarstan, and lasted 51 months. This project was monitored by the present writer along with the High Commercial Management School in Moscow and two other projects in Kazakhstan (KIMEP and a programme for the training of young entrepreneurs).
10. This was the 'Establishment of a training programme for young entrepreneurs' in Alma-Aty which was evaluated by C. H. Laugesen and the present writer.
11. The most common source of complaints concerned the purchased equipment: often the beneficiary stated that they could have obtained better items for the money; sometimes the equipment did not corresponded to what the beneficiaries wanted or the chosen suppliers did not provide servicing or spare parts.

11

Cross-Cultural Comparison between Hungarians and Expatriates

Henriett Primecz

Introduction

The past decade has brought with it fundamental economic and political changes in Central and Eastern Europe. These countries opened up their doors to foreign investments. My study is about a green field investment. Generally speaking, we know how difficult the collaboration between newcomer Western owners and local employees is, because of the two totally different mind setups: market vs. planned economy.

My story is however different. It starts immediately after 1990, when Hungary encouraged foreign investors to bring capital into the country. This, in theory, should have been easier than a process of privatization with foreign capital, as the new investor did not have to fight the ineffective production of existing companies as well as and the *we-know-it-better-we-lived-here-in-the-last-forty-years* attitude of the local staff. The green field investment recruited young professionals, mainly freshly graduated, enthusiastic young people, who spoke good English. In the beginning, the company paid better salaries than any other companies in the area, so it could afford to employ only the best people; thus, not only office employees, but also production workers[1] were well educated.

The company offered better working conditions than others; and the possibility to travel abroad, to embark on training and, in general, a great deal of educational support. One could start as a production worker (semi-skilled), and end as a production engineer or an HR specialist with an MBA degree in this plant. Above all, Hungarians felt that something new started and something better was going on in Hungary, as they participated in building up a company, which was different from the others that they worked for before, or than those companies their parents worked for.

This overwhelmingly positive picture may be 'true', but there are many layers of the same phenomenon. I try to analyse some layers of this complex organization from a cultural view. I am especially interested in cross-cultural issues, where we define Hungarians as one culture, and the expatriates as the other culture. In so doing, I make use of the framework provided by Joanne Martin (1992) regarding three perspectives on organizational culture. I believe we can learn much more about expatriate and local cultures, when we use all three perspectives in a synergetic fashion.

Perspectives on culture

Before describing Martin's three perspectives let me define what I mean by culture, and what cross-cultural means. I embrace the interpretative approach, which understands culture as a system of shared meanings and symbols (Allaire and Firsirotu, 1984, p. 221). It is important to emphasize that 'shared' has two contrary meanings. The meaning most of us immediately think of has to do with common experience; when we share we are directly involved with others in a way that emphasizes our *similarity*. However, sharing also means the opposite: we divide something into individual pieces (shares) and distribute them among themselves. This second meaning emphasizes our *separateness* (Hatch, 1997, pp. 204–5).

'Cross-cultural' is a term that has sprung from comparative studies, namely cross-cultural research, which analyses practices of one culture in order to compare them with another culture (Barinaga, 1998, p. 15). In my research cultural differences are presented through one culture's eyes. Expatriates have been placed into Hungarian culture (context), and their experiences and opinions highlight cultural differences between them and the locals.

Martin (1992) introduced three perspectives on culture: the integration, the differentiation and the fragmentation perspective. These perspectives help us to understand the complexity of culture. Although, she writes mainly about organizational culture, her three perspectives are useful lenses for any kind of culture.

From an integration perspective organizations are described as a cultural unity that has no place for doubt, uncertainty, or collective dissent. According to Martin (1992, p. 45) the main three characteristics are:

> First, a set of content themes (usually values or basic assumptions) are described as being shared by all members of a culture, in an organization-wide consensus. Second, these content themes are said to be enacted, consistently, in a wide variety of cultural manifestations. Third, cultural members are described as knowing what they are to do and why it is worthwhile to do it. In this realm of clarity, there is no place for ambiguity.

Integration stresses harmony and homogeneity within organizations. In contrast, Parker (1995; p. 544) emphasizes that 'culture, like organization, is a process that is never stable and never homogenous.' He argues that 'culture was all too often viewed as a normative consensus that performed functions for the organizational system' (1995, p. 518). Munro (1995; p. 437) emphasizes the dangers of viewing organizational culture as an integrated mechanism as this would put a gloss over heterogeneity. Willmott (1993) also criticizes the integrative view on culture, as being built upon the mistaken assumption of a spontaneous consensus between individual needs and corporate objectives.

The second perspective, *differentiation,* presupposes that cultural manifestations are at times inconsistent. Consensus occurs only within boundaries of subcultures which often conflict with one another. Ambiguity is channelled:

> Differentiation views of organizational culture have three defining characteristics. First, interpretations of content themes, practices and forms are often inconsistent. Second, the differentiation perspective is suspicious of claims of organizational-wide consensus. To the extent that consensus exist, it is seen as located primarily within subcultural boundaries. Third, within subcultural boundaries, clarity reigns, while ambiguity [is] relegated to the periphery. (Martin, 1992, p. 83)

The third perspective emphasizes ambiguities:

> Contemporary life inside and outside is permeated with ambiguities. In part, these ambiguities stem from societal problems that we do not fully understand and we cannot seem to solve ... Juxtapositions of symbols, people, issues, policies and actions are poorly understood, perhaps random. As possible interpretations multiply, and discontinuities of change become transformed into ceaseless flux, ambiguities seem inescapable and pervasive. (Martin, 1992, p. 131)

More and more scholars, and practising managers accept the fact that contemporary life is ambiguous and fragmented. If something is ambiguous, it means it is unclear, highly complex and/or paradoxical. Information flows can solve the problem of lack of clarity or help to understand complex things, but paradoxes rarely can be solved only by information. 'Ambiguity is perceived when lack of clarity, high complexity or paradox makes multiple (rather than single or dichotomous) explanation plausible' (Martin, 1992, p. 134). When a member of the organization encounters situations that are ambiguous or undefined, it is necessary for him/her to make sense of the situation (Brown, 1986; p. 73).

Ambiguity may be conceived as environmentally determined, as something 'out there' to be managed (Munro, 1995; p. 441). In general ambiguity has a negative connotation, something to be improved, developed, clarified. Munro argues that ambiguity can also be a productive resource which can form a counterpart to dominant agendas (1995, p. 456). From a *fragmentation perspective,* culture is

> A web of individuals, sporadically and loosely connected by their changing positions on a variety of issues. Their involvement, their subcultural identities and their individual self-definitions fluctuate, depending on which issues are activated at a given moment (Martin, 1992, p. 153).

A summary of the three perspectives is provided in the Table 11.1.

These three perspectives can also be applied to national culture. Those culture researchers who emphasize the commonalities of certain cultures, strive to the integration perspective. Those researchers who emphasize social strata, or ethnicity for example within a culture, adhere to a differentiation perspective. While those researchers who emphasize ambiguity within a culture, share the fragmentation perspective. These three perspectives are useful lenses as they throw different light on the same concept. I believe that it is a mistake to see culture only from the dominant, integration perspective, which denies features of differentiation and fragmentation.

Another useful framework that can be used to understand culture is provided by Hatch (1997). She talks about the modernist, symbolic-interpretative and postmodernist approach to cultures. Both modernist and symbolic interpretativists believe that assumptions and values influence behaviour through their expression in norms and expectations and communicate identity through symbols, tradition and customs. Modernists, above all, interpret knowledge about culture as a

Table 11.1 Three perspectives on culture

Perspective	**Integration**	**Differentiation**	**Fragmentation**
Orientation to consensus	Organization-wide consensus	Subcultural consensus	Multiplicity of views (no consensus)
Relation among manifestations	Consistency	Inconsistency	Complexity (not clearly) consistent or inconsistent
Orientation to ambiguity	Exclude it	Channel it outside subcultures	Focus on it
Metaphors	Clearing in jungle, monolith, hologram	Islands of clarity in sea of ambiguity	Web, jungle

Source: Martin, 1992, p. 13

tool of management, and culture itself as a variable to be manipulated to enhance the likelihood of achieving desired levels of performance from others within the organization (Hatch, 1997; p. 231). Chia (1995; p. 589) explains that only a postmodern 'weak' style of thinking can deal accurately with the subtle and complex nature of organizing processes (such as culture) as postmodernism problematizes issues of authorship and the authenticity of representations.

On the contrary, modernists believe in scientific detachment from the object of study while symbolic-interpretativists claim that cultural meaning can be only understood from within the cultural system in question. Modernists argue for objective understanding, while symbolic-interpretativists believe that scientific objectivity claimed by modernists is an illusion, and there can be no such thing as an outsider's objective perspective. Modernist studies generally involve looking at statistical relationships between variables representing culture and performance.

Managing culture is another disputed domain. While modernists and symbolic interpretativists believe that top managers can change culture by influencing recruiting and hiring practices in organizations or through the management of meaning, postmodernists warn about the ethics of controlling culture. Changing cultures presupposes the manipulation of people's minds and souls, and this may hurt their individual freedom and democratic processes. The outcomes of changes are unpredictable and sometimes undesirable (thus, increasing employee cynicism towards the cultural change programme). Finally, Hatch advises the manager not to attempt to manage culture as other people's meanings and interpretations are highly unmanageable (1997, p. 235). The success of culture change projects is at best partial, because employees can become trapped in a vicious circle of cynicism and dependence (Willmott, 1993, p. 518).

The case study

The company under study (which for confidentiality reasons shall remain anonymous) is an American multinational production and sales company. It was a green field investment in Hungary, which started its operation in 1992. The limited liability company was launched in two locations in Hungary in 1990; one produces components in a town one hour drive from the capital city, Budapest, and the other deals with sales and credits in the capital, Budapest. My study concentrates only on the production plant.

The plant employs approximately 150 office workers and 1000 production workers. At the time of my investigation nine expatriates worked for this plant, one of them is Gibraltarian British, and the others are Americans. Six of them work in managerial position: plant manager, finance manager, human resources manager, purchasing manager, and two product managers. One works for the HR department, as compensation specialist,[2] and there are two design engineers. Six of them were available for interviews. (The plant manager, the purchasing manager, and one of the design engineers did not answer my questions.)

I know most of them personally, since I used to work for this company myself. This means that it is more difficult to keep an objective distance from the data. But at the same time I have more background information about them: I saw them during work, I know what their subordinates and co-workers think about their work, leadership style, and their personality. And also many company-specific procedures and abbreviations make more sense for me, than it would for an absolute outsider.

The aim of my interviews was to find out how expatriates see their life and work in Hungary. I was interested in their perceptions about differences and difficulties they face while working and living in Hungary. I used semi-structured interviews, which means that I had a loose set of questions, and I asked some additional questions when something was not clear, or further information was needed. Interviews lasted between 40 and 60 minutes.

After analysing the interviews it became clear that expatriates find the *language barrier* the biggest problem of their stay here. Why is this problem? Hungarians do not speak English, and expatriates do not speak Hungarian. Of course, Hungarians who work in the office speak English, since it is a requirement for the job: the working language is English. But many of the shop floor workers do not speak English (their instructions and procedures are written in Hungarian), and common people in the street do not speak English either, for example, shop assistants, clerks, postal officials and so on. There are not many countries of the world where common people speak foreign languages, and Hungary is definitely not among those. Expatriates felt that the working environment is more or less the same as at home, but they have difficulties in every day life, mostly because of the language barrier.

As one interviewee said: 'there are no written signs in English' in Hungary. When they go shopping there are no written labels in

English, they have to 'visually understand' what they buy. In many restaurants you do not find English menus.

There are fewer problems at work, but still the language barrier is present. Interviewees mentioned a so-called *intellectual filter*, because of the language. One respondent said 'I am not aware of many things, because of the language.' Another one said 'I cannot speak with people on the shop floor, I just make decisions. People do not like the person who makes decisions.' One of the product managers mentioned 'I am not able to communicate with shop floor workers. I have to depend on my engineers, and I have the feeling that this information is filtered.'

When asked about returning home one of the interviewees said that 'Here if I do not want to understand, I do not understand, for example a woman yelling in the street. I have a protecting bubble around me. When I return home I will understand everything, there will be a lot of noise around me, my mental peace will go away.'

If the language barrier is one of the main sources of their problem, why did they not start to learn Hungarian? They did indeed. All of them started to study Hungarian, and most of them spoke some. They mentioned that learning Hungarian is difficult. One said 'I expected learning Hungarian to be easier.' The other put it differently 'I did not study hard enough.' One of the respondents clarified 'We are not pushed to learn Hungarian. Management meetings are in English.' Indeed, any time when an English-speaker is present the conversation switches to English.

They also mentioned that their life in Hungary feels very transient: they are here for a few years and then they get posted to some other place. This may explain why some of them feel that investing time and effort to learn Hungarian is not a very attractive option. One of them said 'Everything is so temporary here. I spend a year here, and then I go home.' (Design engineer). Managers spend usually three years in a foreign assignment, which may be enough to feel comfortable in a country but not enough to call it home.

Interestingly, one manager did not mention any problems connected with language and communication; he did not find this a problem, because everybody at work speaks English and outside work, his wife, who learned Hungarian with pleasure, is in charge of their schedules. (Another manager also mentioned that his wife learnt Hungarian, and they enjoy going to restaurants where there is no English menu, so she can practise her Hungarian.) The manager, who does not perceive language as a barrier, is from Gibraltar, and he (and his wife) are bilingual, they speak English and Spanish natively. He seems to be more involved with the Hungarians than the other expatriates, he goes out for lunch with his Hungarian subordinates, arranges parties for his engineers and so on. In contrast, another manager mentioned that 'We go out to the cafeteria separately (Hungarians and English-speakers), because I do not want to force my people to speak English during lunch.'

It seems that the language itself is not a barrier, only people's perceptions and alignments with respect to their language status may be. The Gibraltarian manager said 'I did not think that I would like Hungary so much. But I found friendship here, I feel comfortable with people, I have many common things with Hungarians.' He does not feel frustrated when he cannot communicate with people in the street, and he asks his engineers to help when he is confronted with language barriers at work.

In attempting to find out what is the difference between the Gibraltarian product manager and the other respondents, it became clear that it was a matter of trust. The former said he trusted Hungarians and added: 'I feel more liberated here.[3] I can be rude to my engineers. I would be in trouble in the UK, but here people understand what I mean to be a joke. I have good relationship with my engineers'. In contrast he mentioned that 'you do not know how much you can trust the Americans.'

He added that he was surprised to see that: 'Hungarian people obey Americans.' It is contrary to what Americans perceive. As one American respondent explained 'We are part of a special group, there is no status for expatriates. We do not matter. We are coming and going. We are not part of the social structure. It is hard to say where we fit. Hungarians are not happy with us.' Why might she perceive this?

She describes her arrival in the following terms: 'I came from a good supportive working environment and excellent relationships, and in Hungary peers hated me, my boss was lazy,[4] we did not have shared history'. So she perceived the Hungarian plant as a *hostile environment*. It is difficult to establish trust after this kind of first impression.

While professional competence was not a question in technical fields, foreign HR specialists are not satisfied with Hungarians' HR background in this plant. They believe that Hungarians are not well educated in HR issues: this may indeed be the case since not all of those working in this plant studied Human Resources Management in their college or university.[5] To add one American HR specialist's opinion about Hungarian HR people: 'Here more follow-up is needed, people are less of a self-starter, and they are less experienced in HRM.[6]

Hungarians think that they know the local environment better than the Americans, and their knowledge of Hungarian circumstances and people is equally valuable as is the general knowledge in Human Resource Management. This mutual disregard on each other's knowledge does not help to build constructive co-work.

The further difficulty resides in the different conceptions about time. As one American manager puts it: 'There is not the same appreciation for deadlines, there is *lack of sense of urgency* in Hungary'. She thinks that everything takes much longer here, because her subordinates are too laid back and in general they do not care about deadlines too much. Above all, people go home earlier than in the US. One design engineer also mentioned the difference in timing between Hungarians and Americans. As she explains 'Timing is different: Americans work longer working hours, here people go home earlier.' But she adds: 'work still gets done. I do not understand how, but everything gets done.' These two approaches to time are known from the literature as *sequential and synchronic time-conceptions*. Sequential people do things right after each other in a sequence, deadlines and appointments are highly appreciated, time is seen as money, which can be spent, shared and saved. While synchronic people are not so much concerned with time, they can do different tasks in the same time, and regard deadlines and appointments just as approximate.

The other typical difference between Americans and Hungarians can be mapped out around the *diffuse vs. specific approach*. Americans are very specific, and separate work and private life clearly. Hungarians are more diffuse, for them many things are interconnected. One manager says: 'American people go home without knowing each other. I cannot do it here. There is a kind of community spirit. I have to take time to deal with my people's personal issues. I had to adapt.' The Gibraltarian manager also mentioned 'You know, Americans do not talk about work in their free time. When we go out to a barbecue I am the only one who wants to talk about work. When I go out with my engineers to a pub, for example, I talk to them about work if that comes up'.

The other issue at stake here is *interdependence* between expatriates. The manager also says that 'We[7] have got close to each other: Managers' wives do things together. You are more dependent on others who are similar to you.' Anther manager also states 'You are more dependent on your family. A couple that goes on an international assignment either divorces or gets closer to each other.' Other respondent also said about family: 'We stick more together.' One even mentioned a *gap* between them and the locals. Some mentioned loneliness in Hungary ('You realize you are alone.'), and independence, for example, 'I am on my own.' She also added 'I am more responsible here than at home, I have to do paper work, for example, tax papers, visas and so on, all on my own.'

For many expatriates 'Hungary is not a *land of convenience*.' This signals the lack of service in Hungary. Most of them complained that stores close early, clerks and post officers[8] are not helpful, Hungarians are less customer-focused. There are no English menus, and many service providers try to cheat them when they realize that they are foreigners.

But is Hungary such as bad place for foreigners? Do foreigners just suffer here? Definitely not. Expatriates mentioned many things they appreciated in Hungary. For example, 'I enjoy the richness of culture, I want to see more places, meet other people. To be an expatriate you have to open yourself up.' One American mentioned the cultural side of Europe, such as operas, and 'few hours driving and you can meet other cultures: It is not far to drive to Austria, Italy or Prague, which are wonderful places to see.' One respondent mentioned 'I am happy that my kids saw Michelangelo's David in Florence, where we drove last weekend.' Some mentioned good weather, picturesque landscape, nice wine, good cuisine (though some mentioned that they dislike Hungarian food). They also mentioned that Hungarians are more easy-going and party liking than Americans or British. The Gibraltarian manager said that he really enjoys camp meetings,[9] because 'they last until morning, whereas people would go home at 10 in the UK.'

Another manager mentioned the cosmopolitan atmosphere in Budapest, when I asked about the positive side of his staying. He mentioned that he is from a small town in the USA, where he would never have experienced this mixture of cultures. In Budapest he has neighbours from Taiwan, Ireland and Korea, with whom they have dinner together. Another manager also mentioned that among his friends there are a Belgian and Spanish couple. The finance manager told me that he found excellent an event when he was involved in governmental issues as a representative of a big American corporation. He met ministers and they discussed the future of American multinationals in Hungary. He said 'I would have not experienced it in the US.'

About minor problems all of them mentioned driving. First of all, you cannot drive everywhere in Hungary; downtowns are closed for cars, and people have to walk. And in historical parts of the cities streets are narrow, and it is difficult to find parking places. Above all Hungarians seem to drive more aggressively than Americans and

British. One of them mentioned there is 'no respect for women drivers'. Another one said that he adapted to the local driving style, and he drives crazier here. He says that he can drive fast, because he can pay the fine easily, and there is no police record on him. As he puts it 'I would have lost my license in England.'

Further examples of minor problems include dogs barking, pollution and the number of smokers. Interestingly many of them are annoyed by dogs barking during the nights, as one said 'It seems that every Hungarian has a dog, and they are all barking during the night.' Pollution and dust is especially present in bigger cities, mainly because of old cars, and, of course, because of old power plants. It is almost impossible to find restaurants and pubs which are not totally smoky, which is annoying for the self-conscious, healthy non-smoker.

When I asked about the difference between being a tourist somewhere and living and working somewhere, one of them used an excellent metaphor. 'When you are a tourist somewhere you see only the party dress, when you live somewhere you see the morning dress and bad breath.' The respondent also said he would recommend his friends, who are independent and emotionally intelligent to come to Hungary for international assignments, because it was an interesting experience.

What similarities can we find among expatriates, which we defined as one culture and contrasted against the Hungarian culture? Surprisingly, it seems to be easier to find differences. What is common between a male manager coming from a small town in the USA, now lives in Budapest, surrounded by neighbours from all over the world, and has an all-important job that allows him to negotiates with ministers, and a female subordinate with an MBA, preparing her PhD, moving from New York to a countryside town in an Eastern-European country, where nobody except her colleagues speaks English? These seem to share few similarities: this is why Martin's fragmentation metaphor is especially useful here.

Does it make sense to still talk about 'we' and 'us' when we refer to the locals and the expatriates? To start with there are some common features within the two cultures. There are two language groups, English-speakers and those who have just learned English. Also one group has their relatives and all connections thousands of miles away, the other one is surrounded by such ties at an immediate distance. But the two cultures could have been defined in different ways: men vs. women, office employees vs. production workers, full-time employees vs. contractors, party-people vs. those who dislike parties and so on. To understand these divisions, one could employ Martin's differentiation perspective. Above all, my questions about expatriates and Hungarians, forced me to define two separate cultures; in so doing, I formulated differences which might not really exist, and this way the interviewees reinforced such perceptions of differences and strengthened existing stereotypes.

The integration perspective brings a sense of unity to people working in this plant, and reinforces a sense of community among people working together. The only problem with the integration perspective is that it hides the complexity of the organization and assumes that everybody pulls in the same direction.

Final reflection

The purpose of the study was to examine a green field investment in Hungary, which could show a different picture from a privatized firm. This example is especially timely, because in the future, supposedly, more and more multinational companies will open new sites in Hungary.

Many people expected Western investors to come to Eastern European countries, bringing capital and know-how in order to establish effective production and service firms. At that time nobody thought about possible conflicts and cultural differences. My study is about such differences and potential conflicts.

What we have learned is that there may be some differences, though not very fundamental ones between expatriates and Hungarians. These differences seem to cause problems mainly in the everyday life, but not at work. However, these differences are perceived by individuals differently: some feel there is a large gap between 'us' and 'them', others less so. But we cannot talk about two distinct and opposed cultures, which are unable to cooperate or work together. Perhaps, this is why the two sides did not put too much effort into establishing an integrative common culture which would swipe away the difference. Difference is good: *vive la difference*!

Notes

1. Most of the production workers had a high school degree, while the work itself needed only semi-skilled workers.
2. She came with her husband, who was appointed as manager to this plant, and she did not want to stay at home as housewife, hence the creation of a compensation specialist post.
3. Compared to the UK.

4. The manager was a kind of *lassez faire* type of manager, he did not strongly supervise his subordinates, people were left to work freely.
5. Not all of them have degrees in business or related fields. Moreover, in the 1980s business courses contained only organization behaviour and general management courses, very rarely a personnel management course. HRM is a new concept, and its teaching started in the 1990s in Hungary. HR people in this plant learned the new concept on the job. The situation is changing nowadays, because younger, freshly graduated staff have HR specific degrees (some Hungarians working for the HR department have received their graduate degrees in HR recently).
6. This respondent is highly educated in HRM: she has an MBA with an HR emphasis, and she is doing her PhD in the field of HRM.
7. Expatriates.
8. One of them mentioned that 'there is much more stuff done in the post office', which seems to be very complicated for an outsider. One of them even mentioned 'I try to avoid post offices when it is possible.'
9. Camp meetings are problem-solving procedures in the company's life, when people of one area (managers, middle management, first-line management, and shop floor workers) go out for a day, and discuss all the problems of the area, and they try to solve them together. The purpose of the camp meetings are not only problem solving, but teambuilding as well. These meetings end in a restaurant or in a pub with partying.

12
When Reality Fails: Science Fiction and the Fall of Communism in Poland

Jerzy Kociatkiewicz and Monika Kostera

Introduction: when the walls fell

When martial law was enforced on 13 December 1981 in Poland, after the Solidarity rebellion that lasted for almost one-and-a-half years, it felt like all hope was being buried forever. The system, once again, proved that it was invincible. The massive popular movement, which had reached 10 million members at its peak, was shattered during the following years; the leaders were, once again, imprisoned, censorship tightened anew, and the people subjected to a new wave of unbearably self-righteous propaganda. Its main rhetorical style was named *pan-swinism* by Michal Glowinski (1992): 'we are all swine no one is honest, Party people are swine, but so are the heroes of the Solidarity rebellion. There is no hope.' Communism was here to stay and most people tended to believe that it was permanent; some voiced the belief that it might perhaps end in 100 years.

And then, in 1989, state TV started to show glimpses of a remarkable event: the so-called 'round-table talks'. Representatives of the opposition and Party officials met and discussed possible scenarios for the future. Suddenly, people all over Poland could see famous dissidents: Adam Michnik, Jacek Kuron and other, up to now, totally 'forbidden' faces. On 4 June 1989, the first free elections since World War II were held. The Solidarity candidates celebrated a remarkable victory, gaining more mandates than the limited quotas of the elections deal assigned them. Soon thereafter, a Polish actress and member of the opposition, Joanna Szczepkowska, declared on the state TV: 'On the 4th of June 1989, communism ended in Poland.' A lot of other extraordinary events followed: the Berlin Wall fell, more and more countries of the former communist block declared the return of democracy. We were facing the impossible – the immortal institutions imprisoning individual initiative and belief died before our eyes. Together with the rest of reality, the world of enterprises changed as well – lots of new private companies, small and large, appeared, the big state-owned enterprises were privatized, divided or significantly changed their role; the planned economy was replaced by the free market; many people's jobs were diametrically transformed, administrative cadre (*kadra kierownicza*) became managers (*menedzerowie*). Changes in this field were also unimaginable and they form the main topic of this study. But before we come back to that momentous occasion, let us consider the images of the reality before and after its metamorphosis.

The reality: press accounts

In order to recreate the mood of the communist times, we would like to turn to the press of the period. Obviously, it was not the voice of all (or even the majority) of the social actors, but that of the so-called Power, that is, the largely anonymous voice of the ruling forces. The reality presented through the various censored media was quite different from that encountered by the social actors in their everyday life, contributing to the raging hypocrisy of the social life in these times. Although we are particularly interested in the world of organization and management, it does not and did not exist in isolation from other aspects of lived reality. A review of the images of the organization of social life conjured up by the press and other popular texts will help us to show what kind of incantations by the actors with the initiative and the right to define reality were the common background noise of the life of several generations of people living in Poland before the fall of communism. To these incantations some responded with anger, protest, some with faked faith, few with genuine belief, some with consent, many with indifference. A popular joke circulating among Polish society in the 1960s ties reflected the general atmosphere of deception: 'Are there more bright or good people in the Party? – There are more good people – that's easier to fake.'

The society was depicted as being based on the highest of humanist ideals, however, in their 'new improved' version:

> at the foundations of socialism and the struggle for socialism there lies the concern for man, a great trust in man, based, however, on a realist approach to him, depending on his real transformations – and not on a mythical-falsified one. And so that man of the new

> type will have the full possibility of development, he has to make himself free from the ropes of false individual liberty, [traditional Polish] sovereignty and seeking in another man and nation the elements motivating his distrust (Borejsza, 1949, as quoted in Roman, 1990; 44).[1]

Culture was finally liberated from the 'decadent aesthetics of capitalist societies':

> Socialist culture, being objectively the necessary and in our times highest phase in the development of world culture, erasing the contradictions characteristic of the spiritual creation in the class society, eradicates the one sidedness and constrictions imposed on culture by the relationships of private ownership, creates the conditions favouring the rapid progress of culture and versatile development of human personality (Baller, 1975, as quoted in Roman, 1990, p. 113).

The logic of the new economy was based on statements such as this one, intended to popularize communist economics among the common reader:

> The existence of too many retail shows increases the costs, because every new merchant decreases the turnover – of the already established; every one of them serves in effect a smaller number of clients, and has to increase the prices of the sold articles, because the general costs comprise a smaller quantity of turnover (*Kalendarz Warszawski*, 1947, as quoted in Roman, 1990, p. 13).

The new economic order would solve all such problems. Communism was heaven on Earth:

> The abundance of goods and the way of their distribution will create conditions, under which it will be possible to take on the managerial and subordinate functions successively by everyone – in theory, and in practice – by the majority of the employees of the enterprise (Sawicki, 1962, as quoted in Roman, 1990, p. 23).

The communist enterprise was officially introduced as the most democratic of social realities. Lenin thought that accounting and control were to be handled by the manager only in the first phase of communism. Later, the working class itself would take over these duties

(Kiezun, 1991). Early Russian management theorists such as Gastyev and Jermanski repeated many of the Taylorist principles (such as discipline, order, self-control, and functional control), but under new labels, as a 'truly scientific system of work organization' based on Marx's concept of disalienation of the working class under communism (Gastyev, 1924, as quoted in Kiezun, 1991; Jermanski, 1972). However, empirical research shows that the communist organization was rigid, hierarchic, highly bureaucratic and oppressive for the participants (Kostera and Wicha, 1996; Obloj, 1986).

The communist manager was to be of working class origin (Gomulka, 1945), a defender of the people. The new society was to be reminiscent of a united, uniform, unanimous organization, or 'a single office and a single factory with equality of work and equality of pay' (Lenin, 1981, p. 96) and with absolute equality in living and working conditions. In such a society the manager's role was to embody the ultimate interests of the working class, to be its 'avant-garde', knowing what is 'really' good for the masses.

> A good director is a real treasure for the Party organization. Such a director does not prompt the Party to intervene directly; he guarantees the proper execution of Party and government directives; he takes an active part in Party work and is able to make use of advice from below (of criticism of the working masses); and he can correct his mistakes of 'self criticism'. One can say without hesitation that a good enterprise director and good divisional director solve half the problems of the Party in the factory. (Szyr, 1951, as quoted in Najduchowska, 1976).

The Polish president of the 1950s, Boleslaw Bierut (1953, p. 1) declared that:

> The supervisor should consider the worker, his working conditions, his pay conditions, his security; the supervisor should be friendly to the worker, just as in our people's army the officer is friendly to the soldier.
>
> Secondly, the supervisor should be demanding, should strictly espouse all the regulations ...

Bierut briefly mentioned that the 'supervisor', a term that contextually turned out to refer to the manager, should be skilled (the context implied it was technical skill that Bierut meant), and continued (p. 1):

> The supervisor has to guard his/her authority, his/her dignity as a commander, because those who do not see that all their commands are strictly and well followed, are not worthy the name of commander.

Bierut reminded the managers, (p. 1) that

> Lenin and Stalin pointed out many times that the task of management is not only to foster, to organize the masses, but to learn from them, to take their voice into account.

Field research points out that managers under communism had more responsibility than freedom to act and make decisions, they felt restricted, limited and constantly harassed by the secret police and party aparatchiks (Czarniawska, 1986; Czarniawska-Joerges, 1988; Kostera and Wicha, 1996).

The dissidents, such as Adam Michnik and Jacek Kuron were not only harassed by the police, imprisoned, both they and their relatives had trouble at work, their children pestered at school (and thrown out for some more or less vague excuse), but also depicted as demoralized demons, hateful radicals, ungrateful paranoiacs. The accusations were absurd and sick. For example, Jacek Kuron, the current symbol of personal warmth is depicted as a person 'from whom a great cold emanates' (Roszewski, 1981, as quoted in Roman, 1990; p. 165). The dissidents were often listed in plural and without capitals: 'the kurons and michniks', in a rhetorical trick meant to further degrade, depersonalize and dishonour them.

The general atmosphere we remember of these times was that of futility. The 1980s especially felt like an endless display of hopelessness. 'Real socialism' indeed seemed like the only realistic option, with its newspeak, boring lies and sudden hideous displays of power to 'teach a lesson' to those who were still unable to grasp that there was nothing else to hope or wish for.

The new order

This situation changed drastically after communism fell, to be replaced with a totally different vision, of reality, of organizing, and of a manager. Monika Kostera (1996) has studied the identity transfer of enterprises and managers taking place in Poland in the early 1990s. She has analyzed three magazines read by business people, looking for images of management. She has found that Western enterprises and managers were depicted as heroes, one-sided images of perfection, that some Polish enterprises have come close to imitating. Enterprises other than western and Polish-'westernlike' were typically referred to as a negative 'background' to achieve an effect of contrast between what symbolizes the 'era that had passed' and what is 'modern'. Both western and Polish managers were presented primarily in the categories of 'success' – achieved only through hard work in the economic field, and not political games. The Polish version of the American dream is often in use. Again, the Western managers were idolized. The image of the manager was strongly gendered, and the stereotypization of genders was strong. The stories about Western firms and managers are as one-sided as the Polish contrasting examples: they are simple and with a plain moral. The Western examples are successful because they are what they are (Western and thus successful). Polish negative 'background' examples are, similarly, a failure because they are as they are. The Polish positive examples are different, because they are not the image of perfection, and very often they are problematized: they narrate stories of problems and how they were or are overcome. The images in the press are rather consistent, simple and not leaving much choice. The proposed identity is much more naive than the actual managerial responses to change, which are based on varying rationalities, often either continuing to work from the 'old' one they knew from communist times or composing a suitable mixture of 'old', political, and 'new', economical (Kostera, 1995a). Instead, the identity-image's one-sidedness reminds more of the symbols transferred by the communist Polish press: black-and-white, and always having a simple moral (see, for example Glowinski, 1992). Choosing the 'wrong' identity is unthinkable: there is no acceptable image for 'dissidents', at least not in the press. Even more one-sided and rigid is the image of the woman manager. She is not presented with an identity of her own, but with a re-mix of two others: that of the male manager and that of the traditional female social role. The rhetoric of the press reminded me of the communist style of propaganda. The black-and-white picture does not seem appealing: the one sided critique of the labels of background may evoke protest and rejection by managers who have lived long enough to be presented with various images of villains and 'enemies of the people' by the press. In 1994 and 1995 Monika Kostera asked MBA students and practising managers, students of evening courses in management to comment on the images of managers and of enterprises disseminated by the press in anonymous reviews. Typically, they reacted with open irony and distancing to the images of the organizations, with very subtle between-the-lines irony to the images of managers,[2] except to the role of the woman manager which was not commented at all. We believe this testifies to the blandness of the last image, considered unfit even for irony and caricature.

Elsewhere, Monika Kostera depicted the learning process as a crusade, the one-sided transfer of 'truths' from the West to the East (1995b). The Western consultants acts as missionaries of the old times, converting the Eastern 'heathens' to the new faith of market economy. To this the Polish managers typically respond with private irony and public passivity. They thus act as they have learned under communism: let 'them' do their talking, then try to do one's job (Kostera and Wicha, 1996).

Changing times

Regardless of some similarities in the language used, the two realities – before and after 1989 – are clearly incommensurable. What did, then, happen in 1989 to cause such a drastic change? Here is the first story of the shift.

In 1989 a new daily, *Gazeta Wyborcza* appeared, in which all the heretofore 'forbidden' voices spoke. Articles signed by Jacek Kuron, Adam Michnik, Zbigniew Bujak, Tadeusz Mazowiecki, and others, were published and the paper could be bought in ordinary newspaper stands. The issue of 4 June 1989, published a short statement signed by Lech Walesa, which included the following phrase: 'this is not yet freedom and democracy, but it is an important step towards a free, democratic, economically sane Poland' (Walesa, 1989, p. 1).

The date was a significant one: that of the first semi-free elections[3] since the World War II. The front page also contains instructions on how to cast a valid vote, and an article by Jozef Tischner, a Catholic oppositionist priest and philosopher, declaring that he intends to vote, praising democratic values, courage, and the public good. *Gazeta Wyborcza* of 5 June 1989, was beginning to reflect the realization of the triumph of the opposition:

> Solidarnosc, by organizing and carrying through a successful campaign, has proved that it is a great social power. This [is] the common work of those who had organized this campaign, those who had supported it in different ways, those who manifested an interest in it, and those, or perhaps, in the first place, those who voted for Solidarnosc. They will be rewarded through the results of the elections. (*Gazeta Wyborcza*, 1989b, p. 1)

Another article from the front page explains that the votes are still being counted, but the preliminary unofficial results 'put [us] in a very optimistic mood' (*Gazeta Wyborcza* 1989b: 1). On 6 June it was already more or less certain and almost official: Solidarnosc had won the elections, within the limits set in the preceding negotiations. Leading activists of the opposition speak of a victory – and of responsibility in *Gazeta Wyborcza* of that date. Adam Michnik, in an article about the elections entitled 'Joy ... and a moment of reflection' (Michnik, 1989, p. 1), says:

> Thank you, dear friends. Thanks to all who helped Solidarnosc with the campaign. It is thanks to you, tens of thousands of anonymous friends from every part of Poland that we won the campaign and the elections.

He recognizes the importance of the moment:

> the day of June 4th will be remembered as a **Polish day of celebration**. The Polish people voted for hope (p. 1; original emphasis).

But it is only a beginning. Further, he speaks of the important to build an institutional order under difficult circumstances 'the geopolitical position of Poland has not ... changed, and the ones managing the apparatus of coercion have not changed' (p. 1). 4 June is the day beginning the 'endeavour of all supporters of the idea of an evolutionary transformation from the Stalinist communist system to parliamentary democracy' (p. 1).

While none of these newspaper explicitly talk about changing reality, their very existence, as well as the up till then blacklisted names signing the articles, bear witness to a dramatic metamorphosis taking place at that time in Poland. Official availability of such newspapers was not only unthought of, but downright impossible even a few months earlier. Now, though, the impossible has happened, leaving people to make sense of and deal with the change.

Encounters with the impossible

The miracle of 1989 was a sudden change, in a way it was the end of the world as it was known. For many people it was the fall of the house in which they had lived for many years – a foul house, but a home nonetheless (to use Jacek Kuron's, 1990, metaphor). For a moment, reality was swaying at the edge of chaos. However, soon life got back to normal. When looking back on 1989 from the perspective of the present, time has passed and things happened, there is a story to tell in which the symbolic date can be put into a sensemaking context.

Here we present one narrative interpreting the time of the shift. We have pieced it together from short stories on the events of 1989, collected in 1998 from students on a management course. We will provide more details of this study further on, when we return to the other narratives appearing in the stories we have collected. Now let us turn to what we have called the *nothing much happened* story.

This narrative never registers any of the political events of the year 1989; either they are considered to have never taken place, or are perceived as having no significant impact on the life of the narrator. Instead, personal events are often invoked. Sometimes they denote important occurrences ('I decided to get married' – said one respondent. 'In 1989 I was finishing ground school and had to chose the type of my further education ... the year of one of the great shifts for me – I went to the gymnasium' – said another.) and sometimes only trivialities ('That wasn't a year very different from any other. The family finances allowed us to keep a fair level of life ... Generally quiet.') Some people state the insignificance of the year openly: 'To be honest, I do not associate anything special to me personally with this year'. One respondent excuses him- or herself, why s/he doesn't believe that the year 1989 was anything significant – s/he was only 19, and too young to be interested in politics. The explanation is referring to a logic internal in the text: we know many people who were and are actively interested in politics at the age of 19, and younger.

We would like to compare the *nothing much happened* story to two fictional narratives. The first takes place in a country torn by a sweeping slave revolt. A young male prostitute turned petty smuggler tells his life story, which unfolds against the background of intrigue, battles and espionage surrounding the uprising. The rebellion reshapes the lives of countless people and ends the lives of those who fall in its numerous battles. Still, it never comes to the foreground of the smuggler's story. It is not exactly invisible, either – the protagonist is certainly conscious of it, and is immensely intrigued by the figure of Gorgik, the slave leader. Yet at the same time the revolt never becomes the main focus of the story and the smuggler himself, despite his involvement, does not seem to ascribe any particular significance to it. Pryn, a young girl in the same country, seems even more detached from the historical changes around her even as they continue to reshape the life of the whole continent. She is not unaffected, but she does not regard the rebellion as an important event in the course of her life.

Another story tells of an alien spacecraft crashlanding in the middle of a small Russian town. The ship's pilot survives and is met by the town's inhabitants. Humans' first contact with an alien culture is peaceful and amiable, but the townsfolk quickly decide that the event is of little or no consequence to them, and happily continue with their daily routines. The otherworldy encounter is noticed and accepted, but it is doubtful that it would figure prominently in the life histories of any of the humans involved.

The story of the slave revolt comes from Samuel R. Delany's (1994) *Return to Neveryon* series, the crashing spacecraft is described in Kir Bulytchev's (1983) short story, *Steam engine for the Tsar.* Both belong to the genre of science fiction, and they both mirror one of the narrative types of the systemic shift in Poland in our story collection. The protagonists are immediate witnesses to great changes but in their own narratives these changes are placed in the background of the more mundane plots of their everyday life. It is not by accident that we are turning to science fiction for help in interpreting the sensemaking involved in retelling the story of the fall of Communism. The event is pretty much unprecedented in Western history – not only has the impossible arrived, quite suddenly, but it also was also a change for the better for most of the people involved.

For this reason, the rich literature on people coping with the experience of Holocaust is not very useful in contemplating the changes of 1989, even though it was an unimagineable event, and for its victims it often was very sudden. The differences prevail, however – the Holocaust was unspeakably atrocious and from a societal point of view an extended process. The systemic shift in Poland on the other hand was a sudden change for the better, a potential for liberation and it was associated with the symbolic date of the 4 June 1989. Other events, such as the French revolution are at least much more ambivalent in their valuation, whereas the fall of Communism is almost universally regarded as liberation and a triumphant exercise of the common will of the people of Eastern Europe.

Thus sociology does not provide good patterns for interpreting the experiences of encountering the unimaginable, and so we have turned to literature to furnish us with ideas of possible ways of coping with the arrival of the impossible. The issue is, after all, very similar to the problem of confronting the unspeakable, envisioned by Edward Balcerzan (1998, p. 21) as one of the central themes of literature:

> To maintain that unspeakability is a problem deserving manifestation means to be certain that literary texts are – texts. That is: they mean something in relation to the world, they have their own semantics, they not only inform of fictional reality – which fully realizes itself in word orderings – but also transmit an image of a reality external to the work of art (historical, social, empirical, transcendental, onirical, imaginative, psychological or parapsychological etc.) – experienced not in writing and not in reading.

As we sought literary visions of confrontations with the impossible, we also tried to narrow down the scope of our search. We turned towards the genre of science fiction, in which the theme of encountering the unimaginable, of reacting to extraordinariness, and of witnessing the fall of the seemingly most reliable (though not necessarily beneficial) institutions forms one of the more popular motifs, thus providing us with the obvious resource to peruse for knowledge regarding possible courses of action in the event of sudden reality withdrawal. The stories already quoted demonstrate direct correspondence with the narratives of the Polish shift, while the ones we examine here reveal other possible reactions.

The reasons behind the shock of confronting impossibility can be most varied. In George Alec Effinger's *When Gravity Fails* (1986) which inspired us to the title of this chapter, it is the advanced technologies enabling mass inhabitation of orbital stations; in Philip K. Dick's (1964/1990) *The Three Stigmata of Palmer Eldritch* it is drug-induced hallucinations, and in Andre Norton's (1963) *Witch World*, it is stepping into an alternate universe that causes the meeting with the unthinkable. What interests us in the context of enterprises and the fall of communism in Poland is, however, not so much the causes of impossible events, but stories of how people react to the unknown and the unexpected.

It comes as no surprise that we cannot find one easy answer shining like a beacon from all the different science fiction stories – quite the opposite, what we encounter is a multitude of responses to the intrusion of impossibility. We would like to take a look at a few of the reactions we find the most significant and promising in our attempt to understand the change of 1989. The stories we reference here form by no means a complete list of those pertinent to the issue, they are included rather as examples of the ways of approaching the problem characteristic of the science fiction genre. We have chosen the ones we find the most enlightening in the context of making sense of the fall of communism, though of course this choice involved a considerable amount of arbitrariness. In the present text we are, thus, telling our own story (and choosing a plot) as well as recounting the stories already told.

The first, very prosaic way of looking at the possibilities offered by the appearence of impossibility is to notice all the business opportunities opening up because of the paradigm shift. This line of thinking is represented by a film producer L. M. Greenspan in Harry Harrison's (1967/94) *Technicolor Time Machine*. The author cannot help but be ironic in describing the commercial use of a time machine in film-making (producing cheap but epic Hollywood historical kitsch), although the producer's attitude in itself is far from inconceivable. A more drastic version of the story is presented in Iain M. Banks' (1996) *Excession*, where a discovery of an artefact of highly advanced technology has numerous civilizations vying for the power it might offer. While the unimaginable does not pass unnoticed, it quickly becomes inscribed in the existing pattern of rules and acceptable behaviours.

Simply ignoring the fall of the familiar reality is not always, however, an easy thing to do. Sometimes changes disrupt the established ways of coping, leading to polarity in the attitudes towards the shift and its consequences. On the one hand, we meet with eagerness in embracing the impossible as typified by Daniel Chain from Roger Zelazny's (1980/89) *Wizard World*, who steps into a fantasy world and finds it much more to his liking than the twentieth century he has just left, even though his life up till then was not too miserable. On the other, there is Thomas Covenant (Donaldson, 1977/80), who, in a similar situation, retains considerable reluctance, viewing his new predicament as an obstacle in coping with the problems he had in the 'real' world, although his situation there used to be pretty miserable. These characters perceive changes as completely redefining their situation, they differ only in their reaction to such a drastic transformation of their world. Thomas Covenant is a special case here – he perceives the change, but does not conform to it, denying the new, metamorphosed reality; such behaviour is quite different from that of Bulytchev's townfolk, who accepted the impossible, refusing only to ascribe too much importance to extraordinary happenings.

Let us return, though to the issue of judging which reality should be perceived as more valid, or more 'real'. Such decision tends to present a serious problem to the science fiction characters facing the impossible. Disbelief in one form or another is common enough, either complete as in Thomas Covenant's case, or partial, like that of Arthur Dent

(Adams, 1979/93), who, upon seeing the destruction of Earth, can easily accept the end of New York but not of McDonald's. Cyril M. Kornbluth (1985) adds yet another twist to the idea of disbelieving what contradicts the accepted reality – in his short story *The Silly Season* a long series of apparently absurd events reported by various newspapers causes humans to ignore the news of a Martian invasion until it is far too late. This narrative cautions us, in a Kuhnian tradition, to look closely at all the discontinuitires and paradoxes of the reality we know – any one of them can be a harbinger of its imminent end.

The final reaction to the appearance of the impossible that we would like to present here is the one of wonder at all the possibilities opening up due to the arrival of the unimaginable, possibly accompanied by the relief at seeing all the old worries turning obsolete and unimportant. Such is the case in Samuel Delany's (1966/92) *Empire Star*, where Jo, a teenage boy from a backward planet starts a journey through the whole known universe on an unexpected errand, discovering in the process that reality is much more complex (or, as the author would have it – 'multiplex') than he has ever anticipated. A strong aspect of this revelation is the realization of the manifold points of view contributing to the perceived world (that is more or less the meaning of the word 'multiplexity' as used in this novel), as well as a diffusion of any absolute judgements he held about the universe in general. The impossible in this narrative becomes a source of wisdom, not by itself, though, but through the subversiveness of its message. Kazimierz Bartoszynski (1998, p. 9) comments on a similar theme:

> The feeling of unspeakability has to appear thus as a form of opposition to the domination of that which is socially inscribed as speakable and as a form of opposition to the language usually burdened with discursivity.

In our case unspeakability (a concept close to the one of unimaginability) does not *have to* but *can* manifest its opposition to the dominant form – the main theme of our text is, after all, the multiplicity of possible interpretations – nevertheless it is the questioning of the established reality that leads to deeper understanding.

This brief examination of the attitudes and responses to the unimaginable presented throughout the science fiction genre might provide us with a context for how people (and particularly managers) coped with the changes that took place in Poland. However, in order to correlate science fiction stories and experiences of the Polish systemic shift, we need to relate a few more personal stories discussing the latter.

Stories of the actors

Barbara Czarniawska and Marta Calás (1998) used a narrative method to explore cultural differences in gender construction. Their study was designed around a collection of short stories with a female heroine. These stories were purposefully imprecise and vague. They were distributed to participants of six different cultures to be filled in with details and interpreted. We have used a similar method to see what kind of stories people tell about the shift of 1989. We did not write any narratives ourselves, but asked our informants, students of an MBA level course at a private school of management in Warsaw, to write them themselves. Our respondents are of varied age (mid-20s to late 40s), slightly more men than women, all working as managers, albeit of differing levels (middle to top management, a few CEOs for own business). A friend, teaching one of the courses in the MBA programme, asked the students to write a short story about what, according to them, happened in 1989. They had 30 minutes to accomplish the task. He promised them that the answers would be anonymous, which would encourage them more to write freely about possibly emotionally laden matters. Only one person signed his text. We received in all 24 texts.

None of the students wrote what we would call fiction or consciously metaphoric text. They tended to answer briefly, often as a personal narrative of a biographic kind. We have analysed the material and found that almost all narratives fit into one of three major plots, of which we have already described the most typical one, the *nothing much happened story*. We will now present two other popular narrative types and discuss some non-typical aspects of the stories in our collection.

The second popular plot we have named *the cliché*. It is typically a set of slogans, put together more or less smoothly into a narrative or semi-narrative with an obvious moral sense. 'The year of 1989 is a gate for me and for Poland and a chance for normalcy.' The term 'normalcy' was used very often in the years 1989–90 in the mass media to convey the message that Poland was now on the road to something normal, standard, not very revolutionary or remarkable, from having been 'abnormal', 'sick' and 'wrong'. 'The victory of ideas that I believed in; optimism and hope' – says another, repeating words and sentences we both have heard in the mass media innumerable times. 'It was for me the year of regaining independence and the year of new hopes for better conditions of living' is another sentence we recognize too well from the mass media, although in a slightly distorted version. 'This year turned out to be the year of the retrieving of freedom for millions of beings from Central Europe, and especially from Poland.' The abundance of platitudes used by the respondents is remarkable, phrases once used extensively by media as metaphors communicating the change and its significance were embedded in sentences concerning the change itself. Only the personal narratives of private occurrences, not having to do with the shift, and of business developments, lack such platitudes.

The third plot we have called *the business opportunity narrative*. It is a story of how significant the year 1989 was to the person's economy or how the person made use of the opportunity it presented. One person says:

> That was a time of great change for the individuals who wished to lead their own businesses. My father together with my uncle established a firm, that started as a service enterprise and developed to a trade enterprise.

Another tells about the 'changes in the ways of communication within the company – talking aloud about privatization'. One person tells his story of working abroad in 1989 and how he was disconcerted at first by the change – it made the value of his laboriously earned dollars much less than under communism, but how he then realized that it was, after all, a favourable change: 'Looking from the perspective of the time [that passed], the changes that arrived with the year of 1989 turned out, in my case, beneficial.' He explains that he now 'leads [his] own company, and the incomes from the company are higher than the incomes that [he] would have got from physical labour abroad.' One respondent tells her own, brief but powerful story:

> In 1989 I stopped working in a large firm with a decidedly communist approach to work, people, sales etc. and I started my own construction firm employing 6 people plus a part-time employed book keeper. I bought 2 concrete mixers, a few shovels, trowels, and I lead reconstruction works. It was horrible, no experience, but with great enthusiasm.

This story strikes us as particularly interesting – this person regards founding her own company as a breakthrough; she uses the word 'horrible' to describe the fusion of two elemnts: the lack of experience, probably coupled with the difficulty of making sense of what was happening and the great enthusiasm. This short narrative suggests a mixture of horror and fascination brought about by passion for creation and by encountering the unknowable.

Generally, the stories tell that the year 1989 was either nothing much, or that the significance of the date was obvious, an institution already dressed in platitudes. The business opportunity plot seems to be the most engaging, and contains the most suspense. It is not okay to be reluctant towards the change, some respondents present a story of how they were ambivalent in the beginning, but then realized how good it was: 'The explosion of the new made me anxious at first.' It all happened so unexpectedly, it could mean that 'people from the former system would be held responsible', it could prove to be unstable, once again reversible, the respondent explains. Another person says:

> Unfortunately, the hopes for better living conditions were not real for everyone. It turned out that again political cynicism, theft and corruption entered the stage. But this period should be treated as a time of transition that will end in some time and the situation will be stabilized, as for example in the European Union to which we aspire.

Among the different texts there was especially one, containing just one plain sentence:

> The year of 1989 was to me
> 'The Great Unknown'???

Here we meet a mood similar to the story of establishing the construction company – affirmation of the unknowable, without limiting it to just one sphere of life, or even without limiting it at all.

Another answer, generally faithful to the conventions we have described above, contained one sentence which did not fit into any of our plots very well, but was extremely puzzling and ambiguous: 'For the first time I realized that the problems that concern me are important to many people in Poland.' It may be one of the 'nothing much' stories but it may also be something more than that, a statement about the recognition of the link between the person and society, a link severed under communism (see Nowak, 1979, on the gap between the public and private spheres in communist Poland). Another respondent tells the story of her/his engagement – how s/he participated in the strike of April 1989, and how s/he was engaged in various political activities connected to the campaign and the elections. In a story full of platitudes and private recollections of trivialities, one respondent included the following capitalized sentence: 'PEOPLE SMILED MORE OFTEN AND WERE HAPPIER.' The main plot of the brief narrative then returns into the mixture of trivialities and platitudes, the above statement being something of an emphasized footnote, a sidetrack in the main line of answer.

Our stories

To me, 1989 felt like a personal gift from God, a powerful sign that 'realist' things are not necessarily as inevitable as they seem as long as they last. I was interested in politics, but to a limited degree, and I was a kind of an outsider, having lived in Sweden until the mid-1980s. The political significance of the shift was indeed important to me, but I perceived the symbolic dimension as perhaps much more dazzling than the political. The 'owners of truth' were questioned, the 'only realistic scenario' shattered, my favourite interpreters of social and political reality, such as Adam Michnik, marginalized before, were now allowed their authority and dignity. The lies and the counterfeits of the past suddenly lost the legitimacy they had acquired through being the 'only real presence' among public voices, an empty space for construction of a new social reality was offered us. I had some pictures of a new democratic order, based on a market economy, but I was thrilled by the possibility to experiment, to try out new things – the old, solid, invincible 'one best way' was overthrown – and thus there was no reason to adopt another 'one best way' in its place. Everything was possible, for one beautiful moment. On New Year's Eve of 1989 I went out on the street, shouting 'Free Europe.'

For me, the changes of 1989 felt like an utterly inspired revelation – not so much because of the freedom of expression, of travel, or the introduction of free market economy, although all these were in no way insignificant, but mostly because of the sheer impossibility of what was happening before my very eyes. I guess that it is much easier now to see causes leading inevitably to the downfall of Communism, but in 1989 such a shift seemed utterly impossible and unbelievable, at least to me. Actually, the dreamlike haze of unreality still hangs about my impressions of the event, a strong testimony to the malleability of basic fabric of reality. Gone was the aura of futility, not because I did anything much, but because I could see that there were some results, after all, of other people's actions. All the colours starting to appear on the streets felt deeply symbolic, as the dreary sameness of the Communist propaganda made place for the multiplicity of voices – some wise and joyful, others stupid or hateful, but none of them as inescapable as the weighty voice of the system in the Communist years.

Making sense of the stories

Now we would like to return to the comparison between the actors' interpretations of the Polish systemic shift and science fiction plots by looking at our own narratives as told above. From all the motifs we have described, we feel the strongest kinship to Jo, the hero of Samuel Delany's *Empire Star*. The lesson we have learned from the events of 1989 also concerns the nature of reality – we found out about the multiplicity of possible actions and about the fragility of unbreakable institutions. At the same time our sense of wonder parallels the similar feelings experienced by all the children drawn into the magical world of Narnia in C. S. Lewis' classic novel series (1950/85), and our situations were not dissimilar from that of the characters of these novels – a chance meeting followed by a lesson of a scope stretching far beyond the limits of the one reality. But such experiences were not numerous – most of the stories followed quite a different plot.

For most of the authors of the stories we have collected the change of 1989 turned out to be nothing much, people tell same old stories incorporating some new language, new clichés etc. The magic of the moment is no longer there, the new reality is as solid as the old one, the shift itself has been a one time event, and besides – the old reality was destined to fall, it was *ab*normal and there was no way it could hold together any longer[4]. Furthermore, the new reality has surprisingly many points in common with the old one.

The narratives we have collected thus seem to speak about a deflected change. The actors interpret reality after 1989 in a way as similar as possible to their mind frames from before that date. In the same vein, reality from before change is interpreted as the sole cause of the current situation. Like the townsfolk from Bulytchev's short story, Polish managers do not see anything important in the change. *Plus ça change, plus c'est la meme chose* – they read symbols and signals in a way that enables them to continue acting according to the same basic schemes. Of course, some of them follow the example of L. M. Greenspan, enthusiastically embracing new economic possibilities, but they did not change or, as we suspect, assume that they did not change the basic patterns of behaviour. They are still being subjected to a streamlined and unidirectional transfer of identity and images of what is 'good' and 'right' in management, usually in the form of more or less corrupted images of what the West is like. The managers sometimes stress their distance from the new images, in a way they are used to using from the communist times – in ambiguous, subtly ironic statements, or silence. The Polish managers' freedom to act within the frames is, however, currently much more significant than before. Therefore their responses to change are, in practice, mixed, and the results of their actions are definitely more varied than before, and some are also more successful in the economic domain (Kostera, 1995a; Kozminski, 1993). A majority of the MBA students' stories that we have presented above are of a similar kind. They either trivialize the change through accounting it as if 'nothing much happened', or through defining it with the use of platitudes and clichés. It seems that Baudrillard (1992/94, p. 43) was right in noticing that

> we are not at all threatened by the totalitarian (Stalinist) rewriting of the past, but the democratic rewriting of history: the very images of Stalin and Lenin swept away, streets and cities renamed, statues scattered, soon none of all that will have existed.

The past is indeed being rewritten to maintain continuity with the present; it is not eradicated, only remoulded in the image of the current reality. Only by retroactively eliminating impossibility can a 'nothing much' story be successfully told (see also Kelemen's chapter).

This process of domesticating radical changes and institutionalizing the new reality using tools drawn from the previous context brings to mind yet another concept already appealingly presented in a science fiction form, in Robert Sheckley's (1966/95) *Mindswap*. The hero of this novel, travelling through rapidly changing and increasingly bizarre realities, attempts to order and understand all the incomprehensible events taking place all around him and, as a result, begins using genre templates already available to him, and seeing in the surreal worlds around him scenes from kitschy western, romance, detective or adventure stories. Although at times he manages to regain his senses and to see the fallacy of all these ascriptions, the final change of reality catches him by surprise, and at the end of the novel we find him in a dramatically altered copy of modern-day planet Earth, oblivious to all the drastic changes that have taken place all around him. Much like the authors of the *nothing much* stories, we might say, but to do so would be to slip into the trap of ascribing our own ready-made templates. Of course, all typologies commit the same reductionist error as reality construction depends upon its ordering. We thus do not see a mistake in comparing stories of the Polish changes to science fiction plots, but now we would like to ponder over the banality of MBA students' answers, regardless of their similarities to literary predecessors. It is here that we see a chance for using ideas straight from science fiction stories, which represent alternative ways of interpreting radical social change seen as an encounter with the impossible. It does not have to be seen exactly like in the books, but it can be seen in as many ways and it can be acted upon accordingly (and, once again, in a multitude of varied ways). As many authors before us have already pointed out (for example, Czarniawska-Joerges and Guillet de Monthoux, 1994; Philips, 1995), it is well worth analysing literary plots in the course of organzation theory research. We believe that science fiction has a lot of things to say on social change – mostly by broadening the pool of acceptable (or imaginable) behaviours, by overstepping the boundaries of accepted clichés and conventions in interpreting radical shifts. This genre can thus prove useful in staging new realities and in filling 'empty spaces', the creation of which is, as Czarniawska-Joerges (1993) notes, at the heart of all reforms. This emptiness can be populated by interpretations taken from the past, providing a sense of continuity in which life simply goes on, or it can be filled with new experiments and reconfigurations of past experiences, and so on. We also believe that the empty space can be reclaimed through problematizing established definitions. It is here that we hope to use our access to as large a number as possible of alternative ways of interpreting reality, as well as openness to the unimaginable and impossible qualities of the worlds around us.

We prefer to curb ourselves to pointing out the similarities between the 1989 situation in Poland and the plight of Sheckley's protagonist, suggesting that responses from science fiction stories augment and parallel those presented in the narratives we have collected, forming together a richer background for understanding social change than any of them would on their own.

Another type of plot is represented in the MBA students' 'business opportunity' stories. They are also depicted in field material: Kozminski (1993) tells of a multitude of new firms that emerged after 1989, as well as of new forms that the old ones begun to take. So does Kostera (1995a) – through the reading of her field material she tells the story of a business opportunity. By placing these narratives alongside those from science fiction, some of which, as we have already mentioned, deal with the very issue of entrepreneurs striving to exploit a drastic reality change, we enrich our ability to make sense of and interpret these stories. This does not mean that stories exactly like those of the MBA students have already been told before by science fiction writers, but only that the issue is not one completely unheard of, and all these new stories can be treated as new voices in an ongoing discussion. In other words, science fiction literature seems to have many stories to tell about change – some similar, and some completely different than those of the actors participating in the shift of 1989 in Poland. There is no reason why the insights they offer should be left out of the discourse of the social studies.

Science fiction as a genre seems to be a way to explore different dimensions in social change, which may be helpful in enacting the reality and filling in the 'empty space' – the emergence of which is, as Czarniawska-Joerges (1993) put it what reforms are all about. These blanks can be inscribed by modes of interpretation and writing from the past (as if life continued as usual), by new experiments, by reconfigurations of past experience and so on. Discussing radical change with the aid of science fiction literature may help to make mental and emotional experiments in how to make sense and use of the change. Finally, the appearance of the blank is, in itself, a wonder – a point we would like to make as a final conclusion to the present text.

Notes

1. Andrzej Roman (1990) collected press clippings and other texts from the communist era, mainly Polish, and published them with short ironic comments to expose their utter absurdity and malignancy in his book *Paranoja: Zapis choroby – Paranoia: A note on illness.*
2. It is worth noticing that 'between-the-line' comments were a typical strategy of resistance and semi-resistance during communism. Ambiguous allusions were either 'too intelligent' for the censor to grasp, or the risk of ridicule was too high for the opponent to dare attacking such a statement frontally. Also, if the author happened to be confronted by those in power s/he could always point to another, politically acceptable interpretation of what s/he had said or written and thus avoid being held responsible.

3. Negotiations between the communist government and the opposition resulted in an agreement stating that the opposition may take seats in the parliament if they gain a sufficient share of the votes but the seats allowed them were *ex ante* limited and could not constitute a majority.
4. It might be interesting to compare such a stance with *The Endgame*, a book by Michal Glowinski (1999), in which he presents his analyses of the Polish language, conducted in the late 1980s.

Bibliography

Aaltio-Marjosola, Iiris (1991) 'Cultural Change in a Business Enterprise. Studying a Major Organizational Change and its Impact on Culture', *Acta Academiae Oecenomicae Helsingiensis* Series, A, 80.

Aaltio-Marjosola, Iiris (1994) 'From a "Grand Story" to Multiple Narratives? Studying an Organizational Change Project', *Journal of Organizational Change Management*, vol. 7, no. 5 pp. 56–67.

Acker, Joan (1990) 'Hierarchies, Jobs, Bodies: A Theory of Gendered Organizations', *Gender and Society*, vol. 4, pp. 139–58.

Acker, Joan (1992) 'Gendering organizational theory', in Albert J. Mills and Peta Tancred (eds), *Gendering Organizational Analysis* (London: Sage) pp. 248–60.

Adams, Douglas (1979/1993)*The Hitchhiker's Guide to the Galaxy* (London: Heinemann).

Adler, Nancy J. (1992) *International Dimensions of Organizational Behavior* (Belmont: Wadsworth Publishing Company).

Ajani, Gianmaria, Dallego, Bruno, and Grancelli, Bruno (eds) (1992) *Privatization and Entrepreneurship in Post-socialist Countries* (London: St Martin's Press – now Palgrave Macmillan).

Allaire, Yvan and Firsirotu, Mihaela E. (1984) 'Theories of Organizational Culture', *Organizational Studies*, vol. 5, pp. 193–226.

Alonso, Ana Maria (1998). 'The Effects of Truths: Re-presentations of the Past and the Imagining of Community', *Journal of Historical Sociology*, vol. 1, pp. 33–57.

Altmann, Franz-Lothar (1987) 'Employment Policies in Czechoslovakia', in Jan Adam, *Employment Policies in the Soviet Union and Eastern Europe* (Basingstoke: Macmillan – now Palgrave Macmillan), pp. 78–103.

Amann, Klaus and Hirschauer, Stefan (1997) 'Die Befremdung der eigenen Kultur. Ein programm', in: Stefan Hirschauer and Klaus Amann, K. (eds) *Die Befremdung der eigenen Kultur. Zur ethnographischen Herausforderung soziologischer Empirie (The alienation of culture: the ethnographic challenge of sociological empirical research)* (Frankfurt/M.: Suhrkamp) pp. 7–52.

Amann, Kluas and Knorr-Cetina, Karin (1990) 'The Fixation of (Visual) Evidence', in M. Lynch and Stephen Woolgar (eds) *Representation in scientific practice*. (Cambridge: MIT-Press) 85–121.

Arrington, C. Edward and Francis, Jere R. (1993a) 'Giving Economic Accounts: Accounting as Cultural Practice', *Accounting, Organizations and Society*, vol. 18, no. 2–3, pp. 107–24.

Arrington, C. Edward and Francis, Jere R. (1993b) 'Accounting as a Human Practice: The Appeal of Other Voices', *Accounting, Organizations and Society*, vol. 18, no. 2–3, pp. 105–6.

Arthur, Michael B., Hall, Douglas T. and Lawrence, Barbara S. (eds) (1989) *Handbook of Career Theory* (Cambridge: Cambridge University Press).

Attwood, Lynne (1996) 'The Post-Soviet Woman in the Move to the Market: A Return to Domesticity and Dependence?', in Rosalind Marsh (ed.), *Women in Russia and Ukraine* (Cambridge: Cambridge University Press) pp. 255–66.

Azhgikhina, Nadezhda and Goscilo, Helena (1996) 'Getting Under Their Skin: The Beauty Salon in Russian Women's Lives', in Helena Goscilo and Beth Holmgren (eds) *Russia, Women, Culture* (Bloomington: Indiana University Press, 1996), pp. 94–121.

Baecker, Dirk (1988) *Information und Risiko in der Marktwirtschaft (Information and risk in the market economy)* (Frankfurt am Main: Suhrkamp).

Baglione, Lisa A. and Clark, Carol C. (1997) 'A Tale of Two Metallurgical Enterprises: Marketization and the Social Contract in Russian Industry', *Communist and Post-Communist Studies*, vol. 2 pp. 153–81.

Bailey, Derek T. (1988) 'Introduction', in Derek T. Bailey (ed.), *Accounting in Socialist Countries* (London: Routledge) pp. 1–18.

Balcerzan, Edward Niewyrazalne (1998) 'Czy niewyrazone?' (Unexpressed or inexpressible?) in Wlodzimierz Bolecki and Erazm Kuzma (eds) *Literatura wobec Niewyrazalnego (Literature in the face of the Unspeakable).* (Warszawa: Wydawnictwo IBL PAN) pp. 5–17.

Banks, Iain M. (1996) *Excession* (London: Orbit).

Barinaga, Ester (1998) 'Criteria for the Analysis of Cultural Issues: "Cultural Diversity" Revised', in L. Busati (ed.), *Managing Across Borders: Cross-cultural Issues in Management Studies*, proceedings of the Third AIDEA Giovanni International Conference (Milano: CUEM).

Bartoszynski, Kazimierz (1998) 'Miedzy niewyrazalnoscia a niepoznawalnoscia (Between unspeakability and unknowability)', in Wlodzimierz Bolecki and Erazm Kuzma (eds), *Literatura wobec Niewyrazalnego (Literature in the Face of the Unspeakable)* (Warszawa: Wydawnictwo IBL PAN) pp. 19–30.

Baudrillard, Jean (1992/1994) *The Illusion of an End (L'illusion de la fin)* (Cambridge: Polity Press).

Bauman, Zygmunt (1988) *Freedom* (Oxford: Oxford University Press).

Beckert, Jens (1997) *Die Grenzen des Marktes. Die sozialen Grundlagen wirtschaftlicher Effizienz* (Frankfurt/am Main: Campus) [*Beyond the Market. The Social Foundations of Economic Efficiency* (Princeton: Princeton University Press, Forthcoming 2002).

Berger, Peter and Luckmann, Thomas (1966) *The Social Construction of Reality: A Treatise in the Sociology of Knowledge* (Garden City: Doubleday & Company).

Bierut, Boleslaw (1953) 'Wykonanie zadan planu – to najwyzszy obowiazek kazdego robotnika, technika, inzyniera, kierownika (The accomplishment of tasks – the highest duty of the technician, engineer, manager), *Trybuna Ludu*, 1459/33, p. 1.

Bloom, Paula Jorde (1997) 'Navigating the Rapids: Directors Reflect on their Careers and Professional Development', *Young Children* vol. 7, pp. 32–8.

Boisot, Max Henry (1994) 'Learning as Creative Destruction: the Challenge for Eastern Europe', in Richard Boot, Jean Lawrence, John Morris (eds) *Managing the unknown by creating new future* (London: McGraw-Hill).

Bommes, Michael and Wright, Patrick (1982) '"Charms of Residence": The Public and the Past', in Richard Johnson, Gregor McLennan, Bill Schwarz and David Sutton (eds), *Making Histories: Studies in History Writing and Politics* (Minneapolis: University of Minnesota Press) pp. 253–302.

Bond, George C. (1976) *The Politics of Change in a Zambian Community* (Chicago: Chicago University Press).

Bond, George C. and Gilliam, Angela (eds) (1994) *Social Construction of the Past: Representation as Power* (London: Routledge).

Borda, Maria and McLeay, Stuart (1996) 'Accounting and Economic Transformation in Hungary', in Neil Garrod and Stuart McLeay (eds), *Accounting in Transition* (London: Routledge), pp. 28–42.

Bourdieu, Pierre (1979) *Entwurf einer Theorie der Praxis auf der ethnologischen Grundlage der kabylischen Gesellschaft* (Frankfurt/am Main: Suhrkamp, 1979). [*Outline of a Theory of Practice.* (Cambridge: Cambridge University Press, 1977)].

Bourdieu, Pierre (1982) *Ce que parler veut dire. L'économie des échanges linguistique* (Paris: Fayard). [*Language and symbolic power. The economy of linguistic exchanges* (Cambrige: Polity, 1991)].

Bridger, Sue (1992) 'Young Women and Perestroika', in Linda Edmondson (ed.), *Women and society in Russia and the Soviet Union* (Cambridge: Cambridge University Press), pp. 178–201.

Bridger, Sue and Kay, Rebecca (1996) 'Gender and Generation in the New Russian Labor Market', in Hilary Pilkington (ed.), *Gender, Generation, and Identity in Contemporary Russia* (New York: Routledge, 1996) pp. 21–38.

Brown, Mary Helen (1986) 'Sense Making and Narrative Forms: Reality Construction in Organization', in Lee Thayer (ed.), *Organization –Communication: Emerging Perspectives* (New Jersey: Ablex Publishing Corporation).

Bruno, Marta (1996) 'Employment Strategies and the Formation of New Identities in the Service Sector in Moscow', in Hilary Pilkington (ed.), *Gender, Generation, and Identity in Contemporary Russia* (New York: Routledge) pp. 39–56.

Brzezin, Wlodzimierz and Jaruga, Alicja (1988) 'Accounting Evolution in a Planned Economy', in Derek T. Bailey (ed.), *Accounting in socialist countries* (London: Routledge) 41–58.

Buck, Trevor and Cole, John (1987) *Modern Soviet Economic Performance* (Oxford: Basil Blackwell).

Buckley, Mary (1992) 'Glasnost and the woman question', in Linda Edmondson (ed.), *Women and Society in Russia and the Soviet Union* (Cambridge: Cambridge University Press) pp. 202–26.

Bulytchev, Kiryl (1983) *Retrogenetyka i inne opowiadania (Retro-genetics and other stories)* (Warszawa: Iskry).

Buono, Anthony F., Bowditch, James L. and Lewis, J. W. III (1985) 'When Cultures Collide: The Anatomy of a Merger', *Human Relations,* vol. 38, pp. 477–500.

Burawoy, Michael and Lukács, Janos (1992) *'The Radiant Past: Ideology and Reality in Hungary's Road to Capitalism* (Chicago: University of Chicago Press).

Burr, Vivien (1998) *Gender and Social Psychology* (London: Routledge).

Burrell, Gibson and Morgan, Gareth (1979) *Sociological Paradigms and Organizational Analysis* (London: Heinemann).

Chia, Robert (1995) 'From Modern to Postmodern Organizational Analysis', *Organization Studies*, vol. 16, pp. 579–604.

Clark, Ed and Soulsby, Anna (1995) 'Transforming Former State Enterprises in the Czech Republic', *Organisation Studies*, vol. 2, pp. 215–42.

Clark, Ed and Soulsby, Anna (1999) *Organizational Change in Post-communist Europe: Management and Transformation in the Czech Republic* (London: Routledge).
Clark, Kate (1994) 'Translator's Preface', in Anastasia Posadskaya (ed.), *Women in Russia: A New Era in Russian Feminism* (London/New York: Verso) pp. ix–xiii.
Collin, Audrey (1986) 'Career Development: The Significance of the Subjective Career', *Personnel Review*, vol. 2, pp. 22–8.
Collingwoord, Robin George (1961) *The Idea of History* (Oxford: Oxford University Press).
Colville, Ian D., Waterman, Robert H. and Weick, Karl E. (1999) 'Organising and the Search for Excellence: Making Sense of the Times in Theory and Practice, *Organization*, vol. 1, pp. 129–48.
Conger, Jay A. (1990) 'The Dark Side of Leadership', *Organisational Dynamics*, vol. 2, pp. 44–55.
Cooke, Bill (1999) 'Writing the Left out of Management Theory: The Historiography of Management of Change', *Organization*, vol. 1, pp. 81–125.
Corvellec, Hervé (1997) *Stories of Achievements: Narrative Features of Organizational Performance* (New Brunswick–London: Transaction Publishers).
Coulson, M. R. (1987) 'In the Matter of Class Intervals for Choropleth Maps: With Particular Reference to the Work of Georg F. Jenks', *Cartographica*, vol. 24, pp. 16–39.
Cox, Taylor H. and Harquail, Ceila V. (1991) 'Career Paths and Career Success in the Early Career Stages of Male and Female MBAs', *Journal of Vocational Behavior*, vol. 39, pp. 54–75.
Czarniawska, Barbara (1986) 'The Management of Meaning in the Polish Crisis', *Journal of Management Studies*, vol. 23, no. 3, May, pp. 313–31.
Czarniawska, Barbara (1997) *Narrating the Organization: Dramas of Institutional Identity* (Chicago-London: The University of Chicago Press).
Czarniawska, Barbara (1998) *Narrative Approach in Organization Studies* (Thousand Oaks: Sage).
Czarniawska, Barbara (1999) *Writing Management* (Oxford: Oxford University Press).
Czarniawska, Barbara (2001) 'Is it Possible to be a Constructionist Consultant? On the Complex Relation between the Logic of Theory, the Logic of Practice and the Logic of Representation', *Management Learning*, vol. 32, no. 2, pp. 253–66.
Czarniawska, Barbara and Calás, Marta (1998) 'Another Culture: Explaining Gender Discrimination With "culture"', *Administrative Studies*, vol. 4, pp. 326–41.
Czarniawska, Barbara and Sevón, Guje (eds) (1996) *Translating Organizational Change* (Berlin-New York: de Gruyter).
Czarniawska-Joerges, Barbara (1988) *Ideological Control in Non-ideologic Organizations* (New York-Westport-London: Praeger).
Czarniawska-Joerges, Barbara (1992a) 'Nice Work in Strange Worlds: Anthropological Inspiration for Organization Theory', in Thomas Polesie and Inga-Lill Johansson (eds) *Responsibility and Accounting: The Organizational Regulation of Boundary Conditions* (Lund: Studentlitteratur), pp. 59–77.
Czarniawska-Joerges, Barbara (1992b) *Exploring Complex Organizations: A Cultural Perspective* (London: Sage).

Czarniawska-Joerges, Barbara (1993) *The Three-dimensional Organization: A Constructionist View* (Lund: Studentlitteratur).
Czarniawska-Joerges, Barbara (guest editor) (1994a) 'Painful Transformations: Privatization in East and Central Europe', *Industrial and Environmental Crisis Quarterly*, vol. 8, no. 1.
Czarniawska-Joerges, Barbara (1994) 'Narratives of Individual and Organizational Identities', in Stan A. Deetz (ed.), *Communication Yearbook 17* (London-Thousand Oaks-New Delhi: Sage), pp. 193–235.
Czarniawska-Joerges, Barbara (1995) 'Narration or Science? Collapsing the Division in Organization Studies', *Organization*, vol. 2, no. 1, pp. 11–33.
Czarniawska-Joerges, Barbara and Guillet de Monthoux, Pierre (eds) (1994) *Good Novels, Better Management: Reading Organizational Realities* (Chur: Harwood).
Danielsson, Albert (1989) 'On Accounting and Management Information', in Bo Fridman and Lars Östman (eds), *Accounting development – some perspectives: A Book in Honour of Sven-Erik Johansson* (Stockholm: EFI) pp. 11–21.
Davis, Stanley W., Menon, Krishnagopal and Morgan, Gareth (1982) 'The Images that Have Shaped Accounting Theory', *Accounting, Organizations and Society*, vol. 7, no. 4, pp. 307–18.
Delany, Samuel R. (1966/1992) *Gwiazda Imperium (Empire Star)* (Gdansk: Phantom Press).
Delany, Samuel (1994) *Return to Neveryon* (Hanover–London: Wesleyan University Press, 1994).
Dent, Bordon D. (1990) *Cartography. Thematic Map Design* (Dubuque, IA: Brown).
Dent, Jeremy F. (1990) 'Strategy, Organisation and Control: Some Possibilities for Accounting Research', *Accounting, Organizations and Society*, vol. 15, pp. 3–25.
Desrosières, Alain (1993) *La politique des grands nombres. Histoire de la raison statistique* (Paris: La Découverte) [*The Politics of Large Numbers: A History of the Statistical Reasoning* (Cambridge; Harvard University Press, 1998)].
Desrosières, Alain (1994) 'Le territoire et la localité. Deux langages statistiques (The territory and locality: Two statistical languages)', *Politix. Travaux de science politique*, vol. 25, pp. 46–58.
Deutsch-Polnische Wirtschaftsförderungsgesellschaft (1996) *Investitionschancen und -risiken in Polen (German-Polish Society for the promotion of economics: chances and risks for investment in Poland)* (Gorzow).
Dick, Philip K. (1964, 1990) *Trzy Stygmaty Palmera Eldritcha (The Three Stigmata of Palmer Eldritch)* (Poznan: Amber).
DiMaggio, Paul J. and Powell, Walter W. (1991) 'The Iron Cage Revisited: Institutional Isomorphism and Collective Rationality in Organizational Fields', in Walter W. Powell and Paul J. DiMaggio (eds), *The New Institutionalism in Organizational Analysis* (Chicago: The University of Chicago Press), 63–82.
Donaldson, Stephen (1977/1980) *Lord Foul's Bane* (Glasgow: Fontana).
Douglas, Mary (1991) *Wie Institutionen denken.* (Frankfurt/am Main: Suhrkamp, 1991) [*How institutions think.* (London: Routledge & Kegan Paul, 1987)].
Drost, Helmar (1993) 'The Great Depression in East Germany: The Effects of Unification on East Germany's Economy', *Eastern European Politics and Societies*, vol. 7, no. 3, pp. 452–81.

Dubin, Robert (1956) 'Industrial Workers' Worlds: A Study of the Central Life Interests of Industrial Workers', *Social Problems*, vol. 3, pp. 131–42.

Dubin, Robert, Champoux, Joseph E. and Porter, Lyman W. (1975) 'Organizational Life Interests and Organizational Commitment of Blue-collar Workers', *Administrative Science Quarterly*, vol. 3, pp. 411–21.

Dunn, Elizabeth (1998) *Privatization and Personhood: Transforming Work in Postsocialist Poland*, Doctoral dissertation (Baltimore: Department of Anthropology, Johns Hopkins University).

Dyer, W. Gibb Jr (1994) 'Toward a Theory of Entrepreneurial Careers', *Entrepreneurship: Theory and Practice*, vol. 2, pp. 7–21.

Eberwein, Wilhelm and Tholen, Jochen (1997) *Market or Mafia: Russian Managers on the Difficult Road Towards an Open Society* (Aldershot: Ashgate).

Eco, Umberto (1973) *Dzielo otwarte: Forma i nieokreslonosc w poetykach współczesnych (Opera aperta: Forma e indeterminazione nelle poetiche contemporanee)* (Warszawa: Czytelnik). Published as *The Open Work* (English translation by Anna Cancogni – Cambridge, Mass.: Harvard University Press, 1989).

Edgar, Don and Glezer, Helen (1994) 'Family and Intimacy: Family Careers and the Reconstruction of Private Life', *International Social Science Journal*, vol. 139, pp. 117–39.

Edmondson, Linda (ed.) (1992) *Women and Society in Russia and the Soviet Union* (Cambridge: Cambridge University Press).

Effinger, George Alec (1986) *When Gravity Fails* (New York: Baen Books).

Elster, Jon (1991) 'Rationality and Social Norms', *Archives Européennes de Sociologie*, vol. XXXII, no. 2, pp. 84–108.

Elster, Jon, Offe, Claus and Preuss, Ulrich K. (1998) *Institutional Design in Post-communist Societies: Rebuilding the Ship at Sea* (Cambridge: Cambridge University Press).

Euromoney (1994) 'Coopers and Lybrand Responds to Individual Country Needs', vol. 4, no. 4, p. 25.

Erofeev, Viacheslav (1990) 'Sex and Perestroika', *Liber*, vol. 1, p. 17.

European Training Foundation (1996) 'A Short Description of the Methodological Approach', *Evaluation of Activities in the Field of Management Training in the NIS* (Torino).

Evans, Martin G., Gunz, Hugh P. and Jalland, Michael R. (1997) 'Implications of Organizational Downsizing for Managerial Careers', *Canadian Journal of Administrative Sciences*, vol. 4, pp. 359–71.

Ezzy, Douglas (1997) 'Subjectivity and the Labour Process: Conceptualising "good work"', *Sociology*, vol. 3, pp. 427–43.

Federowicz, Michal, Dabrowski, Janusz and Levitas, Anthony (1992) '*State Owned Enterprises in the First Year of Economic Transformation* (Warsaw: Institute for Philosophy and Sociology Press).

Federowicz, Michal, Dabrowski, Janusz and Levitas, Anthony (1993) *State Owned Enterprises in the Second Year of Economic Transformation* (Warsaw: Institute for Philosophy and Sociology Press).

Feldman, Martha S. and March, James G. (1988) 'Information in Organizations as Signal and Symbol', in James G. March (ed.), *Decisions and Organizations* (Oxford: Blackwell), pp. 409–28.

Fernler, Karin (1996) *Mangfald eller likriktning? Effekter av en avreglering* (*Diversity or isomorphism? Effects of deregulation*) (Stockholm: Nerénius och Santerus).

Fiol, C. Marlene (1991) 'Seeing the Empty Spaces: Towards a More Complex Understanding of the Meanings of Power in Organisations', *Organisation Studies*, vol. 4, pp. 547–66.

Foucault, Michel (1977) *Discipline and Punish: The Birth of the Prison* (Harmondsworth: Penguin).

Fournier, Valerie and Kelemen, Mihaela (2001) 'The Crafting of Community: Recoupling Discourses of Management and Womenhood', *Gender, Work, Organisation*, vol. 8, no. 3, pp. 267–90.

Gal, Susan (1978) 'Peasant Men Can't Get Wives: Language Change and Sex Roles in a Bilingual Community', *Language in Society* 7, pp. 1–16.

Gazeta Wyborcza (1989a) 19, p. 1.

Gazeta Wyborcza (1989b) 20, p. 1.

Gazeta Wyborcza (1989c) 21, p. 1.

Garrod, Neil and McLeay, Stuart (1996) *Accounting in Transition. The Implications of Political and Economic Reforms in Central Europe* (London: Routledge).

Geertz, Clifford (1996) *After the Fact. Two Countries, Four Decades, One Anthropologist* (Cambridge, MA: Harvard University Press).

Gergen, Mary M. and Gergen, Kenneth J. (1993) 'Narratives of the Gendered Body in Popular Autobiography', in Amia Lieblich and Ruthellen Josselson (eds), *The Narrative Study of Lives. Vol. 1* (Thousand Oaks: Sage), pp. 191–218.

Gherardi, Silvia (1995) *Gender, symbolism and organizational cultures* (Thousand Oaks: Sage).

Giddens, Anthony (1991) *Modernity and Self-identity: Self and Society in the Late Modern Age* (Cambridge: Polity Press).

Giddens, Anthony (1995) *Die Konstitution der Gesellschaft. Grundzüge einer Theorie der Strukturierung* (Frankfurt/am Main: Campus, 1995). [*The Constitution of Society. Outline of the Theory of Structuration* (Cambridge: Polity Press, 1984)].

Glinka, Beata and Ludwicki, Tomasz (1997) *Marriage in Post-industrial Realities* (Warsaw: SCOS conference paper).

Glowinski, Michal (1992) *Rytual i demagogia: Trzynascie szkicow o sztuce zdegradowanej (Ritual and Demagogy: Thirteen Sketches on Degraded Art)* (Warszawa: Open).

Glowinski, Michal (1999) *Koncowka (Endgame)* (Krakow: Wydawwnictwo Literackie).

Golden-Biddle, Karen and Locke, Karen (1997) *Composing Qualitative Research* (Thousand Oaks-London-New Delhi: Sage).

Gomulka, Wladyslaw (1945) 'Nowe zadania i nowe metody pracy ruchu zawodowego (New Tasks and Work Methods of the Working Class Movement)', *Glos Ludu*, List 19, p. 1.

Goode, William J. (1957) 'Community Within the Community: The Professions', *American Sociological Review*, vol. 22, pp. 194–200.

Gorbachev, Mikhail (1987) *Perestroika: New Thinking for our Country and the World* (New York: Harper & Row).

Goscilo, Helena (1996) 'Perestroika or Domostroika? The Construction of Womanhood under Glasnost', in Helena Goscilo, *Dehexing Sex: Russian Womanhood During and After Glasnost* (Ann Arbor: The University of Michigan Press) pp. 5–30.

Grabher, Gernot (1992) 'The Elegance of Incoherence: Institutional Legacies in the Economic Transformation of East Germany and Hungary', in Eckhart

J. Dittrich, Gert Schmidt and Richard Whitley (eds), *Industrial Transformation in Europe: Process and Contexts* (London: Sage).
Grabher, Gernot and Stark, David (eds) (1997) *Restructuring Networks in Post-socialism: Legacies, Linkages and Localities* (Oxford: Oxford University Press).
Grancelli, Bruno (1997) *Training and Education Centers in the Region of Urals*, Individual Report (TACIS-ETF, Torino and Brussels).
Grancelli, Bruno (1998a) *Soviet Management and Labor Relations* (Boston: Allen & Unwin).
Grancelli, Bruno (1998b) 'Post-Soviet Management: From State-dependency to Entrepreneurship?', in Steward Clegg, Eduardo Ibarra-Colado and Luis Bueno-Rodriguez (eds), *Global Management: Universal Theories and Local Realities.* (London: Sage) pp. 111–27.
Grancelli, Bruno (1995a) 'Organizational Change: Toward a New East–West Comparison', *Organization Studies,* vol. 16, no. 1, pp. 1–25.
Grancelli, Bruno (1995b) 'Who Should Learn What?', in Bruno Grancelli (ed.), *Social Change and Modernization: Lesson from Eastern Europe* (Berlin: de Gruyter), pp. 3–41.
Gray, Frenacibe du Plessix (1989) *Soviet Women: Walking the Tightrope* (New York: Doubleday).
Grey, Christopher (1994) 'Career as a Project of the Self and Labor Process Discipline', *Sociology,* vol. 2, pp. 479–97.
Gunz, Hugh P. and Jalland, Michael R. (1996) 'Managerial Careers and Business Strategies', *Academy of Management Review,* vol. 3, pp. 718–56.
Guillet de Monthoux, Pierre and Czarniawska-Joerges, Barbara (1994) 'Introduction: Management Beyond Case and Cliché', in Barbara Czarniawska-Joerges and Pierre Guillet de Monthoux (eds), *Good Novels, Better Management: Reading Organizational Realities* (Harwood Academic Publishers), pp. 1–16.
Hall, Edward T. (1983) *Dance of Life: The Other Dimension of Time* (New York: Doubleday).
Hampden-Turner, Charles (1990) *Corporate Culture from Vicious to Virtuous Circles* (London: The Economist Books).
Hampden-Turner, Charles and Trompenaars, Fons (1998) *Riding the Waves of Culture* (London: Nicolas Brealey).
Harley, J. Brian (1989) 'Deconstructing the Map', *Cartographica,* vol. 26, pp. 1–20.
Harrison, Harry (1967/1994) *Filmowy Wehikul Czasu (Technicolor Time Machine)* (Warszawa: Amber).
Harsanyi, Doina Pasca (1993) 'Women in Romania', in Nanette Funk and Magda Mueller (eds), *Gender Politics and Post-communism* (London: Routledge) pp. 39–52.
Hatch, Mary Jo (1997) *Organization Theory: Modern, Symbolic, and Postmodern Perspectives* (Oxford: Oxford University Press).
Hausleitner, Maria (1993) 'Women in Romania: Before and After the Collapse', in Nanette Funk and Magda Mueller (eds), *Gender politics and Post-communism* (London: Routledge), pp. 53–61.
Hayashi, Reiko (1997) 'Hierarchical Interdependence Expressed Through Conversational Styles in Japanese Women's Magazines', *Discourse and Society,* vol. 8, no. 3, pp. 359–89.
Heidrich, Balázs (1999) *The Change of Organizational Culture in the Transition Period in Hungary,* doctoral dissertation (Miskolc: University of Miskolc).

Hermes, Joke (1995) *Reading Women's Magazines: An Analysis of Everyday Media Use* (Cambridge: Polity Press).
Hertzfeld, Michael (1987) *Anthropology Through the Looking Glass: Critical Ethnography in the Margins of Europe* (New York: Cambridge University Press).
Hewett, Ed A. (1988) 'Soviet Central Planning: Probing the Limits of the Traditional Model', in Josef Brada, Ed A. Hewett and Thomas A. Wolf (eds), *Economic Adjustment and Reform in Eastern Europe and the Soviet Union* (Durham, NC: Duke University Press), pp. 305–39.
Hobsbawm, Eric (1984) 'Mass-producing Traditions: Europe 1870–1914', in Eric Hobsbawm and Terence Ranger (eds), *The Invention of Tradition* (Cambridge University Press), pp. 263–307.
Hobsbawn, Eric J. (1992) *Nationalism since 1780. Programme, myth, reality,* (Cambridge: Cambridge University Press).
Hobsbawm, Eric and Terence, Ranger (eds) (1984) *The Invention of Tradition* (Cambridge: Cambridge University Press).
Hofstede, Geert (1991) *Culture's consequences* (Beverly Hills: Sage).
Hopwood, Anthony G. (1992) 'Accounting Calculation and the Shifting Sphere of the Economic', *European Accounting Review,* vol. 1, pp. 125–43.
Hughes, Everett Cherrington (1958) *Men and their work* (Glencoe: Free Press).
Husserl, Edmund (1950/1992) *Cartesianische Meditationen. Gesammelte Schriften Band 8 (Cartesian meditations: collective writings: Vol. 8)* (Hamburg: Meiner, 1963/1992).
Ingersoll, Virginia Hill and Adams, Guy B. (1987) 'Beyond Organizational Boundaries: Exploring the Managerial Myth', *Administration and Society,* vol. 18, no. 3, pp. 360–81.
Inkson, Kerr (1995) 'Effects of Changing Economic Conditions on Managerial Job Changes and Careers', *British Journal of Management,* vol. 3, pp. 183–94.
Jankowicz, A. D. (1993) 'Worlds in Collusion: An Analysis of an Eastern European Management Development Institute', *Management Education and Development,* vol. 24, no. 1, pp. 93–104.
Jankowicz, A. D. (1994) 'Parcels from Abroad: The Transfer of Meaning to Eastern Europe', *Journal of European Business Education,* vol. 3, no. 2, pp. 1–19.
Janyska, Petr (1992) 'Imperfect but Right', *East European Reporter,* vol. 1, 59–60.
Jaruga, Alicja (1996) 'Accounting in Socialist Countries: The Beginnings of Reform', in Neil Garrod and Stuart McLeay (eds), *Accounting in Transition* (London: Routledge) pp. 12–27.
Jeffries, Ian (1993) *Socialist Economies and their Transition to the Market* (London: Routledge).
Jenkins, Keith (1991) *Rethinking History* (London: Routledge).
Jermanski, O. (1972) 'Elementy Systemu Taylora (Elements of Taylor's system)', in Jerzy Kurnal (ed.), *Tworcy naukowych podstaw organizacji (The Makers of the Scientific Foundation of Organization)* (Warszawa: PWE).
Jones, C. S. (1985) 'An Empirical Study of the Role of Management Accounting Systems Following Take-over or Merger', *Accounting, Organizations and Society,* vol. 10, pp. 177–200.
Josselson, Ruthellen and Lieblich, Amia (eds) (1993) *'The Narrative Study of Lives. Vol 1* (Thousand Oaks: Sage).

Kalleberg, Arne and Stark, David (1993) 'Career Strategies in Capitalism and Socialism: Work Values and Job Rewards in the United States and Hungary', *Social Forces*, vol. 1, pp. 181–198.

Kalthoff, Herbert (2000) 'The inventory of firms: How banks analyze risk in Central Europe', in Herbert Kalthoff, Richard Rottenburg and Hans-Juergen Wagener (eds) *Facts and Figures. Economic representations and practices.* (Marburg: Metropolis) 59–85.

Kanter, Rosabeth Moss (1977) *Men and Women of the Corporation* (New York: Basic Books).

Katz, Ralph, Tushman, Michael and Allen, Thomas J. (1995) 'The Influence of Supervisory Promotion and Network Location on Subordinate Careers in a Dual Ladder RD and E Setting', *Management Science*, vol. 5, pp. 848–63.

Kavan, Jan (1992) 'Imperfect but Wrong', *East European Reporter*, vol. 1, January–February, p. 61.

Keane, John (1999) *Václav Havel: A Political Tragedy in Six Acts* (London: Bloomsbury).

Keesing, Roger (1993) *Cultural Anthropology: Contemporary Perspectives* (New York: Harcourt Brace College Publisher).

Kelemen, Mihaela (1999) 'The Myth of Restructuring, Competent Managers and the Transition to a Market Economy: The "Romanian case', *British Journal of Management*, vol. 10, no. 3, pp. 199–208.

Kelemen, Mihaela and Hristov, Latchezar (1998) 'From Egalitarian Culture to Entrepreneurial Culture: The Example of Romanian and Bulgarian Organizations', *Journal of Enterprising Culture*, vol. 5, no. 2, pp. 155–70.

Kelemen, Mihaela and Lightfoot, Geoffrey (2000) 'Organizational and Individual Identities in Transition: The Case of the Romanian Small and Medium Sized Enterprise', *Journal of Southern Europe and the Balkans*, vol. 2, no. 1, pp. 89–103.

Kennedy, Susan (1994) 'Unclassed Choropleth Maps Revisited: Some Guidelines for the Construction of Unclassed and Classed Choropleth Maps', *Cartographica*, vol. 31, pp. 16–25.

Khotkina, Zoya (1994) 'Women in the Labour Market: Yesterday, Today and Tomorrow', in Anastasia Posadskaya (ed.), *Women in Russia. A New Era in Russian Feminism* (London–New York: Verso), pp. 85–108.

Kieser, Alfred (ed.) (1994) *Organizationstheorien (Theories of organization)* (Stuttgart: Kohlhammer).

Kiezun, Witold (1991) *Management in Socialist Countries: USSR and Eastern Europe* (Berlin: de Gruyter).

Klimenkova, Tatiana (1994) 'What Does Our New Democracy Offer Society?', in Anastasia Posadskaya (ed.), *Women in Russia. A New Era in Russian Feminism* (London-New York: Verso), pp. 14–36.

Klüter, Helmut (1986) *Raum als Element sozialer Kommunikation (Space as an element of social communication)* (Giessen: Justus-Liebig-Universität).

Knight, L. E. (1967) 'Czechoslovakia's Fading Old Guard', *East Europe*, November, pp. 15–17.

Knorr-Cetina, Karin (1999) *Epistemic Cultures. How the Sciences Make Knowledge* (Cambridge, MA: Harvard University Press).

Knorr-Cetina, Karin and Bruegger, Urs (2002) 'Global microstructures: The interaction practices of financial markets', *American Journal of Sociology*, vol. 107, no. 4 (forthcoming).

Kociatkiewicz, Jerzy and Kostera, Monika (1999) 'Templates of Ideas: The Charm of Storytelling in Academic Discourse', *Knowledge Transfer,* vol. 2, no. 1 pp. 49–69.

Kornai, János (1992) *The Socialist System: The Political Economy of Communism* (Princeton, NJ: Princeton University Press).

Kornbluth, Cyril M. (1985) *Sezon ogorkowy (The Silly Season)* (Warszawa: Iskry), pp. 7–20.

Kostera, Monika (1995a) 'Differing Managerial Responses to Change in Poland', *Organization Studies,* vol. 16, no. 4, pp. 673–97.

Kostera, Monika (1995b) 'The Modern Crusade: Missionaries of Management Come to Eastern Europe', *Management Learning,* vol. 26, no. 3, pp. 331–52.

Kostera, Monika (1996) 'The Manager's New Clothes: On Identity Transfer in Post-1989 Poland', in Monica Lee, Hugo Letiche, Robert Crawshaw and Michael Thomas (eds), *Management Education in the new Europe* (Thomson Business Press), pp. 194–211.

Kostera, Monika (1997) 'Personal Performatives: Collecting Poetical Definitions of Management', *Organization,* vol. 4, no. 3, pp. 345–53.

Kostera, Monika and Wicha, Maciej 'The "Divided Self" of the Polish State Owned Companies: Culture and Environment', *Organization Studies,* vol. 17, no. 1, pp. 83–105.

Kostera, Monika, Kurczak, Piotr and Kociatkiewicz, Jerzy (1995) *Art or Science? Collapsing Another Division,* working paper (Warszawa: Warsaw University, Faculty of Management).

Kozminski, Andrzej K. (1993) *Catching Up? Organizational and Management Change in the ex-Socialist Bloc* (New York: State of New York University Press).

Kozminski, Andrzej K. (1995) 'From the Communist Nomenclatura to Transformational Leadership: The Role of Management in the Post-communist Enterprises', in Bruno Grancelli (ed.), *Social Change and Modernization: Lesson from Eastern Europe* (Berlin: de Gruyter), pp, 83–106.

Krejci, Jaroslav (1972) *Social change and stratification in post-war Czechoslovakia* (Basingstoke: Macmillan – now Palgrave Macmillan).

Kunda, Gideon (1992) *Engineering Culture* (Philadelphia: Temple University Press).

Kuron, Jacek (1990) *Moja Zupa (My soup)* (Warszawa: BGW).

Kušin, Vladimir V. (1978) *From Dubcek to Charter 77 A Study of "Normalisation' in Czechoslovakia 1968–1978* (Edinburgh: Q Press).

Kvande, Elin and Rassmussen, Bente (1995) 'Women's Careers in Static and Dynamic Organizations', *Acta Sociologica*, vol. 38, pp. 115–30.

Latour, Bruno (1986) 'The powers of association', in John Law (ed.), *Power, Action and Belief. A New Sociology of Power?* (London: Routledge and Kegan Paul).

Latour, Bruno (1988) 'The politics of explanation: an alternative', in Steve Woolgar (ed.), *knowledge and Reflexivity: New Frontiers in the Sociology of Knowledge.* (London: Sage).

Latour, Bruno (1990) 'Drawing things together', in Michael Lynch and Steve Woolgar (eds) *Representation in Scientific Practice* (Cambridge: MIT-Press) 19–68.

Latour, Bruno (1999) *Pandora's Hope: Essays on the Reality of Science Studies* (Cambridge: Harvard University Press).

Lehmbruck, Barbara (1999) *Managing Uncertainty – Hierarchies, Markets and 'Networks' in the Russian Timber Market – 1991–1998*. Discussion Papers 4 (Helsinki: Bank of Finland, Institute for Economics in Transition).
Leicht, Kevin T. and Fennell, Mary L. (1997) 'The Changing Organizational Context of Professional Work', *Annual Review of Sociology*, vol. 23, pp. 215–31.
Leidner, Robin (1993) *Fast Food, Fast Talk: Service Work and the Routinization of Everyday Life* (Berkeley–Los Angeles–London: University of California Press).
Lejeune, Philippe (1989) *On Autobiography* (Minneapolis: University of Minnesota Press).
Lenin, Vladimir I. (1981) *The State and Revolution: The Marxist Theory of the State and the Tasks of the Proletariat in the Revolution* (Moscow: Progess Publishers).
Levinson, Daniel J. (1978) *The Seasons of a Man's Life* (New York: Ballantine Books).
Lewis, Clive Staples (1950/1985) *The Lion, the Witch and the Wardrobe* (London: Fontana).
Leyshon, Andrew, Thrift, Nigel and Pratt, Jonathan (1998) 'Reading Financial Services. Texts, Consumers, and Financial Literacy', *Environment and Planning D: Society and Space*, vol. 16, pp. 29–55.
Lilley, Stephen J. and Platt, Gerald M. (1994) 'Correspondents' Images of Martin Luther King Jr: An Interpretive Theory of Movement Leaderships', in Theodore R. Sarbin and John I. Kitsuse (eds), *Reconstructing the Social* (London: Sage), pp. 65–83.
Linde, Charlotte (1993) *Life Stories* (New York: Oxford University Press).
Lipovskaya, Olga (1994) 'The Mythology of Womanhood in Contemporary "Soviet" Culture', in Anastasia Posadskaya (ed.), *Women in Russia. A New Era in Russian Feminism* (London-New York: Verso), 123–34.
Lissyutkina, Larissa (1993) 'Soviet Women at the Crossroads of Perestroika', in Nanette Funk and Magda Mueller (eds), *Gender Politics and Post-communism: Reflections from Eastern Europe and the Former Soviet Union* (New York-London: Routledge), pp. 274–86.
Liuhto, Kari (1999) *The Organizational and Managerial Transformation in Turbulent Business Environments: Managers' Views on the Transition of Their Enterprise in Some of the European Former Soviet Republics in the 1990's*, series A-9 (Turku: School of Economics and Business Administration).
Llewellyn, Sue (1994) 'Managing the Boundary. How Accounting is Implicated in Maintaining the Organization', *Accounting, Auditing and Accountability Journal*, vol. 7, pp. 4–23.
Luhmann, Niklas (1981) *Soziologische Aufklärung. Band 3 (Sociological enlightenment. Vol. 3)* (Opladen: Westdeutscher Verlag).
Luhmann, Niklas (1984) *Soziale Systeme. Grundrisse einer allgemeinen Theorie (Social Systems: Foundations of a general theory)* (Frankfurt am Main.: Suhrkamp).
Luhmann, Niklas (1994) *Die Wirtschaft der Gesellschaft (The economy of society).* (Frankfurt am Main: Suhrkamp).
Lynn, Susan A., Cao, Le Thi and Horn, Betty C. (1996) 'The Influence of Career Stage on the Work Attitudes of Male and Female Accounting Professionals', *Journal of Organizational Behavior*, vol. 2, pp. 135–49.
Lyotard, Jean-François (1979/1984) *The Postmodern Condition. A Report on Knowledge* (Manchester: Manchester University Press).

Mackevicius, Jonas, Aliukonis, Juozas and Bailey, Derek (1996) 'The Reconstruction of National Accounting Rules in Lithuania', in Neil Garrod and Stuart McLeay (eds), *Accounting in Transition* (London: Routledge), pp. 28–42.

Majone, Giandomenico (1996) 'Regulation and its Modes', in Giandomenico Majone (ed.), *Regulating Europe* (London: Routledge).

Major, Iván (1993) *Privatization in Eastern Europe: A Critical Approach* (London: Edward Elgar).

March, James G. (1994) *A Primer on Decision Making: How Decisions Happen* (New York: Free Press).

Mark, David M. and Csillag, Ferenc (1989) 'The Nature of Boundaries on "Area-class Maps"', *Cartographica*, vol. 26, pp. 65–78.

Marsh, Rosalind (ed.) (1996a) *Women in Russia and Ukraine* (Cambridge: Cambridge University Press).

Marsh, Rosalind (1996b) 'Introduction: Women's studies and Women's Issues in Russia, Ukraine and the Post-Soviet States', in Rosalind Marsh (ed.), *Women in Russia and Ukraine* (Cambridge: Cambridge University Press), pp. 1–28.

Martin, Emily (1989) *The Woman in the Body: A Cultural Analysis of Reproduction* (Milton Keynes: Open University Press).

Martin, Joanne (1992) *Cultures in Organizations: Three Perspectives* (Oxford: Oxford University Press).

McCloskey, Deirdre N. (1998) *Knowledge and Persuasion in Economics* (Cambridge: Cambridge University Press).

McRobbie, Angela (1994) *Postmodernism and Popular Culture* (London-New York: Routledge).

Meyer, John W. and Rowan, Brian (1977) 'Institutionalized Organizations: Formal Structure as Myth and Ceremony', *American Journal of Sociology*, vol. 7, pp. 340–63.

Mezentseva, Yelena (1994) 'What Does the Future Hold? (Some Thoughts on the Prospects for Women's Employment)', in Anastasia Posadskaya (ed.), *Women in Russia: A New Era in Russian Feminism* (London–New York: Verso), pp. 74–84.

Michnik, Adam (1989) 'Radosc ... i chwila namyslu (Joy ... and a moment of reflection)', *Gazeta Wyborcza*, vol. 21, p. 1.

Miller, Peter (1994) 'Accounting as a Social and Institutional Practice: An Introduction', in Anthony G. Hopwood and Peter Miller (eds), *Accounting as Social and Institutional Practice* (Cambridge: Cambridge University Press), pp. 1–39.

Miller, Peter and O' Leary, Ted (1987) 'Accounting and the Construction of the Governable Person', *Accounting, Organizations and Society*, vol. 12, pp. 235–65.

Miller, Peter and O'Leary, Ted (1993) 'Accounting Expertise and the Politics of the Product: Economic Citizenship and Modes of Corporate Governance', *Accounting, Organizations and Society*, vol. 18, no. 2/3, pp. 187–206.

Mintzberg, Henry (1975) 'The Manager's Job: Folklore and Fact', *Harvard Business Review*, July-August, pp. 49–61.

Mishra, Aneil K. (1996) 'Organizational Responses to Crisis: The Centrality of trust', in Roderick Moreland Kramer and Tom R. Tyler (eds), *Trust in Organizations: Frontiers of Theory and Research* (Thousand Oaks: Sage), pp. 246–60.

Morgan, Gareth (1983) 'Social Science and Accounting Research: A Commentary on Tomkins and Grives', *Accounting, Organizations and Society,* vol. 8, no. 4, pp. 385–88.

Morgan, Gareth (1987) *Accounting as Reality Construction: Towards a New Epistemology for Accounting Practice,* working paper (Toronto: York University).

Morgan, Gareth (1993) *Imaginization: The Art of Creative Management* (Newbury Park-London-New Delhi: Sage).

Mount, Michael K. (1984) 'Managerial Career Stage and Facets of Job Satisfaction', *Journal of Vocational Behavior,* vol. 24, pp. 340–54.

Munro, Rolland (1995) 'Managing by Ambiguity: An Archeology of the Social in the Absence of Management Accounting', *Critical Perspectives on Accounting,* vol. 6, pp. 433–82.

Myant, Martin (1989) *The Czechoslovak Economy 1948–1988: The Battle for Reform* (Cambridge: Cambridge University Press).

Najduchowska, Helena (1976) 'The Selection of General Directors of Industrial Enterprises and the Changing Role of the Industrial Enterprise in Poland', in J. J. Boddewyn (ed.), *European Industrial Managers: East and West* (White Plains, NY: IASP), pp. 416–48.

Nelson, John S. (1993) 'Account and Acknowledge, or Represent and Control? On Post-modern Politics and Economics of Collective Responsibility', *Accounting, Organizations and Society,* vol. 18, no. 2/3, pp. 207–29.

Newell, Helen and Dopson, Sue (1996) 'Muddle in the Middle: Organizational Restructuring and Middle Management Careers', *Personnel Review,* vol. 4, pp. 4–20.

Nilsson, Karin (1996) 'Practice, Myths and Theories for Change: The Reconstruction of an East German Organization', *Organization Studies,* vol. 17, pp. 291–09.

Norton, Andre (1963) *Witch World* (New York: Ace Books).

Nowak, Stefan (1979) 'System wartosci spoleczenstwa polskiego (The Value System of the Polish Society)', *Studia Socjologiczne,* vol. 4, pp. 155–73.

Nurmi, Raimo (1982) 'Cross-Cultural Comparisons of Organization: Methodological Reflections', in Piha K. (ed.) *Docial Responsibility in Marketing.* (Turku: Turku School of Economics) A-2, 264–77.

Nurmi, Raimo and Uksvärav, Raoul (1995) 'Estonia and Finland: Culture and Management, A Conjectural Presentation', series A-9 (Turku: Turku School of School of Economics and Business Administration).

Obloj, Krzysztof (1986) *Zarzadzanie: Ujecie praktyczne (Management: A Practical Approach)* (Warszawa: PWE).

Obloj, Krzysztof and Kostera, Monika (1993) 'The Polish Privatization Program: Remarks on Action, Symbolism and Cultural Barriers', *Industrial & Environmental Crisis Quarterly,* vol. 7, no. 3, pp. 7–21.

Ochberg, Richard L. (1994) 'Life Stories and Storied Lives' in Amia Lieblich and Ruthellen Josselson (eds), *The Narrative Study of Lives. vol. 2. Exploring Identity and Gender* (Thousand Oaks: Sage), pp. 113–44.

OECD-Development Assistance Committee on Aid Evaluation (1993) *Principles on Effective Aid* (Paris: OECD).

Ol'shanskaya, Yelena (1998) 'Sexual Harassment – The Russian Way', *Cosmopolitan,* April, pp. 84–8.

Orwell, George (1949/1976) *Nineteen eighty-four* (Toronto: Penguin).

Orzack, Louis H. (1959) 'Work as a "Central Life Interest" of Professionals', *Social Problems,* vol. 6, pp. 125–32.

Pahl, Jan M. and Pahl, Ray E. (1971) *Managers and Their Wives: A Study of Career and Family Relationships in the Middle Class* (London: Penguin Press).

Pankov, Dmitri (1998) 'Accounting for Change in Belarus', *Management Accounting,* vol. 76, no. 10, pp. 56–8.

Parker, Martin (1995) 'Working Together, Working Apart: Management Culture in a Manufacturing Firm', *The Sociological Review Sociological Review,* 43/3, 518–47.

Paul, David W. (1979) 'The Cultural Limits of Revolutionary Politics: Change and Continuity in Socialist Czechoslovakia', *East European Quarterly,* vol. 48, pp. 186–7.

Peltonen, Tuomo (1998) 'Narrative Construction of Expatriate Experience and Career Cycle: Discursive Patterns in Finnish Stories of International Careers', *International Journal of HRM,* vol. 5, pp. 875–92.

Petukhov, Sergei (1998) 'Paradoxes of a Woman's Mind', *Ona,* 3 March pp. 18–20.

Philips, Nelson (1995) 'Telling Organizational Tales: On the Role of Narrative Fiction in the Study of Organizations', *Organization Studies,* vol. 16, no. 4, pp. 625–49.

Pilkington, Hilary (ed.) (1996) *Gender, Generation and Identity in Contemporary Russia* (London–New York: Routledge).

Ploszajski, Piotr (1995) 'Polish Reforms: The Fine Art of Learning and Forgetting', in Bruno Grancelli (ed.), *Social Change and Modernization: Lesson from Eastern Europe* (Berlin: de Gruyter), pp. 197–212.

Polesie, Thomas and Johansson, Inga-Lill (eds) (1992) *Responsibility and Accounting: The Organizational Regulation of Boundary Conditions* (Lund: Studentlitteratur).

Polkinghorne, Donald E. (1988) *Narrative Knowing and the Human Sciences.* (Albany, NY: State of New York University Press).

Porter, Theodore M. (1995) *Trust in Numbers: The Pursuit of Objectivity in Science and Public Life* (Princeton: Princeton University Press).

Portes, Alejandro (1998) 'Social Capital: Its Origins and Applications in Modern Sociology', *Annual Review of Sociology,* vol. 24, pp. 1–24.

Posadskaya, Anastasia (ed.) (1994a) *Women in Russia: A New Era in Russian Feminism* (London–New York: Verso).

Posadskaya, Anastasia (1994b) 'Introduction', in Anastasia Posadskaya (ed.), *Women in Russia: A New Era in Russian Feminism* (London–New York: Verso), 1–7.

Posadskaya, Anastasia (1994c) 'Women as the Object and Motive Force of Change in Our Time', in Anastasia Posadskaya (ed.), *Women in Russia: A New Era in Russian Feminism* (London–New York: Verso), pp. 8–13.

Posadskaya, Anastasia (1994d) 'A Feminist Critique of Policy, Legislation, and Social Consciousness in Post-socialist Russia', in Anastasia Posadskaya (ed.), *Women in Russia: A New Era in Russian Feminism* (London–New York: Verso), pp. 164–82.

Potter, Jonathan and Wetherell, Margaret (1987) *Discourse and Social Psychology: Beyond Attitudes and Behaviour* (London: Routledge).

Power, Michael (1994) 'The Audit Society', in Anthony G. Hopwood and Peter Miller (eds), *Accounting as Social and Institutional Practice* (Cambridge: Cambridge University Press), pp. 299–316.

Power, Michael (1997) *The Audit Society: Rituals of Verification* (Oxford: Oxford University Press.

Primecz, Henriett (1996) *The Archimedian Point of the Post-modern Society: How to do Business in the Contemporary World?* (Warsaw: CEU).

Puffer, Sheila (ed.) (1992) *The Russian Management Revolution: Preparing Managers for the Market Economy* (New York: Sharpe).

Renner, Hans (1989) *A History of Czechoslovakia since 1945* (London: Routledge).

Ries, Nancy (1997) *Russian Talk: Culture and Conversation during Perestroika* (Ithaca, NY: Cornell University Press).

Ritzer, George (1993) *The McDonaldization of Society* (Newbury Park: Pine Forge Press).

Ritzer, George (1996/1997) *McDonaldyzacja spoleczenstwa (Macdonaldization of society)* (Warszawa: Muza).

Roberts, John (1991) 'The Possibilities of Accountability', *Accounting, Organizations and Society*, vol. 16, pp. 355–68.

Rogers, Annie, Brown, Lyn Mikel and Tappan, Mark Bennett (1994) 'Interpreting Loss in Ego Development in Girls: Regression or Resistance, in Amia Lieblich and Ruthellen Josselson (eds), *The Narrative Study of Lives. vol. 2. Exploring Identity and Gender* (Thousand Oaks: Sage), pp. 1–36.

Roman, Andrzej (1990) *Paranoja: Zapis choroby (Paranoia: A Note on Illness)* (Paris: Spotkania).

Rose, Nikolas (1989) *Governing the Soul: The Shaping of the Private Self* (London: Routledge).

Rose, Nikolas and Miller, Peter (1990) 'Governing Economic Life', *Economy and Society*, vol. 19, no. 1, pp. 1–31.

Rosenbusch, Adam (1980) *Radio Erywan odpowiada (Radio Eryvan answers)* (Warszawa: Przedswit).

Rosenwald, George C. and Ochberg, Richard L. (eds) (1992) *Storied Lives: The Cultural Politics of Self-understanding* (New Haven, CT: Yale University Press).

Rottenburg, R. (1991) '"Der Sozialismus braucht den ganzen Menschen" Zum Verhältnis vertraglicher und nichtvertraglicher Beziehungen in einem VEB', *Zeitschrift für Soziologie*, vol. 4, pp. 86–112.

Sackmann, Sonja A. (1991) *Cultural knowledge in organizations: Exploring the collective mind* (Newbury Park: Sage).

Sarbin, Theodore R. (1986) *Narrative Psychology: The Storied Nature of Human Conduct* (New York: Praeger).

Schein, Edgar H. (1974) 'The Individual, the Organization and the Career: A Conceptual Scheme', *Journal of Applied Behavioural Science*, vol. 4, pp. 401–26.

Schein, Edgar H. (1978) *Career Dynamics* (Massachusetts: Addison-Wesley).

Scheppele, Kim Lane L. (1999) 'The New Private Spheres' (15 March 1999) (http://www.ceu.hu/sun/new.htm).

Schneider, Susan C. and Barsoux, Jean-Louis (1997) *Managing Across Cultures* (London: Prentice-Hall).

Schoenberger, Erica (1997) *The Cultural Crisis of the Firm* (Oxford: Blackwell).

Schultz, Hans-Dietrich (1989) 'Fantasies of Mitte. Mittellage and Mitteleuropa in German Geographical Discussion in the 19th and 20th Centuries', *Political Geography Quarterly*, vol. 8, pp. 315–39.

Schultz, Majken and Hatch, Mary Jo (1996) 'Living with Multiple Paradigms: The Case of Paradigm Interplay in Organizational Culture Studies', *Academy of Management Review*, vol. 21, pp. 529–57.

Schumann, Jochen (1992) *Grundzüge der mikroökonomischen Theorie(Outline of Micro-Economic Theory)* (Berlin.: Springer).

Schütz, Alfred (1971) *Das Problem der sozialen Wirklichkeit. Gesammelte Aufsätze, Band 1*. (The Hague: Nijhoff). [*The Problem of social reality. Collected papers I.* (The Hague: Nijhoff 1962)].

Schwartz, Barry (1996a) 'Reading the Gettysburg Address: Social Change and Collective Memory', *Qualitative Sociology*, vol. 3, pp. 395–422.

Schwartz, Barry (1996b) 'Introduction: The Expanding Past', *Qualitative Sociology*, vol. 19, no. 3, pp. 275–281.

Scott, James (1985) *Weapons of the Weak* (New Haven: Yale University Press).

Setterson, Richard A. Jr and Mayer, Karl U. 'The Measurement of Age, Age Structuring, and the Life Course', *Annual Review of Sociology*, pp. 233–61.

Shack, William A. (1994) 'The Construction of Antiquity and the Egalitarian Principle: Social Construction of the Past in the Present', in George C. Bond and Angela Gilliam (eds), *Social Construction of the Past: Representation as Power* (London: Routledge), pp. 113–28.

Shearer, Teri L. and Arrington, C. Edward (1993) 'Accounting in Other Wor(l)ds: A Feminism Without Reserve', *Accounting, Organizations and Society*, vol. 18, no. 2–3, pp. 253–72.

Sheckley, Robert (1966/1995) *Zwichrowany swiat (Mindswap)* (Warszawa: Amber).

Shim, Jae K., Siegel, Joel G. and Simon, Abraham J. (1986) *The Vest Pocket MBA* (Englewood Cliffs, NJ: Prentice Hall).

Shreeves, Rosamund (1992) 'Sexual Revolution or "Sexploitation"? The pornography and Erotica Debate in the Soviet Union', in Shirin Rai, Hilary Pilkington and Annie Phizacklea (eds), *Women in the Face of Change. The Soviet Union, Eastern Europe and China* (New York-London: Routledge), pp. 130–46.

Shrivastava, Paul (1986) 'Postmerger Integration', *Journal of Business Strategy*, vol. 7, 65–76.

Siklová, Jirina (1996) 'Lustration or the Czech Way of Screening: The Case Against Decommunization', *East European Constitutional Review*, vol. 1, pp. 57–62.

Silbiger, Steven (1993) *The Ten Day MBA: A Step-by-step Guide to Mastering the Skills Taught in America's Top Business Schools* (New York: Quill/William Morrow).

Silverman, David (1993) *Interpreting Qualitative Data* (London: Sage).

Simecka, Milan (1984) *The Restoration of Order: The Normalization of Czechoslovakia* (London: Verso).

Simmel, George (1900/1991) *Philosophie des Geldes* (Frankfurt am Main: Suhrkamp [*The Philosophy of Money*. (London: Routledge and Kegan Paul, 1978)]

Simmel, Georg (1908/1992) *Soziologie. Untersuchungen über die Formen der Vergesellschaftung* [*Sociology. Investigations of Forms of Socialization*] (Frankfurt am Main: Suhrkamp).

Smart, Roslyn and Peterson, Candida (1997) 'Super's Career Stages and the Decision to Change Careers', *Journal of Vocational Behavior*, vol. 3, pp. 358–74.

Sochaka, Renata and Malo, Jean-Louis (1996) 'Emerging Capital Markets, Securities Regulation and Accounting: A Systems Perspective', in Neil Garrod and Stuart McLeay (eds), *Accounting in Transition* (London: Routledge), pp. 28–42.

Sonnenfeld, Jeffrey A. and Peiperl, Maury A. (1988) 'Staffing Policy as a Strategic Response', *Academy of Management Review,* vol. 13, pp. 588–600.

Soulsby, Anna and Clark, Ed (1998) 'Controlling Personnel: Management and Motive in the Transformation of the Czech Republic', *The International Journal of Human Resource Management,* vol. 1, pp. 79–98.

Stark, David (1991) 'Path Dependence and Privatization Strategies in East Central Europe', *Eastern European Politics and Societies, vol.* 6, no. 1, pp. 17–54.

Staniszkis, Jadwiga (1991) 'Political Capitalism in Poland', *East European Politics and Societies,* 5, 127–41.

Stark, David (1994) 'Capitalismo su progetto? Nuove combinazioni fra pubblico e privato nell'Europa dell'Est (Capitalism's Project? New Public–Private Partnerships in Eastern Europe)', *Stato e Mercato,* vol. 42, pp. 301–21.

Stishova, Elena (1996) 'Full frontal': Perestroika and Sexual Policy', in Rosalind Marsh (ed.), *Women in Russia and Ukraine* (Cambridge: Cambridge University Press), pp. 188–95.

Stoner-Weiss, Kathryn (1997) *Local Heroes: The Political Economy of Russian Regional Governance* (Princeton: Princeton University Press).

Strandgaard Pedersen, Jesper (1998) 'Organisatorisk integration (Integration of Organizations)', in Jesper Strandgaard Pedersen (ed.), *Fusioner pa tvaers – fra plan til praksis (Horizontal Mergers – From Plan to Practice)* København: Jurist og Økonomforbundets Forlag).

Strathern, Marilyn (1999) *Bulletproofing.* unpublished manuscript.

Strauss, Anselm and Corbin, Juliet (1990) *Basics of Qualitative Research: Grounded Theory Procedures and Techniques* (London: Sage).

Stroh, Linda K. and Reilly, Anne H. (1997) 'Loyalty in the Age of Downsizing', *Sloan Management Review,* vol. 4, pp. 83–8.

Stuart, Robert C. (1972) *The Collective Farm in Soviet Agriculture* (Lexington: Lexington Books).

Super, Donald (1957) *The Psychology of Careers: An Introduction to Vocational Development* (New York: Harper and Row).

Suvorov, Viktor (1995) *Kontrola (Control)* (Warszawa: Adamski & Bielinski).

Svedberg Nilsson, Karin (1999) *Effektiva företag? En studie av hur privatiserade organisationer konstrueras (Efficient Firms? A Study of the Construction of Privatized Organizations)* (Stockholm: EFI).

Sztompka, Piotr (1996) *La fiducia nelle società post-comuniste. Una risorsa scomparsa? (Trust in Post-communist Societies: A Diminishing Resource?)* (Soveria Mannelli: Rubettino).

TACIS-European Training Foundation (1998) 'Evaluation of Activities in the Field of Management Training in the NIS', *Final Report* (Torino).

Talbot, Mary (1995) 'A Synthetic Sisterhood: False Friends in a Teenage Magazine', in Kira Hall and Mary Bucholtz (eds), *Gender Articulated: Language and the Socially Constructed Self* (New York–London: Routledge), pp. 143–65.

Thrift, Nigel and Olds, Kris (1996) 'Refiguring the Economic in Economic Geography', *Progress in Human Geography,* vol. 20, pp. 311–37.

Tintor, Janko (1997) 'Company Restructuring and Business Analysis', in Soumitra Sharma (ed.), *Restructuring Eastern Europe* (Cheltenham: Edward Elgar), pp. 167–76.

Toma, Luigi (1998) 'Main Differences between Romanian Accounting and International Accounting Standards', *Focus Romania Outlook* (March) (http:www.finance.ro/mar1998/1.html).

Turnbull, David (1996) 'Cartography and Science in Early Modern Europe: Mapping the Construction of Knowledge Spaces', *Imago Mundo,* vol. 48, pp. 5–24.

Turnpuu, Lembit, Aaltio-Marjosola, Iiris and Kooskora, Mari (2000) *Finnish Business Students are More Tolerant and Democratic Compared to Estonian peers* unpublished paper).

Tyner, Judith (1992) *Introduction to Thematic Cartography* (Englewood Cliffs: Prentice-Hall).

Uksvärav, Raoul and Nurmi, Raimo (1993) *Estonian Economy and Management in the Early 1990s,* series A-4 (Turku: School of Economics and Business Administration).

Ulc, Otto (1978) 'Some Aspects of Czechoslovak Society Since 1968', *Social Forces,* vol. 2, pp. 419–35.

Van Maanen, John and Gideon Kunda, Real Feelings: Emotional Expression and Organizational Culture', *Research in Organizational Behavior,* vol. 11, pp, 43–103.

Van Zon, Hans (1996) *The Future of Industry in Central Eastern Europe* (Aldershot: Avebury).

Verdery, Katherine (1996) *What was Socialism and What Comes Next?* (Princeton: Princeton University Press).

Voronina, Olga (1994a) 'The Mythology of Women's Emancipation in the USSR as the Foundation for a Policy of Discrimination', in Anastasia Posadskaya (ed.), *Women in Russia: A New Era in Russian Feminism* (London–New York: Verso), vol. 37–56.

Voronina, Olga (1994b) 'Virgin Mary or Mary Magdalene? The Construction and Reconstruction of Sex During the Perestroika Period', in Anastasia Posadskaya (ed.), *Women in Russia: A New Era in Russian Feminism* (London–New York: Verso), pp. 135–45.

Voszka, Eva (1994) 'An Attempt at Crisis Management and the Failure of the Spontaneous Privatisation', *Industrial and Environmental Crisis Quarterly,* vol. 8, pp. 23–40.

Wada, Shuichi (1995) 'The Status and Image of the Elderly in Japan: Understanding the Paternalistic Ideology', in Mike Featherstone and Andrew Wernick (eds), *Images of Aging: Cultural Representations of Later Life* (London: Routledge), pp. 48–60.

Walesa, Lech (1989) 'Mili Panstwo! Drogi Wyborco! (Dear Ladies and Gentlemen! Dear Voter!)', *Gazeta Wyborcza,* 19/1, p. 1.

Warner, Malcolm and Cambell, Adrin (1994) How Russian Managers Learn', *Journal of General Management,* vol. 19, no. 4, pp. 69–88.

Weick, Karl (1995a) *Sensemaking in Organizations* (Thousand Oaks: Sage).

Weick, Karl E. (1995b) *Der Prozeß des Organizierens* (Frankfurt am Main: Suhrkamp) [*The Social Psychology of Organizing.* (Reading, MA: Addison-Wesley, 1979)]

Weil, Simone (1978) *The Need for Roots* (London: Routledge).

Welc, Pawel (1994) *Monografia ZPOW 'Alima' w Rzeszowie (od 1992 r. 'Alima-Gerber SA') (A Monograph on ZPOW 'Alima' in Rzeszów)* Master's thesis (Rzeszów: Szkola Glówna Handlowa w Warszawie, Wydzial Spóldzielco-Ekonomiczny w Rzeszowie).

Whitley, Richard (1999) 'Firms, Institutions and Management Control: The Comparative Analysis of Coordination and Control Systems', *Accounting, Organizations and Society,* vol. 24, pp. 507–24.

Whitley, Richard, Henderson, Jeffrey and Czaban, Laszlo (1997) 'Ownership, Control and the Management of Labour in an Emergent Capitalist Economy: The Case of Hungary', *Organization,* vol. 3, pp. 409–32.

Willmott, Hugh (1993) 'Strength is Ignorance; Slavery is Freedom: Managing Culture in Modern Organizations', *Journal of Management Studies,* vol. 30, pp. 515–52.

Wittgenstein, Ludwig (1984) 'Philosophische Untersuchungen', in Ludwig Wittgenstein, *Werkausgabe Band 1 (Collective Writings: Volume 1).* (Frankfurt am Main: Suhrkamp) 225–580 [*Philosophical Investigations* (Oxford: Basil Blackwell 1953)].

Wolfram Cox, Julie R. (1997) 'Manufacturing the Past: Loss and Absence in Organisational Change', *Organisation Studies,* vol. 4, pp. 623–54.

Wong, Raymond Sin-Kwok (1996) 'The Social Composition of the Czechoslovak and Hungarian Communist Parties in the 1980s', *Social Forces,* vol. 1, pp. 61–90.

Wubben, Emeil F. M. (1993) *Markets, Uncertainty and Decision-making: A History of the Introduction of Uncertainty into Economics* (Amsterdam: Thesis Publishers).

Zelazny, Roger (1980/1989) *Wizard World* (New York: Baen Books).

Zernbavel, Eviatan (1996) 'Social Memories: Steps to a Sociology of the Past', *Qualitative Sociology,* vol. 3, pp. 282–99.

Index of Names

Note: page numbers in **bold** type refer to authors of chapters in this book.

Subject Index